MODERN ALLEGORY AND FANTASY

Also by Lynette Hunter

GEORGE ORWELL: THE SEARCH FOR A VOICE

* G. K. CHESTERTON, EXPLORATIONS IN ALLEGORY

* RHETORICAL STANCE IN MODERN LITERATURE

* *Also published by Macmillan*

Modern Allegory and Fantasy

Rhetorical Stances of Contemporary Writing

Lynette Hunter

*Lecturer, Institute for Bibliography
and Textual Criticism
University of Leeds*

CHESTER COLLEGE

ACC. No. 893477 'DEPT ♂

CLASS No. 809.915 HUN

LIBRARY

M

MACMILLAN
PRESS

© Lynette Hunter 1989

All rights reserved. No reproduction, copy or transmission
of this publication may be made without written permission.

No paragraph of this publication may be reproduced, copied
or transmitted save with written permission or in accordance
with the provisions of the Copyright Act 1956 (as amended),
or under the terms of any licence permitting limited copying
issued by the Copyright Licensing Agency, 33–4 Alfred Place,
London WC1E 7DP.

Any person who does any unauthorised act in relation to
this publication may be liable to criminal prosecution and
civil claims for damages.

First published 1989

Published by
THE MACMILLAN PRESS LTD
Houndmills, Basingstoke, Hampshire RG21 2XS
and London
Companies and representatives
throughout the world

Printed in Hong Kong

British Library Cataloguing in Publication Data
Hunter, Lynette
Modern allegory and fantasy : rhetorical
stances of contemporary writing.
1. Western European literatures, 1950–1987.
Allegory & fantasy
809′.915
ISBN 0–333–45370–0

Contents

Acknowledgments

This work has been shared by many and these acknowledgments act as a dedication.

The writing took place while I was a Research Fellow at the University of Liverpool, and more recently a lecturer at the University of Leeds. I thank those institutions for giving me the opportunity to begin and to complete this work; I would also like to thank Angela Archdale for her patient secretarial help.

Those people who read versions of the work and provided acute criticism are Stephen Bygrave, Shirley Chew, Lesley Johnson, Diane Macdonnel, John Thompson and an unknown publisher's reader. Their help has been beyond value. I am grateful to Christopher Dewdney for permission to begin with the extract from *Fovea Centralis*. And I must particularly thank Peter Lichtenfels and Hilary Rose who beat the unwieldy metal of my thinking into shape, with strength resilience and resistance.

Lynette Hunter

From a Handbook of Remote Control

2. Individual to Individual

The remote control personality constructs a meticulous lie around another being. Particle by particle the solid reality that composed the allegorical ground he stood on is replaced by fantasies and lies. (fossilization) This work, once attained creates a time loophole, a backwater where reality and time stand halted. The remote control agent hides in this cul de sac until he builds up enough energy to attempt a group control situation. At any point a skillful agent can reverse the process and replace fantasy with reality so smoothly the individual does not even know his feet ever left the ground.

from Christopher Dewdney, *Fovea Centralis*

Introduction

The impetus to write this book comes from two sources, the confusion in critical theory about the terms fantasy and allegory and the wildly contradictory readings that emerge from books labelled with either term. The confusion exists not just because the terms are relatively new to criticism but because the theory of genre, which could be expected to help with definition, is itself in turmoil and inadequate to describe the activity of these writings. The concept of genre as a fixed kind tied to a set of techniques has recently been changed to incorporate historically specific strategies that relate writing to epistemology and ideology – the theories of knowledge, culture and perception – pertinent to the time of writing and the time of reading. These changes have led to genres being defined in terms primarily of mode, with the recognition that techniques are still important because at particular times they will be more or less appropriate to a modal strategy.

However, I would suggest that the confusions arising between fantasy and allegory are rooted in materiality and belief – in other words in rhetoric. Only in looking at rhetorical stance, which tries to describe the interaction between writer, reader and words in the text, can we arrive at an activity which begins partially to illuminate the confused nature of the readings.

In part two of this book begins with fantasy and follows early twentieth-century attempts to define it in terms of two apparently different strategies: games and desire. As these modes of fantasy are taken up and extended by theorists in the post-war period it becomes increasingly clear that each strategy attempts a separation from the material world by claiming either neutrality or purity. At the same time a number of theorists in the 60s and 70s begin to recognise that the strategies of games and desire, and the techniques they use in twentieth-century writing, are in effect covert attempts at authoritarian power which can be employed in a pragmatic way in state politics. But these more recent theorists never fully articulate the strategy for a covert persuasion that is held to enable both writer and reader to assume a disinterested, in other words neutral or pure, neither subjective nor objective, relationship.

Only by looking at the rhetorical implications of the mode can we discern the persuasive effect of the techniques used within the current ideological and epistemological set of western humanism. What we discover is first that the theorists of fantasy need an audience fully conscious of the rules of the game being played or the ends of the desire being effected, simultaneously with an audience which can reject this consciousness in order to maintain the separation of the writing from the world necessary to its neutrality and purity. The rhetorical implications of a stance that simultaneously is conscious of and yet rejects the effects of technique and strategy are grave.

The stance of fantasy is end-directed and can achieve substantial short-term effectiveness. In terms of the practicality of how we live our lives within individual and state politics, the stance is enormously useful. However, the long-term effect is that no radical change can ever take place because the ideological and epistemological basis for action is never questioned. More than this, if a skilful rhetor employs the stance she or he may maintain an apparent consistency in politics while covertly manipulating the audience. It only takes one part of the writer, reader, writing interaction to ignore the rejection of the conscious agreement to the rules or ends, and the action immediately loses its supposed neutrality and purity. In effect this rejection of consciousness is not possible. The fantasy stance becomes a series of covert manipulations engaged in competition toward success or failure: with all the opportunities for exploitation, aggression and domination that are attendant.

These two faces of fantasy, the pragmatic short-term end and the authoritative long running domination, are to a certain extent reflected in the criticism of writings that have come to be called fantasy: the stand-off between those who view fantasy as morally definite and those who view it as a temporary seduction. What is unnervingly apparent is that critics who claim moral definitiveness rarely question the rigid basis of such stasis and those who claim temporary seduction are unable to enjoy it. In terms of short-term entertainment or long-term domination, both of indicating a reader willing to take on the positive side of fantasy, the stance is still too covert, too manipulative for political acceptance within the present ideology on the part of both writer and reader. I look briefly at the impasse of critical assessment reached on Tolkien's *The Lord of the Rings*, which delineates arguments within fantasy theory; and at the extraordinary intensity of reaction for and against Orwell's *Animal Farm* and *Nineteen Eighty-Four* which concerns the opposition between fantasy and allegory.

Interestingly, theorists of fantasy have a peculiar blindness to the activity of allegory. Most perceive the allegorical mode as limited and emblematic because they are used to looking for the end-directed, ideologically defined rules or desires of fantasy. But theorists of allegory, although agreeing on little else, do agree that allegory is not only realised in mode but firmly based in an overt stance: one that directs itself to ways of interacting with the external world rather than dominating it.

Beginning once more, this time with theories of allegory, part three of this study looks at the theoretical work on allegory as generic technique, mode and stance. I then move on to discuss approaches to allegory which are defined by their attitude toward the external world and possible interactions with it. The majority of these approaches moves toward a definition of truth as, variously, apprehendable, polysemous or oppositional. Although not treating truth as the fixed absolute which fantasy finds necessary, these theories do tend toward such fixity; and insofar as they do so their discussion of mode, strategy and technique overlaps with the theory of fantasy. But there is continually a straining away from definitions of truth toward definition in terms of activity, of interaction with and difference from the material world, and of the generation of value.

What is of considerable importance is that theorists of allegory do not shirk the need to look at both techniques and strategies appropriate for maintaining the activity involved. Recognition of and interaction with the material world necessitates as full an awareness as possible of the ideological and epistemological basis for one's historical involvement, so that one can act with as wide a recognition as possible of the social and political implications of individual, group or state action. Recent theorists of allegory are often dismissed as relativists, put on the deconstructionist junk-heap of weak-minded liberals: particularly by people looking for ends and specific answers. But what allegory offers is long-term effectiveness, skills in the continual activity of life, action and value.

The study continues in part four with a survey of the terms fantasy and allegory, noting the similarity in generic technique yet rather different strategies of mode that each employs within current ideology and epistemology and that cause the critical confusion. A summary is then provided for the radically different rhetorical stances effective in each which go some way to accounting for the divergent readings. Finally the complexity of the issue is taken up in the concluding discussion of women's writings about alternative worlds. The stances of both fantasy and allegory infuse alternative worlds, and this particular group of writings has come in for a large share of the negative and confused criticism which tends to read it as a single well-defined genre. By restricting itself to genre and mode, by neglecting rhetorical stance, this criticism not only denies the probability of allegorical readings but also hides the other face of fantasy, leaving itself open to the dangers of a text controlled blindly by a single ideology. By examing stance, readings of alternative worlds may go on to engage in the historical specificity of the text, and emerge with practical skills relevant to day to day actions.

1 Genre

I THEORIES OF GENRE

Evolution

During the last thirty years, particularly the last fifteen, there has been increasing interest among readers, writers, critics and theorists, in the genres variously called fantasy or allegory. In the process there has been much discussion of the generic make-up of these ways of writing which has been both rigorous and generative. But the discussion has also, at times, been at cross purposes, limiting its own scope with oddly prescriptive statements that claim 'this is not allegory because ... '. Such claims have often been turned to polemic use, as a weapon to bludgeon humanists and non-humanists alike. A development of far greater interest derives from this latter area – the tacitly ignored but highly evident concern with value, politics and literature – which just because it is so ignored often becomes the source for restricting textual activity rather than extending it and opening it up (F: 272)[1].

The present study will address itself to the question of genre, a much neglected but important topic which is a special concern of criticism and theory in this area, and to the relationship of genre with rhetoric. I would suggest that genre, which has been carefully removed by recent theory from the fixed definitions of prescriptive technique to be described in terms of kind and mode against the background of historical, epistemological and ideological strategies, is effected even in that removal in another manner by the stances of rhetorical activity. And I would also suggest that in the rhetorical activity that infuses the generic strategy of kind or mode, a beginning may be made toward a way of discussing politics in the evaluation of writing.

Much of what follows will be based on the interconnection between rhetoric and genre, so to start it is appropriate to outline a brief background to my use of the word 'rhetoric'. Rhetoric is the art of persuasion: such pleasing simplicity of definition has generated many and often opposing interpretations. Its broad application suggests that in the face of the variousness of human beings and their resistance to predictable definition, we all persuade each other, ourselves and the things around us, in all that we do or say. To put it bluntly, without persuasion, without necessary communication, we would not exist. From this wide perspective, rhetoric itself is an elusive topic concerned with the attitude people have to the world which puts into effect the way that they persuade: it is elusive because the moment the attitude is manifested, it has become involved with something other than human beings, in other words it has already become part of a material external world. Pure rhetoric is impossible to describe, although it may be approached through belief. But, in the process of realising itself rhetoric takes on stance and employs strategy, and stance and strategy can be described.

For example, the rhetoric of a piece of writing is intrinsically part of the materiality of language and literature at the moment of its realisation. The belief that underlies the writing has permeated the current ideology and epistemology by means of the activity of its stance. Rhetorical stance is not a static position. From the earliest recorded rhetoricial studies it has been noted that stance involves the rhetor, the audience and the medium into a relationship that, communally taken, is a stance. In language and literature it involves the writer and the reader into the central body of the writing; it manifests a text and in doing so generates value – for all activity generates value. The strategies that a stance manifests are inextricably tied to the history, the epistemology and ideology of the writer and reader. Again, since the earliest rhetorical studies, there has been an insistence upon the combined presence of moral purpose and knowledge in strategy. The value generated by rhetorical stance is different from its moral purpose or knowledge, because these latter are strategies which can be attributed to each of the components involved in the persuasion rather than to the persuasion as a whole. As a result the strategies taken, or perceived to be taken, in a piece of writing may differ wildly/widely from each other even though the techniques used are identical.

During a conversation I once had with an acquaintance concerning some writing by G.K.Chesterton, a number of these aspects became quite clear. Both of us were discussing Chesterton's use of analogy: I perceived the strategy as one of difference, the indication of something impossible to describe by the use of an obviously inadequate comparison, whose stance was one of involvement into the activity of bridging that indescribable gap. For my acquaintance the strategy was one of severance, the removal of the possibility of any link between a humanly conceived comparison and the indescribable; here the stance was one of a contemplative recognition of the impassable gulf between human being and the indescribable. And interestingly, in this case, the belief beyond both stances indicates the impossibility for human beings to sufficiently describe and in doing so, impose upon, the external world.

This is not to say that the use of analogy by another writer would or would not create the same strategy for either myself or another reader. The writer, the writing and we as readers are all open to the accretions and attritions of our current environment. It is worth pointing out now, at the start, that I am not sure whether stance is realised by means of specific techniques and strategies or not – whether the techniques and strategies are inherently more or less likely to manifest one particular stance – although as I shall recount certain techniques and strategies have traditionally been firmly allied with certain stances. This may not be a testable question. The contingency of history may be so pervasive that it is difficult in such a short time span, for example the last 400 years, to know whether metaphor is inherently symbolic and experiential or whether it is just that for the last 400 years we have been historically set to read it in this way. Certainly the medieval reading of analogy as correspondence is radically different from the surrealist and absurdist readings of analogy in the 1920s and 30s. I just don't know whether it is possible to be normative even within one chronological period. And it is quite possible that history makes a mockery of the very phrasing of that question.

It is the strategies and techniques of rhetoric that are most obviously linked with those of genre, and the rigidity of genre definitions is part and parcel of the problems which have faced attitudes to rhetoric since the seventeenth century and have often reduced it to handbooks of techniques alone. The history of those attitudes to rhetoric is becoming fairly well documented (H). What is apparent is that for various reasons the triumvirate of rhetoric, logic and grammar is split up during the 1600s. One key occurrence is the emergence of a dominant rational analytical logic that, partly by its linear progression and partly by its associative internal structure, tends to forget the hypothetical bases for its assumptions, begins to take things 'for granted'. In doing so it becomes a logic that orders but does not test its mode of ordering. Its stance attempts to control the external world through a number of strategies that take its own processes and perceptions as self-evident, and in doing so claims some kind of neutral objectivity in its dealings.

For the relationship between logic and rhetoric the implications are wide. Because the stance denies the need for 'persuasion', logic becomes separated from rhetoric. Because it is assumed that 'truth' is an absolute quantity, a commodity to be acquired by logic alone, rhetoric's persuasion is simply a matter of success and reward gauged by usefulness; or it is demoted to mere ornament or decoration. That rhetoric might lead to knowledge is denied. The implications of this development of logic spread also to poetic. Poetic now can have nothing to do with 'truth' and has no need of logic. By the end of the seventeenth-century, the poetic is often defined either as emotive or as speaking of sublime topics.

The separation has a background in the split between fact and value in moral philosophy and it generates a concept of morality as a rigid code, prescriptive and limiting. From the predominance of a logic aimed at 'truth', emerges the idea of a univocal language with direct reference between word and thing and an exact grammar to match it. Truth is not only an absolute commodity that can be found, but it can also be expressed. For this to be possible the external world must be without any power of its own and neutral. Human beings control it and impose definitions upon it because it displays no resistance, it is simply there to be discovered and codified. As a result value becomes either fact, neutrally objective and ascertainable 'truth', or subjective 'feeling', backing up the split between rhetoric and poetic as the neutralities of factual information and sublime art, and rhetoric and poetic as the questionable persuasions of decoration and emotion. The neutrality of stance that is claimed for the strategies that result, arises from that initial 'forgetting' and taking for granted; but just because of this there is a clear persuasive element to the stance that is based on hiding its initial assumptions. In effect this attitude denies the existence of rhetoric, as the meeting of human being and the world to which the early books of 'commonplace' phrases attest. The world is simply a neutral object that can be documented and finally understood by the accumulation of fact.

At the same time, during the late seventeenth century, definitions for genre which had abounded throughout the preceding two centuries, were encouraged to become prescriptive. And this limitation is shifted during the nineteenth and early twentieth centuries in a manner curiously similar to the history of rhetoric, logic and poetic. The straining toward a useful rhetoric and a pure poetry manifested itself in terms of two distinct analogies.

Analogies for poetic and rhetoric

The nineteenth-century saw, as Alfred Einstein documents in *Music in the Romantic Era*, an enormous amount of commentary on the purity, autonomy and neutrality of music [2]. He notes that Novalis held the final aim of language to be 'its emancipation into music' (345) which is pure 'precisely *because* it could not communicate any notional perceptions' (345), and this idea gained considerable currency through Shelley [3], Poe's essay 'The Poetic Principle'[4] and the famous statement in Pater's *Renaissance* that music and poetry have 'their fortune in the modern world. Let us understand by poetry all literary production which attains the power of giving pleasure by its form as distinct from its matter ... '[5]. The position was consolidated during the early twentieth century by A.C. Bradley whose address 'Poetry for Poetry's Sake' (1901) among other things stresses the need for autonomy, neutrality and purity in poetic as in music and again relates it to its supposedly 'non-representational' notation[6]. George Whalley describes this school of thought as based on 'an error that leaves music conveniently unexamined in order to avoid the incorrigible *im*purity of language' (W: 196). But despite any erroneous base,

the possible purity of language and literature had been firmly
established and later had spin-offs in aspects of imagism or George
Moore's manifesto of 'Pure Poetry' (1924) which had nothing to do
with the musical analogy[7].

Twentieth-century attempts to restore rhetoric to its former
influence began by trying to incorporate logic back into rhetoric.
Ironically, the kind of logic being reintroduced was invariably
rational and analytical and the aim was to keep rhetoric neutral, to
exclude questions of value. The predominant analogy used was
that of map, and indeed the 1971 *Encyclopaedia Britannica* refers to
classical rhetorics, and twentieth-century revivals of them, as
mapped (H: 1). However, during the 1930s and 40s the dominant
motif for rhetoric shifts, courtesy first of John Huizinga and then of
Wittgenstein, into the 'game', and later into its dual roles of use
and pleasure, design and desire. Here the repeated analogy is that
of the chess game, with its own attempted neutrality.   In 1911 de
Saussure, in the *Course in General Linguistics* , makes an explicit
analogy between language and chess, saying that values in both
depend above all else on an unchangeable convention, the set of
rules that exists before a game begins and persists after each move[8].
He goes on to add that while these values are synchronic, both
language and chess also have a diachronic movement which
extends the implications of an action throughout the entire system.
de Saussure himself recognises the weakness of the analogy noting
that in both cases 'human intention' intervenes to emphasise the
difference between synchronic and diachronic; but no clear
distinction is drawn between rule-bound designed response
throughout the diachronic system, and the reactions of intentional
'human' desire.

The main populariser of the image of game for all forms of
human expression from adolescent initiation rites to poetry and
philosophy, was J. Huizinga in *Homo Ludens*. For him the
underlying current of games is the desire to win (HU: 101). One
satisfies this desire in language by conforming to a 'system of play-
rules which fix the range of ideas and symbols to be used' and
which 'presuppose a circle of initiates who understand the
language spoken' (133). Although the realisation of desire needs
megalomania and infatuation, it is never dangerous or harmful
because it is always a game which everyone recognises as such:
'there is always a tacit understanding to take the validity of the

terms and concepts for granted as one does the pieces on a chess-board' (153). Here again the writer does not separate carefully enough the design of the game from the desire of the person. The only thing that maintains the neutrality of game is its exclusion from reality as it is indicated by the stance; yet the effective point about games is their usefulness and their pleasure giving qualities that are necessarily part of our daily lives. At the start of his *Brown Book* Wittgenstein extends the image of chess in a significant way. He says:

> Suppose a man described a game of chess, without mentioning the existence and operation of the pawns. This description of the game as a natural phenomenon will be incomplete. On the other hand we may say that he has completely described a simpler game. In this sense we can say that Augustine's description of learning the language was correct for a simpler language than ours.[9]

Here one not only has the fusion of a man-made game with language – raising by analogy all the questions of what exactly language is, but also the immediate reversal of the analogy by defining them both as 'natural': A technique and an instinct at one and the same time. Lewis Carroll displays the problem in a curiously precise manner in *Alice Through the Looking Glass*, where characters are continually being brought up short and their grammar corrected at the same time as they move from one chess position to the next in rule-bound actions. Both correct grammar and correct moves appear arbitrary and despotic and the characters react with their own wild anarchy. Of course, for Alice it is all a dream. Once again the neutrality of the analogy depends upon its separation from reality.

Yet the ambivalence of the analogy was soon under attack. The two faces of game presented, games as use and as pleasure, have the problem in practice of continually falling off into each other and losing their neutrality. The writings of Plato, who is an insistent figure in the revival of modern rhetoric (H: 21), note the ambivalence within the analogy of the game in *Phaedrus*. There it is suggested that people must continually struggle against the simple gratification of plausible design or of satisfied desire which are both self-based arrogantly essential[10]. They lead to a negative stance, negative because of the limitations that are put on relationship with the world, because they are founded on a denial of rhetoric. An artist, to counter this, must either be mad or dangerous. But another stance, that of the continuous interaction and dialectic of the philosopher, is proposed as an alternative. The ambivalence of the analogy has been taken up by a number of commentators on rhetoric[11], and they have increasingly turned to analogies that do not claim neutrality, that positively reach out to indicate value. In doing so they have also moved toward a recognition of the importance of stance, and of the 'necessity' for indicating and being aware of the value it generates[12].

Analogies for genre

Just as in rhetorical theory, so the criticism and theory of genre in the nineteenth century spawned two attitudes: the first of genre as a map with rigid functions, which A. Fowler has recently called a 'chimera' (F: 248), and the second of genre as non-existent or fused into the purity of poetic[13]. Plato includes in his discussion of the limitations of rhetoric, comments on the effects of such analogies that extend also to genre. In *Phaedrus* Socrates' discussion of 'writing' concentrates on the stasis of negative stances. If literary genre is limited to technical elements alone it does indeed become mapped, static and lacking the ability to engage each unique audience. Literature with no conventions, even if it were possible, would be similarly isolated and unable to communicate. Works must be able to allow the audience to engage actively or they will remain either permanently closed and incommunicable, or so conventional that they tie themselves inextricably to an ideology, becoming inaccessible to later readers.

These analogies of map and purity have moved quickly to the idea of genre as a game. Some theorists such as Northrop Frye perceive the game as ritual, satisfying desire by putting words and structure into a recognisable form (FR: 99); and others define generic elements specifically as the way desire is manifested (J: 8). The design aspects have also been emphasised in the analogy of problem-solving models (G and F: 31) that are functional (F: 38), and again in the analogy of the chess game (H and F) – although in this latter analogy Fowler indicates some of the limitations when he suggests that we need to know who is playing in order to extend and clarify the game (F: 49). But the chess game has the double accretion of the analogy of *langue* and *parole* which in one direction has developed into areas of linguistic theory. In this respect it is interesting that Winterowd, who sees rhetoric as a mediator between pleasure and 'reality'[14], has suggested that the strategies of rhetoric may be fundamentally linked to the positive deep structures of Chomskyean linguistic theory[15]; at the same time M.L. Ryan notes that the study of deep-structure constraints may indicate the rhetorical strategies that bind together grammatic, semantic and surface rules into generic options[16].

In turning to the model of the game, these theories turn implicitly toward rhetorical strategy but tend to neglect stance. The early writings of Wayne Booth, significantly situated rhetoric and poetic together in a positive stance[17], and presented genre as consisting of continually flexible patterns of expectation and gratification neither static nor arbitrary. *The Rhetoric of Fiction* argues that genre sets a specific distance between writer and reader without which understanding and value is lost[18]. Other recent studies of genre have begun to move away from the dual neutrality of game and incorporate an understanding of the evaluative activity of genre particularly in their study of the activity of 'modes'. But modes are a central problem in genre theory at the present. There is considerable disagreement about what a mode is, about how it differs, or indeed if it differs, from generic kind. These questions lead to others concerning the distinction between intrinsic and extrinsic aspects of genre, between form and structure. Can a literary or linguistic element survive historical shift, and if it does, does this imply that genres evolve? Evolution is a primary analogy in genre description but the implications are rarely discussed. If the analogy is to be taken seriously we should ask: Is genre a biological thing, can it be inherited, how can we deal with the consequent determinism and the social implications of the structure and hierarchy of genres that result?

Because the rest of this essay concerns modern allegory and fantasy, and because most of the critical and theoretical studies of these writings are wrapped up in concern with genre, I have concentrated on writers in this field. A bias will obviously be created by this decision and I hope that readers will remain attentive to it, but it is my intention to try to understand more about genre by way of specific readings within allegory and fantasy.

As T. Todorov has pointed out in his study of the fantastic which begins with a commentary on the genre theory of N. Frye, all such theory founds itself on the one or two aspects that the critic or theorist finds most important. Most theorists of genre are in agreement only upon the denial of the claim that there are no genres, because to write in a manner different from previous writings you need a norm from which to depart (T: 24, F: 18, G: 119). Within that framework the significance accorded to such a norm varies widely. Despite Todorov's insistence on the need to indicate one's point of departure, his own presentation of verbal, syntactic and semantic norms means that any historical or social importance to be derived from careful reading, is implicit rather than explicit. A. Fowler is more definite and speaks about the role of literary norms to either challenge or answer society's needs (F: 17). Northrop Frye, in *The Secular Scripture* and elsewhere, relates generic norms specifically to 'social function' (FR2: 8). But as we shall see the emphasis laid by each critic upon the structural or social aspect of genre, has little to do with the tendency each has toward theory or history. The attitude toward 'norms' has an immediate effect upon the theorists, and they all adjust the concept of genre to lie in accordance with it. In *Anatomy of Criticism* Frye suggests that naive and sentimental literature, which he later describes as popular, is in closest accordance with the norms; it is conventional. Todorov echoes this idea, straightforwardly stating that popular literature is pure convention, the complete norm. Other writers shift the distinctions and claim that popular literature in effect represents the only pure genre[19], but in distinct contrast A. Fowler says that writing only has literary significance and generic import if it has been modified or altered, hence popular writing is neither generic nor literary.

The persistent problem underlying discussions of a norm, is the question of how the writer, reader and the writing itself, relate to it. Genre is clearly not a static presence; it changes with individual history. On the other hand it is just as clearly not arbitrary, otherwise it would not be chosen by a writer or interacted with in specific ways by the reader. In a vocabulary that attains retrospective significance Kenneth Burke pointed out the dual problem, first of the manipulation of the reader's (and writer's) desires by genre, and second of the individuation of universal forms which brings them into jeopardy[20]. Burke goes on to discuss the position of forms in general within the complexities of rhetorical stance. And it is here in the relationship between rhetoric and genre, that the theorists begin to express their differences.

Developing Burke's line of argument, Frye perceives genre as a presentation. Genre describes the 'possibility' of form within a rhetorical situation (FR1: 94), but the idea is not taken further into discussion of the specific interaction of reader, writer and writing in either *Anatomy of Criticism* or *The Secular Scripture* although one or two other theorists have attempted to do so (JA1). However the result for Frye is that his writing does emphasise strategy at the expense of stance. Seizing on this lack of development Todorov takes Frye to task for imposing his proposed genres on writing, and says that works manifest genres rather than exist in any particular one. By doing so he opens up the way for a full study of rhetorical interaction, even though he confines himself to the workings of the fantastic. The problems of definition that result from Frye's emphasis mean that description of genre shuttles continually between its practical effects and its theoretical abstraction (T: 26). In a rather different manner Fowler suggests that works are modifying genres rather than 'being' them. Here it is implicit that strategy is more important than stance, and indeed for Fowler, genre cannot be fully rhetorical for two reasons: first, he defines rhetoric primarily in terms of strategy even though his definition of genre as a combination of value and epistemological desire runs close to the classical definitions of rhetoric as a combination of moral purpose and knowledge (F: 16). And second, he states that literary genres are not discourse because discourse deals with words not works, and there is an extensive group of writings that are not works and have no genres (17), but are legitimately subjects for study by rhetoric.

Commenting more precisely on the rhetorical structure of the relationship between reader and writer Robert Scholes has said that genre indicates an author's 'position' (S), Frye notes that it indicates the author's 'intention' (FR1: 79) and E.D. Hirsch claims that it manifests the 'will and intention' of the writer (HI1: 101). For Hirsch, the reader responds to genre as to a guide to correct interpretation (86), and Fowler extends this by restating that genre conveys an authorial privilege of meaning that the reader does not complete (F: 268). These attitudes, by default or design, limit the relationship of rhetoric and genre to the technical or the strategic.

But Claudio Guillen, in suggesting that a genre provides a 'history of changing theoretical systems' (G: 134), looks on it both as a reader searching backward for form which when found achieves authority, and as a writer looking forward to form to achieve expression (109). He suggests an 'interaction model' rather than a 'domination model' (507), the former leading to genre being defined as 'institutions', 'contracts' between a writer and his readers (JA1: 135).

In *Genesis of Secrecy*, Frank Kermode takes up several of the implications of this idea and separates between institutional and spiritual readings. The former treats genre as a constraint upon interpretation (K: 18) that ensures 'value' (53) by calling upon the authority of the institution. Yet this 'value', although similar to the defined canonical value in Fowler's scheme, indicates by its prevalence the ideological pressure toward an individual desire for closure, for fixed and formal genre. In studying it Kermode uncovers a series of stances that underlie generic strategy; however, the implication in the writing is that spiritual readings can avoid the constraints of genre. Whether these readings interact with genre in a different manner, or what kind of stances are involved in them, is left vague and elusive.

Behind these diversions of opinion is a long-running argument over the status of theoretical and historical studies of genre, which returns us to the question of norms. Theoretical writings are supposed to concentrate on synchronic aspects of genre, the stable identifiable aspects that allow one to classify a work. In contrast, historical writings focus on diachronic aspects that present a chronological sequence of works. The synchronic/diachronic vocabulary runs hand in hand with the theoretical/historical throughout the literature although the partnership develops subtle complications. In effect each writer is aware of the dichotomy and attempts to reconcile the two sides, even though the attempts may tend toward one or the other direction – but this does not stop considerable in-fighting. Fowler castigates Kermode for the activity of completion allowed to the reader (F: 266) because he believes in the historical determinism of a work, yet he also criticises Hirsch for the fixity of the 'heuristic' form of his genre. Hirsch himself goes out of his way to underline the 'arbitrary' nature of heuristic forms, comparing them to Frye's which he perceives as 'constitutive' (HI1: 111). Frye is also accused by

Todorov of being theoretical rather than historical. Yet Christine Brooke-Rose corrects Todorov and says that the archetypes are in effect historical, and F. Jameson reiterates this point of view, although pointing to the ease with which Frye may be read as theoretical (JA1: 156). And although Frye does indeed present the archetypes as historical and does claim that his genres explore the 'possible', he moves toward the theoretical in the rhetoric of his work.

Todorov's analysis of the obscured assumptions in Frye's *Anatomy of Criticism* demonstrates this tendency all too clearly, as does the assertive vocabulary with which Frye criticises the very tautological and assertive style he exhibits (FR1: 17, 18, 19, 36, etc.). Todorov himself claims to have fused the theoretical and historical into 'genres théoriques complexes' (T: 26) by treating theory itself as history. Guillen and Jameson are even more explicit in their fusion of the two: the former emphasises the literary system which is historically stable but chronologically changing, and the latter suggests that genres form historically defined generic systems (diachronic) into which the genre of the work itself (synchronic) emerges.

By way of Althusser's re-structuring of Marxist theory, Jameson is able to present a three-fold discussion of reading, the third part of which is specific to genre. He argues that the classic base-superstructure division caters specifically to a synchronic-diachronic paradox. Althusser's argument for a systematic rather than existential mode of production allows for a 'new synchronic' that incorporates the diachronic movement of chronicled happenings in time, with the more synchronic sense of 'constitutive tension and struggle between classes'. The 'new synchronic', incorporating both, is history – but history cannot be perceived without mediation and genre provides that mediation, the:

> field of force in which the dynamics of sign systems of several distinct modes of production can be registered and apprehended ... *ideology of form*, that is, the determinate contradiction of the specific messages emitted by the various sign systems which co-exist in a given artistic process as well as in its general social formation. (JA2: 99)

This provides for formal processes of the literary genre to be considered as 'sedimented content in their own right' (99).

The analogy that most of these critics employ to describe their perception of the theory/history, synchronic/diachronic dichotomy is one of genus and species, and the predominantly evolutionary interpretations that arise reflect their various dilemmas. Claudio Guillen separates the Renaissance concept of fixed forms from his own attempt at literary system by initially commenting on the Renaissance idea of 'a species resulting from the introduction of certain particulars or differentiae into the genus' (G: 117). Hence the genus is static and fixed; one simply adds to or subtracts from it. Guillen also suggests that we call such forms, which he designates as lyric, dramatic and narrative, 'universals', reserving genus for a 'structural model' that will evolve not 'as the evolution of independant norms, nor as the survival of timeless 'structure' ', but as the history of changing theoretical systems' (134). In other words he displaces the question of change to a much broader historical canvas, that makes it more difficult to assess whether generic structures are immutable or simply very long-lived. Paul Hernadi makes a similar point about genre having very little in common with the 'unequivocal classification of species' (4), yet he betrays his bias toward such classification when he goes on to draw an analogy with Darwin's discussion of the species 'subject to change' (HE: 41) which needed the prior existence of the Linnaen system.

Rather than renaming genus, Hirsch shifts the analogy from genus and species to species and variety. Genre is not stable but neither is it arbitrary and variable. A literary work is specific to experience but still thought of as a genre, 'just as variety is subsumed under a species' (HI1: 77). Here the opposite movement has occurred, and Hirsch has displaced the question of change to a smaller scale to minimise the importance of variation. Fowler follows Hirsch and when he discusses the necessity for genre to evolve he says that they must do so 'like a biological species', which has a relatively circumscribed existence in both space and time (F: 166).

Todorov explicitly denies to writing the concept that he claims pervades the scientific concept of genus and species. He notes that the birth of a tiger will not alter the species but that in art 'toute oeuvre encore modifie l'ensemble des possibles, chaque nouvel exemple change l'espèce' (T: 10). This note points up the assumption prevalent throughout the discussions of other theorists that evolution is saltationist rather than continually variable. But even Todorov doesn't really move very far in this critical direction. Along with the other critics he speaks as if evolution were a matter of inherited 'codes' as Fowler suggests (F: 39); and there is virtually no attention to the analogy of Lamarckian evolution, the inheritance of acquired characteristics, that would appear to be far more suitable particularly to writers who wish to emphasise the historical. Further, there is absolutely no indication whatsoever of the enormous contradictions that exist in such analogy, even within the biochemical study of it, and which make that study into a subtle and generative field[21].

F. Jameson is one of the few writers to attempt to jettison the evolutionary analogy. In an early article he separates genres from 'universals', and goes on to deny that an individual work relates to genre as a species 'belongs to' a genus (JA: 153); rather an individual work emerges into the generic system which is a '*combinatoire*' capable of 'transforming' both and realising a historical situation that makes a literary work semi-autonomous. However, despite this shift toward a mathematical analogy, Jameson returns, in *The Political Unconscious*, at the most crucial moments to the the evolutionary. Not only is generic form 'sedimented content', but as we shall come to later, it is the secreted exoskeleton of a fossil. What Jameson is interested in is the geological remains, the archeological artifact, not the process of change.

Just so, the few non-evolutionary analogies for genre, tend toward mathematics as though it can yield a flexible web, a matrix, that is nevertheless anchored at each radial point to provide stability. Frye situates his entire Anatomy within a mathematical universe that contains the world 'within itself' (FR1: 352). The straining toward an analogy of materiality, either for history or for the individual desire, which is also evident in Frank Kermode's suggestion that the materiality of language itself, its religious import, is best described 'by algebra' (K: 127), leads the writers to neglect the Cartesian methodology of the presuppositions behind the mathematics they employ.

The dilemmas that these analogies push forward become extremely complicated when translated into the current discussions about the activity of mode within genre and the related analogy of *langue* and *parole* which many of these critics specifically

ally with genus and species (F, H). Modes have been introduced
into genre theory specifically to cope with the problem that to
speak of genres one seems to need to speak of essential things
although everyone recognises that they continually change. But
quite what they are or what they do is a moot point.

A. Fowler speaks at length about what modes can do but never
quite clarifies how they do it. In distinction from kind, modes are
'substantive', internal, dealing with attitude, purpose, tone,
subject and audience (F: 55). They are 'adjectival' terms that may
amount to no more than 'fugitive admixtures'; they are
'structurally dependent' having no individual existence. Yet
despite this fusion 'even modes are subject to mutability' (111). In
contrast a writer like F. Jameson treats them as ahistorical. They
are 'a temptation and a mode of expression'. Guillen calls them
creative universals from the poet's 'elementary modes of
experience' (G: 118). All in all, quite a range of elusive not to say
ambivalent suggestions.

Substantial confusion can arise from this ambivalence, and in
my own attempt to understand the implications of mode I turn to
its place in the broader generic systems that are being discussed,
although as the quantity of 'appears' 'seems' 'possibly' and
'perhaps' will indicate, I am far from a resolution of the issues. To
start with an indication of the depth of confusion possible, take first
the systems of Guillen and Hernadi. Guillen initially defines modes
as the 'universals' of lyric, dramatic and narrative, contrasting
them to genres which may be 'modified' because they are historical
(G: 118). But the concluding essay in his collection *Literature as
System* distinguishes between genre: 'like comedy, or a lyric form, or
the historical novel'; mode 'like irony and satire'; theme; and
rhetoric or device of style (503). The looping of previously defined
'universals' back into genre and the lack of definition for the new
concept of mode make it extremely difficult to understand the
interrelationship of genre, mode, theme and style, within the total
synchronic/diachronic study of literature as system.

Another four section system is proposed by Hernadi, who
incidentally provides diagrams of several other systems such as
Frye's but not one for his own. In this case the sections comprise
mode of discourse, which is thematic, dramatic, narrative and
lyric; perspective, which is authorial, interpersonal, dual or
private; scope, which is concentric, kinetic or ecumenic; and mood,

which is tragic, comic or tragicomic. The first thing to be noticed is that even if one suggests Guillen's 'system' corresponds vaguely with Hernadi's use of 'genre' and forgets the 'names' of their individual sections, Guillen's section one contains components of Hernadi's sections one and four and that Hernadi's section one contains only one component from Guillen's section one and completely subsumes section three. No Venn diagram *could* be built, no sets and subsets suggested. There is no way that you can map Guillen's system onto Hernadi's with any significant degree of overlap. Possibly because Hernadi's approach appears to function completely out side Guillen's concept of historical materiality, there is no hope even of attempting to compare the two systems.

Luckily not all systems are so mutually obstructive. Jameson, again working from Althusser's idea of structural causality, appears to suggest specific differences in kind of activity between mode and genre that operate in the historical interrelationship of individual work and generic complex. A mode, in contrast to a genre, is not a 'given type of verbal artifact' nor 'bound to the conventions of a given age' (JA1: 151); it is a 'formal possibility' and not specifically historical. The mode is primarily semantic and governs 'internal questions', whereas genre has to do with the syntactical laws and requirements of a fixed form. R. Jackson, who quotes extensively from Jameson's article, interprets this as a distinction between structure and form. The mode has 'structural features underlying various works in different periods of time' (J: 7). While the distinction between structure as something knitted to meaning and form as convention drained of meaning is helpful, especially with some other writers, Jameson specifically separates mode from syntactic elements and implies that if 'structural features' are at work they are not identifiable as literary strategies. In Jackson's suggestion that genres 'emerge' from modes, there is an unhappy simplification of the activity in Jameson's thought. It seems as though Jackson has fused genre with 'individual work' and mode with 'generic complex', leaving out the 'how' of the interrelationship, or at least leaving it implicit and hence open to ambiguity or even ambivalence.

However, the suggestion that mode is structural and that fixed genre is formal, is widely if variously accepted: as is the separation between individual work and generic complex. In Fowler's *Kinds of Literature* there is a detailed and careful attempt to account for the definitions and modulations of genre as a whole. 'Kinds' are not fixed but they are definitely synchronic, specific to each historical period; they are formal and external including features such as metre and 'structure'. The use of 'structure' here appears to be similar to that of form in Jackson and Jameson, since it refers to syntactical elements and since Fowler also posits a third category of 'constructional types' which are purely formal in a syntactical sense. Modes, as noted above, are substantive, internal, to do with purpose, subject and tone. Yet although they have no individual existence and are dependent upon 'structure' or form, it is unclear whether the dependence is one of symbiosis or synergy, relationship or interrelationship. In other words does (as I suspect here) the form exist as a kind of climbing frame for the mode, vine-like, to penetrate, or is the shape and colour and texture, the material existence of the frame immanent with mode.

In each case it is difficult to distinguish between form and mode, either because Fowler has not specifically suggested a way of recognising mode on its own or because it is intrinsically part of form itself. The activity of constructional types tends to fade away quite quickly after their initial introduction. But Fowler moves on to enlarge on subgenre as the fourth category and suggests that generic change occurs either through hybrid kinds created by subgenre additions, or modal transformation which acts by subtracting specific elements. At this stage, however, the lack of distinction between features of mode and those of form makes it extremely difficult to separate between the two types of change, although Fowler's description of *Amoretti 64* as 'amatory in mode, Elizabethan sonnet in kind, of the blazon subgenre' and of the constructional type 'the collection' (F: 56), is an admirable and helpful attempt at delineation. The problem here may be that the finer workings of these four elements are not laid out in enough detail, possibly through lack of space, but it is undeniable that the idea of accurately delineating 'amatory' is forbidding.

Despite a fairly broad agreement each of these writers relates structure and form, mode and genre, individual work and generic complex in a different manner. Hirsch with his emphasis on authorial determinism, speaks of intrinsic genre as ahistorial, as 'that sense of the whole by means of which an interpreter can correctly understand any part in its determinacy' (F: 86). This could be allied with the insistence on mode as intrinsic, and with the idea of mode as substantive or even as universal. Extrinsic genres which have been defined as fixed forms, are linked by Hirsch to the 'wrong guess', the formal possibility that is an incorrect interpretation of authorial intention. Hirsch also suggests correspondences for the historical status of both individual work and generic system, the former being the particular determination at the end of each interpretation and the latter being his 'heuristic' type which enables the interpreter historically to place and assess the 'Importance of an implication' (HI1: 98) derived from an intrinsic genre. Depending upon the individual theorist's point of view, corresponding ideas each suggest different ways in which the individual work is realised, manifested, modified or interpreted. Todorov, for example, sees the manifestation of genre *as* genre, in other words genre *as* mode, possibly derived from the 'va et vient continuelle entre la déscription des faits et la théorie en son abstraction' (T: 26) which is the individual work as best it can be delineated by 'non-literary' critical language.

What is significant about mode is that it consistently provides the location for the movement, strain or tension away from fixed form. And it is here that the discussion is carried out in terms decidedly not part of 'non-literary' language. Fowler's 'normative' concept of genre, his 'kinds', vary not only with 'substantive' qualities of mode but more importantly with 'values, and ultimately with views of the world' (F: 16). For Hirsch the intrinsic genre is the source of authorial 'will', and the only way that validity in interpretation can be achieved (HI1: 86). Guillen's creative universals are 'elementary modes of experience, of action and reaction in the world' (G: 118). And Jameson's modes are not only 'temptations' but also substitutions of experience for the individual work in question (JA1: 137). And in each case there is a movement away from strategy toward stance and value.

Jameson is one of the few who attempts to account for this experience of value, although Hirsch in *The Aims of Interpretation* attempts to do so by reintroducing the fact and value split, insisting that values are specific things that have fixed causes, and inevitably paving the way, or rather retreading the road, to morality as a rigid code of prescriptive rules that make value and quality sterile. On the other hand, Jameson defines genre studies as active relationships of similarity and difference. For him the generic complex does not cause the work but limits the '*conditions of* possibility of its existence' (JA1: 158). For Hirsch this is tantamount to a relativistic theory, and it is ironic that the structural probabilities that lie beyond this definition should have been held by Frye to have the opposite effect of closure and fixity. An analogy like 'structure' has ambivalent tendencies to both the arbitrary and the absolute, particularly in a statistical and probabilistic framework which is often interpreted as providing the data for the most likely fixed case rather than maintaining a set of probable occurrences. But as Todorov notes, structure is not empirical and diagrammatic but a way of speaking about abstract structure, and hence about the probabilities of a situation. In effect Frye is aware of this. He calls genre a study in possibilities of form; and says of it that noticing such analogies 'forms a large part of our actual experience of literature, whatever its role in criticism' (FR1: 95).

The dilemma is one that Hirsch attempts to address in his more recent Bateson Lecture of 1983, putting the question 'how can meaning be historically constrained by an author's original intention, yet not be limited to the contents of that original intention?' (HI2: 82) He proposes that 'mental content must be considered provisional, whereas referential intent remains rigidly fixed to whatever the referred-to-reality will turn out to be' (87). The enigmatic phrasing of that final verb indicates what Hirsch concludes is a 'trans-mental dimension of reference' (97) which he argues is effected by allegory in connecting fiction with truth. However, the lecture itself does not pursue the detailed procedure of this transcendent allegory. Jameson addresses the same dilemma in different terms as 'This unacceptable option, or ideological double bind, between antiquarianism and modernising "relevance" or projection' (J2: 18). Curiously, he too turns to allegory, but not as a transcendent referent. Rather he emphasises the allegorical immanence of a 'fundamental history': 'the collective struggle to wrest a realm of freedom from a realm of Necessity' (19), that combines respect for the specificity of the past with a solidarity of the 'polemics and passions' within the present day (18). But neither theorist describes an adequate account of value or of stance. Jameson at one point declares that value is, like history, an absence, but spends much of his time searching for the fossilised remains of action, just as Hirsch seeks truth through fiction: both seek for 'things' rather than activities of value, or stance.

To summarise: The problem has been based on the paradox that genres may be recognised as abstractable forms yet tend to shift and change, even to resist recognition, within history. Genres seem to have both synchronic and diachronic aspects. But if they are recognisable how may they be spoken of, and if they change how do they do so? That they might be immutable has been called into question since the Renaissance, and so one asks: are they simply part of current ideology in which case their semantic and syntactic aspects are 'normative'. Further, if they are normative, what does this imply in terms of the relationship between writer, reader and writing? Are these relationships governed by history, by ideology or epistemology? And if so, why do so many theorists – even materialist theorists – think of mode as non-epistemological, pre-ideological and to do with value? There has been a tendency to pay lip-service to the historical aspects yet to stress the effect of the writer: as if ideology were always on the side of the writer and as if it had some fixed meaning. The constant emphasis in genre theory, although it is explored in other theoretical discourses, on the reader's 'need to know the conventions' completely disregards the difficulty of recuperation on the part of the reader. But more important than this, it disregards questions of evaluation and of political effect. Fowler states that the 'best readers' will find a construction 'faithful to the original' (F: 263); and Hirsch insists that the whole process of interpretation is to find the 'will' of the author. Yet other explorations of the reader's active role in reading tend to undermine the possiblity of genre itself.

The relationship between writer, reader and writing in these terms depends in the end upon what one thinks of history, ideology and epistemology. For example, Hirsch and Fowler believe that the institution or canon is recuperable. Whereas for Kermode, the institution or canon is only recuperable as an ideological presentation of another ideology. If you take the former you imply that we can know, not just understand, the definiteness of history, and hence it is possible to emphasise the role of the writer as author. But if you take the latter you need to consider whether one can have a non-ideological or a radically different ideological presentation of another ideology. In either case the reader is put in an entirely different relationship to writer and writing, than to author and book.

I personally do not believe that it is possible to know the material actuality of historical events, although I believe in its occurrence and can attempt to understand it. But the very activity of understanding, standing under and propping up with one's ideas, is subject to ideological and epistemological shift. Having taken this position, the relationship between reader, writer and writing becomes either a question of specific definition, which may be useful as long as one recognises that one is operating within an arbitrary system of absolutes, but which fails to address the problem of generic change; or it becomes a question of avoiding generic definition, which means not only that one cannot address the question of generic recognition but also implies that one cannot speak of or communicate experience of writing at all; or thirdly it becomes a question of the nature of interaction between the three, the politics of the active genre of the text which may best be approached through mode.

The broad interest in and discussion of mode in all of these theorists, is an indication that, despite their avowed positions in some cases, they handker after discussion of genre in these last terms of interaction. Indeed much of the confusion in certain writers may stem from a tension toward the very aspects they overtly reject. Their attempts to relate synchronic and diachronic, theory and history, point to a fundamental paradox of our times: that such things are considered separate in the first place when most people, if pressed, will agree that they impinge upon each other. But if we are to discuss mode, can we do so in slightly less confusing terms? I would suggest that we can, and that to do so we need to turn to rhetoric, with its traditional concern for possibility and probability in terms of quality rather than sophistical plausibility and success; and to the overriding interest of rhetorical stance in questions of value and political action to which each definition of mode, no matter how elusive, eventually turns.

2 GENRE IN FANTASY AND ALLEGORY

The question of mode and how one discusses it is of great importance to critics and theorists concerned with fantasy and allegory. Nearly the only point of agreement among those interested in these writings is the insistence that whatever else they are or do, they have some connection with 'mode'. And even among those who are not specifically concerned with genre theory there is considerable disagreement over the use of the word 'mode', despite an overriding concern with the flexible and elusive activity it signifies. Among the theorists of genre Rosemary Jackson calls fantasy a mode 'from which a number of related genres emerges' (J: 7); and A. Fowler uses allegory as a primary example of 'modulation' (F: 191). Writers specifically concerned with allegory frequently define it as a mode: Gay Clifford notes that it is 'a mode, and capable of subsuming many genres and forms' (C: 5) and Angus Fletcher calls it a 'modal concept' (FL: 1). Just so, Brooke-Rose describes the fantastic within a discussion of Frye's 'modes', as 'not so much an evanescent *genre* as an evanescent *element*' (BR: 63) and Jameson explicitly refers to fantasy as a 'mode' (JA1: 137–140). But there is an imbalance. On the whole it does appear far easier to define fantasy as a generic kind than allegory. This difference is one of the central perplexities of the issue.

In each case the word 'mode' is used in an approving sense, as if to justify the writing being discussed. But the use of the words fantasy and allegory, in the ways that they have become more and more common since World War II, indicates no such consistent evaluation. Various reasons emerge for the growing libraries of books on these topics. It has been suggested that allegory is reaction against the New Criticism (KR); but there is also the suggestion that allegory is a reading of readings, writing of writings (Q) which reflects the linguistic and literary consciousness of the twentieth century, or the suggestion that fantasy starts as a maintenance of pure literature and becomes developed into games and theories of games and desire. Both of these ideas will be discussed in more detail later. Within theories of allegory, apart from earlier work such as C.S. Lewis's *The Allegory of Love*, which certainly alerted readers to the existence of allegory, the first main works were by E. Honig and A. Fletcher in 1957 and 1964 respectively, and were followed in the seventies with a blossoming of related writing. Similarly one finds Tolkien and Huizinga writing in 1937 and 1949 respectively. But it is the enormous popularity of fantasy writing, especially *The Lord of the Rings* in the 60s, and Todorov's book in 1967, that really set things off. Todorov's stab in the dark coalesces and stimulates ideas and reactions in all the recent substantial studies of fantasy, except Manlove's which is not so theoretical, and Northrop Frye's *The Secular Scripture* which, strictly speaking, is about romance, although as we shall discover there are many overlaps between fantasy and romance.

The Critics
But it is the criticism of specific literary works that demonstrates most clearly the extent of the confusion surrounding the terms. For example M. Hodgart classifies *Animal Farm* within 'the genre of allegory, since it has a point to point correspondence with the events of Russian history from 1917 to 1943'[22]. But another recent study claims that it is the ironic allegory in *Animal Farm* that gives it its scope, lifts it out of easy simplistic correspondences[23]. Both C. Small and A. Zwerdling who are concerned with criticism of Orwell's work rather than with definition of terms, decide that *Nineteen Eighty-Four* has primarily to do with fantasy, and that this by itself is unsatisfactory. The former suggests that it is a parody at the same time as being a fantasy[24], and the latter that the fantasy elements only support Orwell's negative criticism and leave his alternatives without support (196). The differences in terminology would not be of much interest in themselves, but judgments are being conveyed by way of words. It is as if the definitions, simply as definitions, pass judgment and are in effect capable of limiting or extending the reading. Yet it is not at all clear that people are disagreeing about the same thing let alone discussing the same thing in different terms.

I have discussed these particular confusions in detail in *George Orwell: The Search for a Voice*. To some extent that book explores a set of practical textual examples for many of the more theoretical issues discussed here, and certainly provides much of the impetus behind my own research. *Animal Farm* does indeed yield a point to point correspondence with the events of the Russian Revolution. Yet even as a satire its metaphorical structure raises questions about its literary form and its processes at the same time as presenting a version of the complex movement of party politics. But the book also functions in broader allegorical terms by discussing the interaction between personal and party politics and the communication that that interaction depends on, by establishing a fundamental separation between the strategies involved within the text itself. The interaction of those strategies provides a guide to or an active analogy for the communication it sees as central (H2: 165).

For example, a primary strategy is that of the fairy story genre which is established early through the sub-title of the book and the conventions of the initial chapters. Gradually the plot of the book calls these conventional literary expectations into question – people do not get the rewards they should and so on – alerting the reader to the issues that are being underlined. Even more explicitly the function of the pastoral scene after the animals' 'confessions' illustrates how the interaction of literary strategies within the text points to different ways of reading. The pastoral can be read as a true pastoral of reassessment in which case it could simply and legitimately conclude a rather negative fairy story. It can also be read ironically, as a more complex fantasy providing an escape into nostalgia by self-deceiving animals. Or it can be read allegorically, concentrating on the reflexivity of the language and structure, as a failed pastoral which succeeds in analysing and commenting on its failure, by establishing the difference in kind between the knowledge and communicating capabilities of the human reader and those of the animals. Read in the first way it will be unsatisfactory, in the second rewarding but cynical, and only in the third will a movement toward positive action be made.

The effect these readings point up is that a single technique can initiate not only different generic modes, but also indicate different rhetorical stances. In a similar manner Orwell's *Nineteen Eighty-Four* often generates the criticism that it is a fantasy about what may go wrong with the state of Britain and western humanism in general. These readings are inevitably pessimistic and allow the readers to condemn the book as 'gloomy', 'sado-masochistic' and so on (H2: 9). without acknowledging that such a judgment implicitly involves the readers who make it by indicating their unwillingness to look for alternatives or to make assessments about the events. By the same token the book also generates much positive commentary that focuses on the implications of its textual strategies that indicate the things that go wrong with the system and how we may face, assess and change them. What will concern me in the critical and philosophical body of this essay and its literary epilogue, is why these different readings emerge and how the vocabulary of genre, mode and rhetorical stance can help in evaluating our readings of such works.

It is also helpful to comment on a work that is contentious in a different way, that arouses mockery and sneers rather than scorn and anger: *The Lord of the Rings*. It is still fair to say with Colin Manlove but ten years on, that 'for most people he [Tolkien] and what they think of as fantasy are synonymous' (M1: 156), yet there is a growing contingent of readers who speak of *The Lord of the Rings* in particular as an allegory. At the same time, there are a number of critics who use *The Lord of the Rings* to illustrate by absence what both fantasies or allegories are *not*. Many of these writers also use the definitions and illustrations as ways of commenting back upon the relationship between the terms fantasy and allegory. And each of these skirmishes is encircled by often hidden and obscured values that lead to the 'conflicting theories' that Bloomfield notes as early as 1963 (B: 161), and have developed in some cases into battles royal as in Jackson's attack on 'humanist' criticism. There are two things here: first I am not trying to be rigidly didactic but to avoid the destruction and restriction of critical warfare; second, I would like to clarify some of the political values inherent in these attacks. Indeed it is noteworthy that in this area of both theory and criticism, many of the unstated but deeply felt political motivations/aspirations/beliefs of literary commentators rise to the surface and play a more obvious role than usual within accounts of genre.

The Lord of the Rings is generally classified as a fantasy. But the reasons for doing so are many and varied, and dominant among them is the opposition made to allegory. In *Tolkien Scholar and Storyteller*, Davie insists that the work is not an allegory because of its 'magic' (D: 266), its enchantment; it completely avoids rigid allegorical emblem (284); yet it is this element of 'magic' that throws forward other contradictory statements. Jackson denies that *The Lord of the Rings* is a fantasy on the grounds of that magic, saying that this specificity places it among the marvellous accounts and out of the realm of the fantastic (J: 9); but A. Wilson denies that it is a fantasy on precisely the opposite grounds that there is no magic in the book – it relates firmly to the external world and is relevant and meaningful (W1: 79). Both these writers are negatively critical of *The Lord of the Rings* because it is not a fantasy and only an allegory, yet there are many who treat it as an allegory and derive considerable comfort from the apparently explicit relation it maintains with either historical, psychological, political or religious events in the real world[25].

The question of realism or non-realism leads to another focus of critical embattlement: In contrast to Wilson and others, both Reilly and Kelly in the Isaacs and Zimbardo collection, *Tolkien and the Critics*, claim that *The Lord of the Rings* presents things definitely not in the 'primary' world [26]; it reminds us of the 'unreal'[27] or as Reilly suggests elsewhere of the 'super-real'[28]. In this it is specifically not allegorical, for allegory deals with relations to the real world, and is rationally reductive[29]. Directly contradicting parts of this definition but upholding others, Brooke-Rose and Helme claim that it is because allegory is indeed related to the real that *The Lord of the Rings* is in fact close to allegory (BR: 254), for it tends toward realism[30]. Others such as Brewer define *The Lord of the Rings* in contrast to 'realistic' allegory, concluding that because it is 'unrealistic' it is not fantasy but romance (BRE: 250); yet Manlove claims that it is fantasy precisely because it derives from romance and is not an allegorical fable which makes a 'rigid skeleton' (M1: 168).

The element of romance points us to another contentious quality of *The Lord of the Rings*: its concern with wish-fulfilment and sentiment. Spacks notes this with reprobation[31] and says that it diminishes the weight of Tolkien's 'fable' (97), but for Helme it is a positive attribute, although it has to be handled with strong self-discipline[32]. In complete contrast, the introduction to *Tolkien and the Critics* suggests that *The Lord of the Rings* is both without wish-fulfilment, without fixed meanings of consolation, and *therefore* an allegory: thus reversing many of the suggested definitions for allegory as well as several dominant readings, and placing it close to Jackson's 'fantastic'. Indeed Brooke-Rose overtly claims that modern fantasy is derived from medieval allegory (BR: 66), even though her definition of allegory shifts as the criticism moves into the modern period (254).

D. Brewer, W. Davie and T. Shippey, each reviewing *The Lord of the Rings* in a single commemorative collection *Tolkien: Scholar and Storyteller*, provide a succinct example of the criticism engendered by fantasy writing. Both Brewer and Davie review the work not for the writing but for the topical importance they find in it and its relationship to events in the external world. Brewer begins by distinguishing in a sharply paradoxical manner between the novel and romance, noting that the former is self-enclosed within 'naturalistic illusion or mimesis' (BRE: 254), while the latter has a 'spontaneous appeal to the natural understanding' and can achieve 'symbolic power'. Although Tolkien succumbs to the twentieth-century prevalence of the former, the strength of the trilogy arises from the latter with its idea that within the nature of the world is a providential order that is 'very consoling' (258), despite the apocalyptic anxiety, the 'cosmic struggle between good and evil' (259). Because the concepts of 'naturalistic' and 'natural' are never sufficiently described, the difference between the symbolic power of providential order and the mimetic power of self-enclosed mankind is never sufficiently argued. Davie does not attempt literary distinctions at all and concentrates on interpreting from arbitrarily selected images the 'symbolic consciousness of the naturally religious man', the transcendent hierarchy 'outside ordinary time and power'. Neither critic is looking adequately at the way the book itself is written, no matter how probing and interesting the topics they discuss. The discussion is carried out in a manner peculiarly common to fantasy criticism in its emphasis on the interpretation of topics. I shall go on to examine the parallel between their stress on the 'natural', in other words unexamined, relationship that the book has to the topics they wish to valorise , and the way that self-enclosed worlds are created by the fantasy stance in the first place in its denial of persuasion and its implicit conveying of truth.

The final critic in the commemorative collection, T. Shippey, is one of the few critics who tries to assess Tolkien's method of writing and does so more fully in an excellent study, *The Road to Middle-Earth*. But while the analysis of Tolkien's role as 'cultural translator' leads to an awareness that the writer is also a man who tries to 'plug gaps', Shippey does not choose to pursue the political implications of the work as for example P. Spacks does in the contribution to Isaacs' and Zimbardo's collection. This writer presents *The Lord of the Rings* as a description of the continual activity of moral choice. Although admirable, the determinism, foretelling, structure of the entrelacement and calcquing, all undercut this activity by introducing suspense and with suspense the idea of completion or reward. The extraordinarily tight control of entrelacement (SH1: 120), the activity of calcquing which creates maps, names, actions, 'isomorphic with reality' (77), separate from reality but which 'betrays influence at every point' (77), are both classic techniques of a stance aimed toward detailed control over the reader's response.

The positive presentation of hierarchy, power and racial discrimination in *The Lord of the Rings* is, from my context, dangerous. I find it difficult to believe that even against the background of World War II it can be accepted, for it maintains the basis of the authoritative power it ostensibly sets out to destroy. It could possibly be read as a critique on exactly that: for example the elves have to destroy themselves if they are to destroy Sauron. But this analogy does not work when translated into the Shire. The potential critique of authority is undercut not only by the superficial glamourising references to kings and things, but also by the very structure of the language which defines its meaning, controls communications to its own ends and creates a totally self-enclosed world.

In positive terms what Shippey does is to establish a very different context for reading by treating the work as 'primarily linguistic in inspiration' (SH2: 286), arguing that while other 'critics think that man is master... Tolkien feels that words have a life of their own' (SH2: 301). From this position the writing does indeed open out a broad and immensely fruitful reading, and one that requires enormous sophistication, indeed all Shippey's scholarship in parallel with Tolkien's. Shippey comments that although he has no idea 'how much of the author's system is apprehended unconsciously by the un-studious reader. The evidence suggests ... , that it is quite a lot' (SH1: 98). Possibly: like most fantasies it has lost its popularity as its grounds have dated, but it certainly has an enormous readership who keep recovering it. However, as Shippey points out, most critics dislike *The Lord of the Rings* for two reasons: the first, restriction to topic (103), can be corrected by study of the writing; but the second 'ideological reluctance' (120) requires a re-setting of context clearly allied to specific sophistication in reading.

Before reading Shippey on *The Lord of the Rings*, I read the writing very much as a straightforward structuring of authoritative techniques. The sophistication of my reading was derived from a rather different literary context. After reading Shippey I am prepared to believe that there could be a positive alternative reading, but Shippey never assesses the implications of the differences his scholarship has opened up. What he has done however, is emphasise the role of reader interaction in the activity of stance when it delimits genre. For fantasy, it is this neglect of the reader that makes the claim either to neutrality or purity so potentially dangerous, because it evades the implications of power and make it possible for its authority to be manipulated.

There are so many problems in tension here that any inter-commentary, or extension of reading is virtually impossible without addressing the detailed context of the criticism, which I shall later go on to do more carefully. But this casual round-up does underline not only the apparent lack of consensus within these discussions but also, and far more importantly, the values implicit in the different stances of each critic.

The Theorists

If we turn away from *The Lord of the Rings* back to the theorists of these two ways of writing, we find that they are often even more confusing. Again, while I shall cover the individual theories in considerable detail throughout the main body of this essay, here I wish simply to provide an overview of the situation. The first thing one needs in order to move through the welter of 'Allegory/Fantasy is...' statements, is to distinguish between apparent clashes within individual definitions and the incompatibilities and contradictions between each and another. For example it is quite common to find allegory defined by a statement in two or more parts, ranging from its function as a representative emblem through to its elusive and enigmatic activity. This may be overt as in George Whalley's *Poetic Process* where he contrasts 'formulated' allegory as cypher to 'allegory as a symbolic mode' (W: 191); it may be implicit as in Clifford's initial definition of allegory as 'overtly moralistic or didactic, ... abstract speculative, and discursive' (C: 7) which is transformed into 'intransigent and elusive' relationships in the 'greatest' works (53); or it may be hidden and obscure in such studies as Fletcher's where allegory is predominantly presented as fixed, controlled and diagrammatic, yet under this presentation runs an insistence on the importance of its 'paradox' and 'obscurity', and its ultimate ability to become 'mythical' (F: 355).

Theories of fantasy are affected by these internal separations rather less. Here it is more common to find definitions that are simply incompatible with each other, or whose grounds are mutually exclusive. Manlove's description of fantasy as 'a fiction evoking wonder and containing a substantial and irreducible element of the supernatural with which the mortal characters in the story or the readers become on at least partly familiar terms' (M1: 1), is quite different from Todorov's 'fantastic' which occupies the time of uncertainty between the imaginary and the real, or Jackson's statement that fantasy 'attempts to compensate for a lack resulting from cultural constraints' (J: 3). To a greater or lesser degree these definitions have little to do with definitions of fantasy exclusively in terms of what it does: such as Irwin's characterisation of fantasy as an 'extended narrative which establishes and develops an artifact, that is, plays the game of the impossible' (I: ix) or Rabkin who defines it as narrative that 'diametrically contradicted' its own ground rules (R: 8).

It is also quite interesting that several theorists of allegory, particularly those such as Kermode and de Man who define that writing almost entirely in terms of its exclusively referential and enigmatic qualities, are just not concerned with talking about fantasy at all. Those allegorists who do mention it tend to think of it solely as a technique that introduces non-naturalistic elements (C: 45). However, many if not all theorists of fantasy make a point of distinguishing this way of writing from allegory, and when they do so they invariably concentrate on its representative and emblematic aspects.

Yet despite these sorties into definition and distinction there is considerable mixing of terms, possibly careless in some cases but in most quite unnoted and probably based on a group of internal self-evident grounds – self-evident to the theorist of course and often not so to the reader. Gerber's book *Utopian Fantasy* defines fantasy as the 'unreal' and at one point goes on to describe specifically allegorical fantasy which is didactic in nature (GE: 83). This is anathema to a writer such as Jackson who goes out of her way to separate fantasy from 'moral allegory' (J: 173), or Brooke-Rose who also makes a point of allying allegory and realism in the opposition to fantasy. At the same time Gerber goes on to refer to 'allegorical symbolism' which sets in motion 'mysterious forces'

(GE: III) beyond fantasy, and as we have seen Brooke-Rose herself speaks of the unresolvable paradoxes of allegory (BR: 66). In contrast to Brooke-Rose's earlier distinction of allegory and realism from fantasy, Apter splits fantasy writing exactly into the two aspects of realistic and allegorical fantasy. In a different manner that is vague rather than contradictory, other critics conflate the terms: referring to aspects of fantasy within allegory (C: 45 and 105), and the apparently fantastic nonsense of allegorical explanations (F: 341), the fantasised energy of allegory (FL: 8) or the allegorical levels of fantasy (MI: 79).

All of this could be the result of poorly delineated genre theory or modal distinctions. The confusions could arise simply because the writers are neither interested in how allegory and fantasy might interact, nor in whether they are being rigorous in their approach to the terms. But they nearly all have the avowed aim to do just those things, so the confusions are more fundamental. This is also apparent in the enormous overlap of claims made for each way of writing, although the same claim is rarely made by the same theorist for both. For example Rabkin claims that the fundamental basis of fantasy is implicitly tied to rationality (R: 28); Scholes claims the same for allegory (S: 60). Given the epistemological structure of western humanism this particular overlap is not surprising, but when it enters the realm of value it takes on broad implications. For example: On the one hand, Jackson also bases fantasy in the rational by claiming that its activity is 'anti-rational', specifically aimed at reversing rationality, and this in her mind is positive because it 'exposes a culture's definitions of that which can be' (J: 23). On the other hand, the 'conceptual' (43) and rational activity of allegory is something that 'legalises', 'neutralises' desire, imposes rather than exposes limitations (110).

When discussions of allegory and fantasy turn to history and the myriad of topics that surround it, values become overt. And the historical specificity of the two ways of writing forms a core for all the theory that leads to questions of ideology, to the extremes of conservative and subversive activity and to the associated but vexed complex of individual psyche, particularly to neurosis. Taking a negative definition of ideology as restrictive and limiting Jameson claims that this lies at the heart of fantasy (JAI: 161), whereas Fletcher claims it for allegory (FL: 368). In contrast, a positive dimension for ideology, its definition of historical determinism, is claimed by Spivak for allegory (SP: 322) and by both Jackson and Habegger for fantasy. Such different attitudes to ideology allow Jackson and Fletcher to warn against allegory as conservative, while elsewhere Jameson, and Frye whose study of romance *The Secular Scripture* has much to add to the theory of fantasy, warn against fantasy as conservative. Subversion is the only alternative that makes any substantial appearance in opposition to conservatism, and is generally held to be a 'good thing' although it can create considerable tension in claiming a constructive aspect (R). Not surprisingly, theorists of fantasy claim it for their writing (J: 91, R: 26 and 75) and theorists of allegory for theirs (WH: 64, HO: 182). Yet the constructive aspects of subversion, the inevitably subject-based realisations of desire, get tangled up in the politics of neurosis which provides a dominant trope that is employed with commendable sense of its danger by Brooke-Rose for fantasy and Fletcher for allegory (FL: 302), although as we shall see much of what Fletcher says about allegory is directly applicable to fantasy instead, and the trope is diverted into the explicitly libidinal by Jackson (J: 70).

Each overlap in definition forms the basis for an acknowledged or hidden conflict – sometimes because the definitions have shifted, but definitions rarely shift without reason. From the fundamental discussions about the relationship between writing and language that preoccupy allegorists, to those about the nature of writing and reality that preoccupy fantasists, the underlying concern is with power, authority and control. Taking their cue from such diverse writers as Tolkien, Huizinga and Sartre, both Todorov and Brooke-Rose attempt to move fantasy into the non-authoritative by cutting it off from reality, denying all connections. Recognising the impossibility of this, both Irwin and Rabkin make a virtue of the separation, presenting it as a conscious acknowledged comment upon specific aspects of the real. However, Jackson in particular senses the danger here and suggests paths of indirect comment upon the reality. Yet in writers such as Frye or Jameson the very attempt at connection with the real is criticised for the implicit relations of power that it enters. In a similar manner, discussions of the differences and similarities between metonymy and metaphor (in BO, HO, or F1), analogy and symbol, (L: 45, W: 191, N: 106) and the activity of language particularly in writing, infuse assessments of allegory with questions of control through reference. The whole of Angus Fletcher's odyssey into allegory and/or fantasy is the discovery of the exercise of authoritative power through language, yet Paul de Man's *Allegories of Reading* totally and completely opposes such an understanding with the claim that 'allegorical representation leads toward a meaning that diverges from the initial meaning to the point of foreclosing its manifestation' (DM1: 74–5).

What is important to emphasise here is that this vocabulary of value is used not just to distinguish between say the writing of Poe and Tolkien – with any one writer placing positive or negative assessments either way – but between two readers of the same work, and sometimes very confusingly, within a single reader apparently reading in different ways at different times. Such radically different evaluation of the work of Ursula LeGuin as either rigidly conservative myth containing and subduing disorder or as continually altering the *status quo* (J: 154, M2: 36), demands some kind of assessment of the theoretical assumptions particularly about genre and mode that lead to these statements: if only because the statements themselves become political fodder for future theorists, and more significantly because they may affect the ways in which a work is read.

Furthermore, it is curious that many writers of both allegory and fantasy arouse deep response, substantial conviction and radical partisanship. The divisions among the critics and theorists are paralleled by an unusually wide rift between academic and non-academic readings from *The Lord of the Rings*, to *Nineteen Eighty-Four*, to the women's writings about alternative worlds to which I turn in the final chapter. Nearly all the recent articles on *The Lord of the Rings* begin by referring to this division, although few go beyond studying it in any detail[33]. This strife torn field does however make use of a series of analogies: games, desire, wish-fulfilment, loss, hesitation, enigma, love, death, neurosis, deceit: which indicate a common set toward the world, the set of common places where the oppositions may fall away a little. I will suggest that many of these oppositions derive from a restricted attitude to the extent of modal activity, and a lack of understanding of the activity of rhetorical stance that informs mode. The descriptions of fantasy and allegory that follow present at least two faces of fantasy and a number of analogies for allegory, that enact the main stances of western humanism in its attitude toward power and control.

2 Theories of Fantasy

1 A BACKGROUND OF GAMES AND DESIRE

Study of literature which has come to be called fantasy has grown exponentially since the middle of the twentieth century, and theory related directly to this literature has exploded ever since Todorov's *Introduction à la littérature fantastique* was published in English in 1970. While admittedly about a very limited chronological period in the development of fantasy, Todorov's work on the fantastic has stimulated others into open discussion of the issues, although many had been clearly pursuing their ideas concurrently with his. And since 1970 the field of fantasy has roughly divided in emphasis into theories of games and theories of desire; more recently theories have emerged that concentrate on the political implications.

Previous to this period there are many writers who discuss the word 'fantasy' yet they do not normally use it to designate a specific group of writings. Coleridge's famous distinction between imagination and fancy, which has generated a vast amount of commentary, referred to ways of looking at the world rather than specific genres. The denigration of fancy explicit in the distinction has influenced many later writers in their evaluation of fantasy; and several modern critics in attempting to re-establish a more positive outlook, begin with Coleridge and either criticise his arguments or start by separating fancy from fantasy[1]. Yet Coleridge was echoing connotations that the word has carried with it from at least the English Renaissance[2].

Both Philip Sidney and George Puttenham, presumably aware of contemporary continental criticism and the distinction in Plato's *Sophist* between the art that copies and art that makes illusions[3], are at pains to distinguish questionable fantasy from the proper pursuit of the poet. Sydney separates between εικαστικη

'which some learned have defined: figuring forth good things' and
φανταστικη : 'which doth, contrariwise, infect the fancy with
unworthy objects'[4]. Here the emphasis lies on the difference
between representation of what is there and presentation of what is
not there. Furthermore, εικαστικη carries with it connotations from
the Greek of indirect comparison even inference[5]. In Puttenham's
The Art of English Poesie the emphasis is different. In defending
poets and philosophers against the charge of having 'busie and
disordered phantasies'[6], it is suggested that there are two sorts of
fantasist, the euphantastiote and the phantastici; the former is
ordered, formal, clear, representing 'appearances of things to the
soule and according to their very truth' (19). While the latter
'breedes Chimeres so monstrous in mans imaginations, and not
only in his imaginations, but also in all his ordinarie actions and life
which ensues' (19). Puttenham's link of a necessary 'invention'
with the activity of the euphantastiote, emphasises more clearly
than Sydney that representation of what is there, 'according to
their very truth', is not a matter of direct imitation.

The classical history of the word fantasy indicates a similar
division in its application. Etymologically, fantasy is derived from
the Greek φαινειν: to make visible, or to show. Yet if we compare
φανταζειν with the related derivative from φαινειν or επιφαινειν,
epiphany: to manifest, show forth, there is a distinct qualification
on its activity. Epiphany makes visible by means of something else;
fantasy lays claim to more immediate and direct skills of showing,
as if it could imitate without the interaction of a medium. This
claim is probably related to a subsidiary connotation in the Greek,
that of boasting and ostentatiousness, in that the boaster is not
aware of the obvious discrepancy between what he or she says and
what the audience perceives. At the same time the middle form,
neither active nor passive, of φανταζειν is defined as 'to imagine'.
What the Greeks meant by imagination is difficult to recover, but
there does seem to be a clear distinction between the active form of
direct imitation and the middle form of a more elusive expression of
perception (ET: 198, 208; OED: 66–68).

The split role of fantasy is related to the history of the words
'delusion' and illusion through the scholastic definition of it as
'mental apprehension of an object of perception; the faculty by
which this is performed' (OED IV: 67). Delusion emphasises
something done to one. It is *de ludere* , to play fully, play false, cajole,

deceive, mock. (ET: 162). In contrast illusion is more something that one does or is done. It is *il ludere* : to play upon, make sport, also to deceive, mock (ET: 287). With illusion there is a sense of teasing, as if the mocked knows what is happening, but with delusion there is a more insidious sense of being deprived of this knowledge. The distinction between the two words is tangled, particularly as attitudes to perception change with history. Delusion, as a 'fixed false opinion or belief with regard to objective things' only becomes viewed as 'mental derangement' in the post-renaissance period, finally taking on the possibility of self-delusion, ultimate deception[7]. During the same period the ability of illusion to suggest a false belief so that reality is attributed 'to what is unreal' is increasingly separated from fundamental perception, so that it now assumes a more familiar sense of the tricks of the illusionist (OED IV: 48).

Here it is timely to return to Coleridge and not only because he notes that 'one of the most common and approved Recipes for Self-Delusion in modern times ... *is* to find out the explanation in an English Dictionary'[8]. Coleridge also makes much of the separation between delusion and illusion, the former leading to 'negative faith' while the latter leads to the suspension of judgment because the actual appearance of things is contrary to experience (BL II: 67). The implication is that in creating art the artist will not be able to imitate the world directly and will inevitably produce something analogous to it; but this analogy may then aim to delude and to claim the status of actuality, or to be illusory, underlining its difference from the actual. Fancy itself emphasises delusion for the reader, if he or she permits, is at the mercy of the writer as 'phantast', yet the phantastical writer is at the mercy of mechanical memory and the law of association. Fancy 'has no other counters to play with, but fixities and definites' (BL I: 281); it attempts the direct representation of the world by 'clear images' (BL I: 288), which Coleridge calls 'passive' and a 'fetisch' (BL I: 288n). On the one hand it is 'emancipated from the order of time and space' and subject to the authority of the author's selection, but on the other the author too can only 'receive all its materials ready made from the law of association' (BL I: 305). In all these activities fancy is subject to an authority that presents an illusion of the actual world but at the same time makes the illusion a source for delusion not only of the audience but of the writer. In

Coleridge's terms fancy is triply passive: reader, writer and writing all subject to the arbitrary authority of association.

At the centre of this circle of authority and passivity lies self-delusion, intimately wrapped up in the subject-centred activity of the writing and reading. And it is the concentration on the individual as authority and source for the action that concerned a number of writers at the turn of the nineteenth century, including Meredith, Stevenson, Barrie, Chesterton and Lawrence, who studied this understanding of authority, subjectivity and self-delusion in terms of a literary expression of fantasy. While they could not be said to form a tradition, they make up an interesting commentary on a kind of 'sentimental' literature far removed from the eighteenth century man of feeling. Individual taste is shifted into egoism, dependent upon the creation of self-contained worlds controlled, as was Coleridge's 'fancy', by a now suspect ability to represent the world directly and bolstered up by the procedures of a rational associationist logic (H1). For these writers sentiment, and the fantasy it generates, is no longer the hand-maid of rationalism but the demeaning of human value, the second-rate sop to a raddled humanism. In this they show an early and marked appreciation of the detrimental effects of the split between fact and value that later critics will note in similar terms of sentiment and rationality[9], and which ally fantasy with 'escapism' in popular jargon.

These diverse writings are noteworthy for the continual opposition they pose to contemporary theories of 'pure art', which for them provides the source of the delusions of fantasy. Indeed Pater's theoretical suggestions in *Renaissance* that the artist should 'burn always with this hard gem-like flame' by 'individual isolation, each mind keeping as a solitary prisoner in its own dream of a world'[10], could be considered the focus of their artistic concerns. But some of the writings are also important for the extent of their political vision, albeit theoretical. Chesterton and Barrie for example both stress first the impossibility for art to be divorced from the material world and second, the dangerous political activity that such attempts engage in. They take one step further Coleridge's statement that 'delirium' is the extended form of fantasy and suggest that the fantasist either develops a monomania that subjects others to itself, finally destroying them, or a madness that is rejected by others and whose private path leads to death: by definition to suicide. Both the illusory, world-creating and sustaining appearance of fantasy, and its deluding capacity to falsely realise belief, are taken up and to varying degrees applied to the broad social and political scene. Some commentators remain within the circle of authority and passivity, urging constant vigilance against its restrictive effects; while others like Chesterton attempt alternatives by removing the individual from the centre of authority.

Theories from the 30s: Tolkien and Huizinga

But these writers were concerned more with their own literary work than with extensive exploration of critical and theoretical issues, nor did the institutions to support the explorations exist in any substantial way. During the 30s however, two major developments took place which provided part of the vocabulary for later theory, J. R. R. Tolkien gave his lecture 'On Fairy Stories' (1938, published 1947) and John Huizinga delivered the lectures that became *Homo Ludens* (published in English, 1944). While Tolkien was not ostensibly speaking of fantasy, the essay provides a central place for it and solves the problem of delusion by justifying it as desire. An interesting equilibrium has developed between Tolkien's idea of Christian desire and Freud's concept of desire within repression and neurosis. Although they derive from slightly different contexts, so that Tolkien's desire is Freud's neurosis, they are similar in their pursuit of wish-fulfilment and the strategies necessary to it. *Homo Ludens* is superficially outwith the concerns of fantasy; but it too deals in the strategies necessary for wish-fulfilment although emphasising their illusory quality, and its comprehensive authority has been used by many theorists of fantasy to justify illusion in the name of the 'games people play'.

Since games and desire are primary fields in which fantasy is currently discussed, it seems sensible to begin a detailed survey of the recent criticism and theory with a study of the work of Tolkien and Huizinga. Tolkien's lecture 'On Fairy Stories' was delivered in 1938 but not published until 1947. In its published form it reflects the fruit of ten years' work on *The Lord of the Rings* as well as a distinguished scholarly career in language and linguistics, and firmly defines fantasy both in the abstract and in practice. First a broad definition of 'Fairy' is given: it is 'the realisation, independent of the conceiving mind, of imagined wonder' (15).

This is intimately linked with fantasy because fantasy is the image-making power that effects the realisation. Fantasy can take 'green', from grass and put it on someone's face; it is:

> An enchanter's power – upon one plane: and the desire to wield that power in the world external to our minds awakes. It does not follow that we shall use that power well upon any plain. But in such 'fantasy', as it is called, new form is made; Faerie begins, Man becomes a sub-creator (TO: 24–5).

Later, fantasy is defined as the 'sub-creative art in itself', and sub-creation is a specific concept introduced by Tolkien as part of his attempt at a Christian aesthetic, that will deal with a dominant problem of *ex nihilo* creativity that concerned many Catholics[11], as well as other writers of the period. Human beings cannot think things into existence, cannot absolutely create nor even try to. Instead creation is of a second order, below that of God's. Yet this very focus on a different order of creativity introduces a range of questions concerned with human control of the external world, and while Tolkien is surprisingly willing to take on these questions of control and power there lies a fundamental ambivalence at the heart of his theory.

The aim of fantasy is to provide patterns of escape, recovery and consolation (TO: 45), through the conscious sub-creation of a world concerned with desirablity, rather than possibility (39–40). Sub-creation 'makes a Secondary World which your mind can enter' (36), which is unlike the 'Primary World' and hence free from the domination of observed 'fact' (45), and which maintains its own, inner consistency of reality' (46) through its image making power. Tolkien now takes an important step; because of this separation from the primary or actual world, fantasy becomes 'a higher form of Art, indeed the most nearly pure form, and so (when achieved) the most potent' (45). Further its power is specifically qualified as 'progenitive' because it is written and is unlike the 'visible' presentations of painting which impose ideas on the audience, as in the case of surrealism which generates morbidity and unease.

Yet this participation of the fantasy audience runs strangely counter to the earlier claim, intrinsically tied to the 'inner consistency' of the secondary or fantasy world, that 'Inside it, what [the narrator] relates is "true"': it accords with the laws of that world. You therefore believe it, while you are, as it were, inside.' The entire relationship 'as it were' between writer, work and audience is called into question by the immediately following discussion of the perception of primary and secondary worlds in children and in adults. The difference between childhood and adult interaction with desire, as realised in the fantasy world, is something that preoccupies many early writers in this field. Tolkien is swift to claim that children quickly learn to distinguish the difference between desire and actuality, and that they know when they escape into another world (TO: 40). He takes up an entire appendix to 'On Fairy Stories' attempting to prove this from his personal experience as a child, but he not only neglects the institutions of adult behaviour that encourage confusion between the two in children but also the pursuit of his own comment that children often cannot judge the difference: Both dilemmas most clearly presented in J. M. Barrie's 'Peter Pan' or in his later plays such as 'Mary Rose' and 'Dear Brutus'.

Tolkien goes on to note that in the adult such 'suspension of disbelief' may appear sentimental, and in this he echoes the warnings of the earlier writers of fantasy. D. H. Lawrence states the case in extreme terms when he writes that sentimentality drapes the attempt to regain 'the rudimentary condition of childhood to obtain the gratification of self-reduction'[12]. He concludes that this is 'all very well for a child' but 'childhood as a *goal* , for which grown people aim: childishness futile and sentimental: this is disgusting' (396). Tolkien's point is that the involvement in fantasy is only apparently sentimental, in effect it has its own rigour for the reader like the writer must exercise a conscious choice parallel to that in the sub-creation of the writer (TO: 37).

Within this context, Tolkien concludes that 'the moment disbelief arises, the spell is broken; the magic, or rather art, has failed' (TO: 36–7). The last is a significant slip of the pen since later on Tolkien distinguishes firmly between magic, fantasy and enchantment. Enchantment is the only form of creation that could fully delude through fantasy, but in any case it is reserved as a skill for elves rather than men. It creates a world 'into which both designer and spectator can enter, to the satisfaction of their senses while they are inside; but in its purity it is artistic in desire and purpose' (50). Magic however tries to produce 'or pretends to produce, an alteration in the Primary World'. It is not an art 'but a technique; its desire is *power* in this world, domination of things and wills' (50). Fantasy aspires to enchantment and

> is inwardly wholly different from the greed for self-centred power which is the mark of the mere Magician ... Uncorrupted it does not seek delusion, nor bewitchment and domination; it seeks shared enrichment, partners in making and delight, not slaves. (50)

The problem here is that such purity is attained only by default, by the fantasist's stated inability to create a world totally consistent and therefore resistant to encroaching actuality, and by the reader's instinctive ability to distinguish between the two worlds. But Tolkien himself goes on to note that 'it would not seem at all impossible' that mankind might become unable to perceive 'truth' in terms of the 'facts' of the actual world. What happens in this situation is that 'Fantasy will perish, and become Morbid Delusion' as do the impositions of the surrealist worlds. This shift of words is an evasion and Tolkien does conclude by admitting that 'Fantasy can, of course, be carried to excess. It can be ill done. It can be put to evil uses. It may even delude the mind out of which it came ... ' (TO: 51).

Yet the shift also focuses on the activity that is being described. We can see here a glimpse of the problems residing in the concept of mode: that a text is a fantasy if it sets up one relationship between writer, reader and words, but that the same text may not a fantasy if there is a different set to the relationship. Despite this qualification there is a fundamental ambivalence in Tolkien's concept of fantasy, that is glossed by a comment at the end of T. Shippey's criticism on the author. Shippey notes the 'No one can expect a fantasy to turn real' (SH1: 211), yet Tolkien held his theory of sub-creation to be implicated in God's creation since human imagination came from God. As a result these Secondary Worlds 'must be fragments of some genuinely if other-worldly truth' (211); they must implicitly create a real world that is just as credible as the actual.

Tolkien's willingness to take up the question of power lies at the heart of his concept of sub-creation. Imaginatively created worlds are morally valid only if the writer is a sub-creator who does not attempt to supplant the real world with a private one. But there is an ambivalence here, for the attempt at supplanting is often made, and intrinsic to the very activity of sub-creations are elements of creation. Yet while the ambivalence of Tolkien's theory lies with the writer, there is a different but just as fundamental ambivalence about the nature of power at the heart of Huizinga's theory of games.

In *Homo Ludens* games are defined by three primary characteristics. First, the game is a voluntary activity 'never imposed by physical necessity or moral duty' (HU: 8). Second, it is never confused with real life; 'Every child knows perfectly well that he is "only pretending"' (8); and even when the game world takes on a cultural aspect it is still disinterested 'outside the immediate satisfaction of wants and appetites ... It interpolates itself as a temporary activity satisfying itself and ending there' (9). Lastly, the distinction from real life is effected by its fixity in time: 'It can be repeated at any time, whether it be "child's play"' or a game of chess ... ' (10), and by its isolation in space which allows it to create order 'absolute and supreme ... [it] casts a spell over us; it is "enchanting", "captivating"'. It is invested with the noblest qualities we are capable of perceiving in things: rhythm and harmony' (10). And because of this nonmoral, disinterested, isolated nature games are neutral; they do not aim for the 'true' but for the pure.

There is here an interesting collocation of key words which have remained tied to the study of fantasy: the child, the game of chess, enchantment, purity and music. And Huizinga is important for his linking of the split history of pure art and music with that of neutral art and games. Elsewhere he notes that game-play 'lies outside the reasonableness of practical life; has nothing to do with necessity or utility, duty or truth. All this is equally true of music' (HU: 158). Neither music nor games involve judgment or logic, their values are held to lie outside reason. Where they reside instead Huizinga does not suggest in this comparison. The non-morality of 'pure' art was put severely to the test during the late 20s and 30s in English writing, and just so the non-morality of the game raises similar questions. The basic problem is simply: how can activity be non-moral? Huizinga solves his problem by defining morality as a system of rigid rules, hence the activity of games is non-moral because it lies outside those rigid standards. But the solution inscribes a number of paradoxical situations. The writer defines games as encompassed by a set of rules which are 'absolutely binding and allow no doubt' (11). So while he denies the validity of a code of morality, a code of another kind is the mainstay of his theory; both take the position that values are quantifiable things, and assume a set of controls over the world from which or toward which people move.

A similar paradox lies in the insistence that the game world is always quite distinct from the actual. The ability of the child to make such a distinction is reiterated throughout the book, although in ambivalent terms. For example it is stated that the child 'almost believes he is such and such a thing, without, however, wholly losing consciousness of "ordinary reality"' (HU: 14). Yet later on an equivalence is set up between the way that a child plays games and the way that an archaic primitive society plays, but the defining quality of the archaic mind is precisely its inability to separate between the game world and the real (129). This is compounded by Huizinga's suggestion that in the civilised world games have become rigid because people have forgotten that they are activities, and they need to cast off the binding of culture and resume the participation in games enjoyed by pre-cultural man. Yet if pre-cultural man could not make the distinction between the game world and the real, he also could not participate in play.

These paradoxes are not particularly profound. They are based on an evasive stance that surfaces continually in the writing, as considerations are sloughed off, difficult queries rejected[13], and the very logic of the argument consciously ignored. In a passage I have quoted elsewhere (H: 94), but which bears quoting again, it is stated;

> We have no wish to go into the deep question of how far the process of reasoning itself is marked by play rules ... May it not be in all logic ... there is always a tacit understanding to take the validity of the terms and concepts for granted as one does pieces on a chess-board? Let others puzzle this out! (HU: 152–3)

But these evasions mark an even deeper rift in Huizinga's presentation. The activity of the game is termed 'agonistic', and the author himself notes that 'the predominance of the agonistic principle does lead to decadence in the long run' (74–5). Games may start off as free and creative but they inevitably 'run down', become stultifying, decadent repetitions that do not renew but wither away and become empty casts of stereotyped opinion.

Huizinga had the opportunity to edit the book for its 1946 English edition, and in the light of immediate history he recast several claims. One of the earliest definitions of the game that he makes is that it 'promotes the formation of social groupings which tend to surround themselves with secrecy and to stress their difference from the common world by disguise or other means' (HU: 13). Yet he also notes that 'at any given moment, even in a highly developed civilisation, the play-"instinct"' may reassert itself in full force, drawing the individual and mass in the intoxication of an immense game' (47). The evident joy with which he views this, this in 1938, is retracted presumably in the light of the events of World War II when he says in the 1946 edition that 'clubs' are acceptable but that it is a 'disaster when whole nations turn into clubs' (205). Indeed, it is this recognition of political danger, of which Chesterton in particular was aware, that leads the writer to a reintroduction of a moral context for game-playing at the end of the book (H1: 96–7).

What Huizinga does not do is to explore the structures that he proposes for games, to work out why they lead to decadence and danger 'in the long run'. And here we need to turn to the strategies that he proposes for effecting his non-moral, separate world: contest and representation. The writer is careful to claim that contest does not aim at power but excellence, and representation does not aim at control by identification but by propitiation. Leaving aside the questionable nature of the activity of each character (H: 93–4), Huizinga insists that they are at the same time pointless and neutral but significant. They are pointless because they occur in a game but significant because they comment upon the real. Yet if they comment upon the world they are related to it; they have lost that essential isolation, so how can they be neutral?

Much of this confusion arises because of the emphasis on strategy rather than stance, and it is illuminated by a study of the activity of the sophist who is Huizinga's ideal games player. In apparently blissful ignorance of the ironic manner in which Plato constructs Gorgias the sophist in his dialogue (H: 21–2). Huizinga places Gorgias centre stage: the orator who preserves his purity by maintaining a regular repeatable repetoire and by charging a fee. In doing so, the sophist makes it clear that the audience is involved in a game not in pursuit of the truth:

> it is only when the sophist ... pursues an instrinsically immoral aim ... that he becomes the falsifier of wisdom, – unless of course it can be maintained that the agonistic habit is in itself immoral and false. (HU: 152)

In light of the earlier comments on the long term decadent effects of the agonistic this is a careless remark. But more important, it assumes too much. If the people listening to the sophist do not realise that he is 'only playing', they may believe that the world that is being presented is not merely a game nor even a comment upon the world, but reality itself. The isolation and fixity of that world are not enough to guarantee its neutrality once an audience is introduced. And if the audience thinks that it is being presented with a form of reality then it is reasonable for it to think that the sophist is pursuing truth after all, and so, within the given definition, be exposed to the immoral.

The ambivalence of Huizinga's theory lies with the audience. Games need a conscious and playing audience so they define their audience as conscious and playing. The inadequacy of this tautological structure is something only brought home to the writer by the disastrous effects of Nazi sophism. And the 1946 version of *Homo Ludens* concludes by saying that although a game, or a set of strategies for creating a fixed isolated world, is 'neither good nor bad', the moment those strategies enter activity, include an audience and become stance, 'moral conscience' must intervene (H: 213). The vagueness with which this is posited is completely inadequate as a way of discussing relationships with power, but it represents a brave shift of ground for the writer, and a shift that many of his readers have ignored.

The common factors in both Tolkien's and Huizinga's theories centre upon purity and neutrality and they are precise about how this is to be achieved. Yet there is a curious dichotomy common to their understanding of the necessary strategies. Tolkien emphasises the ability of words to convey exactly objects or perceptions in the real world at the same time as he uses that absolute correspondence to separate between words and the world to justify the realisation of desire. Just so, Huizinga insists upon the relevance of game-worlds to the real, while also insisting that they remain quite separate from it. Fantasy realises the analogies of desire and games in a similar manner, and what is interesting is that it can only operate fully in a context that has been taught to accept representative language and literature. It needs the possiblity of portraying the external world exactly or it cannot exercise its full power. The history of the writing emerges from medieval romance, through pastorals into the flowering of representation in the post-Renaissance period. Like romance, fantasy deals in the non-real strange terrain of our perception, but representation is what makes it possible for it to linger over their indeterminancy in a world of its own. And the creation of an alternative world is also what makes possible the truncation of pastoral, so that we move away from our own society, but never make the considered return.

Both games and desire hover over a deep chasm. On the one hand the purity of fantasy leans toward realisation of private desire and total denial of the external world . If it severs its connections completely it generates the grotesque and nonsense; if it extends its own world out to supplant the real it ends in magic. Neutral fantasy on the other hand, always remains aware of the external world; it is this awareness that guarantees its neutrality. If it chooses to sever or mutilate the connections as a conscious activity, it engages upon satire; and if it extends its own world it enters the realm of utopia. These generic terms surface with increasing regularity in the writings of post-World War II critics and theoreticians who half-perceive links with fantasy in their pursuit of other topics and I would now like to look at a selection from these writers.

2 ATTEMPTS TO DEFINE FANTASY AS A GENRE

Relationships with romance, fairy tale, satire, utopia, nonsense, the grotesque, pastoral

There are few critics who write directly on fantasy until the 1970s. During the preceding thirty years, relevant criticism arises from studies of genres ranging from satire to nonsense to pastoral. The insistent reference within many of these early commentaries is toward defining the writing of fantasy in terms of an epistemological activity carried out within an ideology that it either depends upon or ignores. When it is dependent, it moves into the realm of games and when it ignores ideology it expresses desire.

The relationship of satire and utopia with the wishful fantasies of human beings is taken up by R. C. Elliott in a study of the golden world, of arcadia (E: 15). The difference lies in that utopia is a better world while arcadia is simply different. Utopias posit desirable wholes in which the writer 'assumes the role of creator himself' (9). This wish to relieve humanity of responsibility, to play God, results in all posited utopian states being totalitarian (96). But within utopia there is always an implicit movement which makes it the positive alternative to the criticism of satire: 'by virtue of its existence alone it casts a critical light on society as presently constituted' (22). The totalitarian states are always deformed by the process of realising them. Utopia has a fundamentally pastoral stance of movement into the other world and return from it. The fictional is stressed, the debate is underlined: In contrast to the idyll which Elliott defines after Schiller as a movement going forward to Elysium where it comes to rest, utopia is a movement back toward Arcadia where it only briefly stays. Utopia always comments on this world.

The relation between utopia and fantasy lying implicit in Elliott's study, was made explicit in R. Gerber's early *Utopian Fantasy*, published in 1955. A source for several of Gerber's theories is *Homo Ludens* and the concept of games. The work studies the aim of the arcadian and scientific utopia which 'not only wants to effect a radical change here, it also wants it now, if possible' (GE: 15). Utopias function by appealing to the reader's desire and creating felicity or pleasure, and power. The concept of arcadia as a place where desires are realised, takes in the concepts of the golden age, the millenium and the earthly paradise. Of particular relevance to utopia is the golden age which is separate from the others because it is humanly conceived and effected. It is a construct in which 'man imposes his will on the imagination' (4), and it concerns people in this actual world rather than the spiritual. Historically, Gerber places the split between the golden age and the earthly paradise or millenium at the Renaissance. The golden age is a supremely humanist concept. It is suggested that before More's *Utopia* people thought of utopian fantasies as actually existing. More turned utopia into:

> the instrument of sophisticated rationalistic hypothesis ... The sophisticated utopian writer ... is clearly aware of the gap between possible and actual reality, but tries to close it by giving to a possibility the appearance of actual reality: he is consciously creative and active. (5)

The change is connected to an epistemological shift from spontaneous imagination and traditional belief toward the .'fictional activity of logical thought' (4). And the shift goes hand in hand with the idea of the artist as creator not imitator. Elliott notes that one later effect of the change is that utopia moves from being a transcendent perfection of the present toward finding its perfection in the future, because the utopian world must adjust to whatever is most plausible for the creation of perfection.

Gerber comes to define utopian fantasy specifically as the definition and achievement of the perfect world by human beings. It is humanist because of its 'conscious, often playful fictiousness' (GE: 5) and its moral purpose is clearly perceptible. In order to fulfill the reader's desires, the utopian world needs to work consistently from a fundamentally acceptable hypothesis. Consistency gains the reader's acceptance of the world, which in turn is necessary to fulfill the utopian's 'desire to create illusions of reality' (86). But Gerber separates between utopia and fantasy when this desire attempts completion. In fantasy alone reality recedes, whereas in utopian fantasy there is always the 'rift between the ideal and the real' (46) that is sophisticated and self-conscious in the Huizingian sense. Because pure fantasy demands that its own reality is not in doubt, the moral pointed by the transition from the ideal to the real is not expressed. Fantasy is basically reactionary; there is no transition to a new point of view. It takes a slice of the present, isolates and amplifies it, but does not permit any adverse criticism. It is this possibility for total control that Elliott suggests is behind the twentieth century fear of utopia (E: 82), a century that has seen that control brought close to totality. But Gerber contradicts this saying that modern utopias attempting the complete world of fantasy achieve only pathos. Great modern utopians know they cannot close the gap between fantasy and reality and turn instead to tragicomedy. His conclusion is that utopias are ultimately spiritual. It is interesting that Gerber calls this overt incompletion allegorical.

Chronologically concurrent with Elliott and Gerber are studies in fantasy as nonsense and magic by writers such as E. Cammaerts, E. Sewell and W. H. Auden. Both Cammaerts and Sewell turn their attention to the tradition of nonsense writing in English, and extend the essays of G. K. Chesterton which are among the earliest critical appreciations of the writing[14]. Chesterton himself notes the duplicity and ambivalence of fantasy in its attempt to remain separate from the world at the same time as deriving from it and commenting upon it. He also distinguishes fantasy from nonsense which severs connections with the world in an explicit and extreme manner, and from magic which attempts an imposition of total control over that world by supplanting it.

A similar distinction is made by E. Cammaerts in *The Poetry of Nonsense*. He allies nonsense and fairy as the 'two ways of escaping the house of Common-sense', but suggests that they move in opposite directions: they escape 'by the magic of Fairyland or by the topsy-turvydom of Nonsense' (CA: 28). Cammaerts also explicitly separates nonsense from satire at a number of points during the essay. Early in the writing he describes parody as a form of satire, and goes on to state that 'Nonsense poems and stories are perhaps the only literary productions which are entirely impervious to parody' (15). Later, he says that whereas the eighteenth century was devoted to the logic of wit, satire and epigram, the Romantics prepared the ground for Lear and Carroll by shifting the emphasis onto the imagination and non-rational connection.

The broad distinction being made here is between genres which clearly refer to and depend upon an external world: satire; and those which do not: nonsense and magic or fairy. The idea that a genre might be able to evade reference to the external world, in itself reflects a kind of faith in the combined absolute and arbitrary nature of representation that Cammaerts seems to be aware of and expresses in terms of the nature of illustrations within nonsense books: He notes not only the arbitrary interpretations of the actual world that illustrations can open up and have 'fun' with, but also the corresponding tendency to absolutism, to 'substitute their own personality for that of the poet's, and to miss the nonsensical quality of the verse' (CA: 64). But he does not apply this to nonsense writing as well. In effect he evades the issue, simply stating rather than explaining that the best nonsense writers pursue the disruption of the actual as far as possible. But even the best nonsense writer has 'to realise that his power is not infinite and that his flight from reality must end somewhere' (52), in other words, must connect with the actual at some point. This faith in the possibility of innocent reference, that reflects exactly or can be detached at will from the actual, also comes to light in the comment that nonsense allows one to 'enjoy once more ... [the] careless irresponsibility' of childhood (37), and in the emphasis on its musical nature (85). Cammaerts concludes that the English have a flourishing genre of nonsense writing precisely because of the Victorian concentration on the music of words.

Much other vocabulary in use here and in Chesterton and Sewell, either feeds into or derives from Tolkien's study of fantasy. Far more explicitly connected is W. H. Auden's *Secondary Worlds*. He takes as a basic assumption that man cannot be a magician, cannot create *ex nihilo* (AU: 50). The poet is a sub-creator, a recreator. But this recreation is a way people have of controlling the suffering and limitations imposed upon them by the real world. We may evade death, be omniscient and omnipotent, may find the sacred and the arcadian (51), yet always in the knowledge that the worlds are not actual. Concealment of artifice may occur, but it always does so for a purpose, it always draws attention to itself (58). Auden concedes that the fantasist's or poet's sense of individuality may turn in upon itself to a narcissism which emerges as necessary to avoid being a 'puppet of fate'; and that this may become idolatry, remaking the poet as God (58). But for the most part the poet is simply enchanted by a topic she or he wishes to share (128), rather than being a black magician who uses power to gain domination. The theory contrasts the conscious and voluntary response to a poet, with the magician's 'tautological echo' eliminating 'consent or dissent' (129) and producing a literature as a simple consumer good. The words are 'idle' because they have been deprived of all value; they are fixed by the author. Auden recognises that the point about Tolkien's fear that people think suspension of disbelief shabby and sentimental, is not that they find the suspension sentimental in itself but that they object to the unquestioning acceptance of someone else's belief instead.

Sentimentality as unquestioning acceptance and as the result of a 'magical' power is the locus for the negative comments on fantasy throughout most of these early commentaries. Wayne Booth defines sentimentality as 'one of the qualities of works based on attitudes that have not survived artistic proof'[15]. I.A. Richards calls it an inappropriate tendency, one that concentrates on only one aspect and tends to hide pain or realise desire[16]. Significantly, Northrop Frye defines it as 'a more extended and literary development of the formulae of naive romance' (F2: 1), making it therefore an unquestioned structure. Sentiment is the manifestation of a restricted point of view and whether it be individual or group, it exhibits all the characteristics of a subjective and isolated negative theoretical stance which cannot be sustained for long (H: 14–20).

However, a more recent and rather odd book by A. Wilson, *Magical Thought in Creative Writing*, continues the connection between magic and fantasy but inverts Auden's initial assumption that man cannot create *ex nihilo* and suggests that 'magical thought (fantasy)' (W1: 7) is a primitive power of absolute creation. It is:

> a form of thinking which is magical in character ... because it is free from the laws and realities of the external world, and therefore operates with special powers to bring things about. These things are brought about in the mind alone, of course ... (15)

and with that last 'of course' the whole definition is evasively qualified. Wilson goes on to mention a number of techniques necessary to this writing. The narrator is not 'detached', in other words cannot be perceived. Hence the protagonist becomes the creator of the narrative. The thoughts and events surrounding the protagonist become 'actual', and the reader is expected 'totally' to identify with him or her, in fact 'readers on the whole never compare its events with what they perceive as external reality' (10). The structure is usually linear, repetitive, mnemonic. The repeated events centre around the conflicts of the protagonist which are not to do with self-reflection, reason or judgment but with 'feelings', and which ultimately end in transformation. And the language is 'primarily pictorial'; it 'does not itself struggle for precision of expression through diction' (13).

Here the critic is picking up on the strategies of conflict and representation suggested by Huizinga, and like him, trying to neutralise or purify them. However, the assumption that mental worlds differ in kind from what we perceive and can therefore be isolated, the idea that the pictorial is absolute and does not have its own diction, and the possibility that an author may avoid presence, are all highly questionable. They place in an awkward position the claim that these magical worlds are acceptable because they have nothing to do with 'period of time' or 'culture'. Indeed other writers such as F. Jameson and N. Frye whose writing we shall come to in detail later, explicitly deny this. In an essay on 'Symbolic Fantasy', G. K. Wolfe notes that fantasy of a mythopoeic variety results from a narrow cultural attitude making it necessary for the individual, loyal to a private sense of value, to expand into other forms of expression[17]. This positive activity is inverted by Frye who remarks on the special, non-literary use of myth to indoctrinate, to impose an individual view (F2: 167), and a similar remark is made by Jameson (JA1: 161).

To move away from myth and back into the critical history of fantasy writing, let us turn to Frye's *Anatomy of Criticism* and examine the broader context for the cultural position of fantasy. In this early work which he expands upon in *The Secular Scripture* twenty years later, Frye places pure fantasy at an extreme of satire near to the genre of naive romance. Romance is defined as humanised myth, with naive romance 'closer to the wish-fulfillment dream' (F1: 17), and the author suggests that romance is necessary to a ruling class because they use it to put forward their desires in terms of a populist wish-fulfilment desire (186). But the activity of all romance is a displacement to a desirable world, an activity of civilisation to 'make a desirable and the moral coincide' (156); and the desirable is always based on analogies with innocence and is organised by chastity or purity and magic. In contrast, pure fantasy attempts the absolute fulfilment of desire which is self-destructive because of the impossibility of excluding the actual, although Frye notes that it is usually pulled back toward satire 'by a powerful undertow often called allegory' (225).

Frye attempts to discuss romance as a modal as well as a generic concept, in that he looks overtly to the broader ideological and epistemological issues that underpin it. Indeed many of these early critics tend toward this approach even though few are as explicit as Frye. A more recent book which also discusses fantasy is P. Marinelli's *Pastoral* , which indicates a trend toward dealing with the distinction more openly when it recognises that pastoral is not just a genre but an informing ethos (MA: 18). The word ethos is taken directly from rhetorical theory and usually refers to the personal strategy of the writer or speaker: whether they wish to appear to be powerful, helpful, charming and so on. As such it is different from stance, which refers to the inclusive situation of reader, writer and text, but it does go some way toward a recognition of the importance of the activity of writing. The concentration upon ethos allows Marinelli a broader historical perspective, underlining the generic links between fantasy and pastoral, formed explicitly in epistemological terms.

It is through ethos that Marinelli is able to locate truncated pastoral or what he calls the libertine, squarely in the mode of fantasy. The movement of pastoral is to examine the complexities of life by moving 'temporarily' to a position of simplicity, and the movement always includes a return to the actual. Without the return, pastoral becomes the illusion of the libertine. Marinelli's concept of the libertine's world is parallel to that of the pastoral: Both are fantasy paradises separate from the actual world. But whereas the pastoral 'recognises Nature for what it is, a fallen state, and calls in the discipline and rule of Art to regulate it' in order to achieve the paradise (22), the ethos of the libertine world tries to be 'natural' and uses art to pretend 'that Nature is innocent and that therefore it has no need of Art to control it ... ' (32). Because it denies that its paradise is artificial, the libertine may look on it as a real alternative and retreat to it permanently. We should note that this is only possible within an epistemology that states some kind of directly representative function for language, for only in that epistemology will we be able to accept that the words we use can fully present an alternative world.

Pastoral and the libertine both attempt escape into the past or future, or into a geographically different present. Pastoral does so specifically in order to examine the present, but the libertine tries to evade the present. In each case the escape is usually in terms of entry into a golden world, without ambition and fulfilling a desire for sinless pleasure incidentally implying that pleasure usually involves guilt: But the libertine attempts to prolong the escape. The alternative fantasy paradise proposed in each case is necessarily realised by artifice which is out of tune with actuality, but the dissonance is ambiguous. It provides a way of 'preserving a dream in the face of the rigours of logic and actuality, an escape-hatch which keeps fantasy alive' (MA: 90). Technically the fantasy is created through an enormous amount of detail that constructs an enclosed world. The ambiguity arises because 'we may not recognize it [the detail] as the product of selection at all' (56). In pastoral the fantasy is short-lived, the selection is noticed and the artificiality clear. But in the libertine, where through an intellectual 'legerdemain' the golden world is supposedly presented without art, in other words as a neutral completely acceptable alternative to actuality, the fantasy is long term, a 'wistful and sentimental hedonism' (34).

It has been observed that from Wordsworth onwards the pastoral myths become private. They are not serious pastoral because they do not stress the return to the actual, and this is connected to their shift from the eighteenth century mock-pastorals of social contentment to the child cults of the twentieth, of which 'Peter Pan' may be the clearest example. But in concentrating on the change in the figures within the golden world, the structural change is neglected. The two-way movement of pastoral is the same in the fourteenth as in the eighteenth century, but it becomes increasingly stopped within the golden world as it approaches the twentieth, and the contemporary attitude to childhood as innocent provides a figure which encourages this truncation. Tolkien himself describes fantasy as 'the pastoral ideal held by youth (without the sense of crisis to sharpen it)' (M1: 157). The child is not held to have the responsibility of the adult to re-examine the world.

Other theories from this period, commenting on fantasy, indicate that contemporary attitudes to children are not quite so straightforward, but they all find the reaction of the child to his world pertinent to defining the term. Viewed from another perspective, Kaplan in *The Passive Voice* notes that the hero as a communicator between God and man in an anthropomorphic world, is a humanist invention today found most often in children's literature[18]. By contrast the modern adult has a scepticism about homocentric illusions. While pastoral documents this change, it is not relevant to its stance. What is important is that the earlier hero had the effective power of returning to change the world after the separation of pastoral, at first carrying out God's will and later on that of human beings. But with the loss of private power, the hero becomes useless to pastoral. This does not mean that the stance of pastoral has changed, but that as prevailing attitudes to human beings within the world have changed, pastoral has turned to different features and generic elements for realisation.

The division and change in the concept of the hero is also relevant to the relationship between folk tale and fantasy. Suvin, in a study of the poetics of science fiction, notes that the hero of fantasy is helpless while that of folk tale is successful. He goes on to say that fantasy, in contrast to science fiction and pastoral, denies the autonomy of physics; the hero is passive in relation to the surroundings. Fantasy is described as 'parasitic' upon science fiction. It is based on fossilised reasoning, the irrational, and magical rather than social forces, in contrast to science fiction which is analogical and extrapolative (T: 31). Yet it is the element of magic, of the possibility of a totally enclosed world of Faerie that Tolkien for example is at pains to separate from fantasy proper. Magic should not be 'an end in itself, its virtue is in its operations ...' (TO: 17).

Throughout the criticism of related genres, each critic views fantasy as taking on a different form from different generic elements. Together their definitions appear to be contradictory. In pastoral fantasy stops the return to reality; in utopia fantasy closes the gap between itself and reality; in romance fantasy replaces reality. Marinelli's libertine pastoral insists on an ideal innocence; Gerber's 'pure fantasy' proposes a perfect alternative world; and Frye's 'naive romance' proposes the imposition of wish-fulfilment. Yet there is wide agreement that fantasy operates not only in the technical terms of generic kind . Most of the fantasy theorists define it with respect to the factors of control, the hiding of artifices and creation of an alternative world and with respect to prevailing attitudes to perception and knowledge. And once more, theorists who define fantasy as a game play upon recognition of the epistemological, while theorists who emphasise desire evade the implications of that recognition. However, the ignoring of the ideological and epistemological within expressions of desire complicates theory enormously, because those elements are clearly present even though being denied.

3 THEORIES OF FANTASY AS A GAME

It may partly have been the difficulty of speaking about desire so clearly delineated in Freud's writings, that turned Anglo-American theorists of written fantasy in the mid-70s toward explication mainly in terms of games, and hence toward the generic relationship with satire and utopia. The major book to appear in this decade was W. R. Irwin's *The Game of the Impossible: A Rhetoric of Fantasy* (1976), the latter part of which is organised around just such generic divisions as those of the preceding chapter. Both Irwin, and E. S. Rabkin in *The Fantastic in Literature* (1976) another important study based on games, are keen to concentrate on satire and utopia, setting aside fairy story in particular from fantasy. The former states that fairy story aims at spiritual truths while fantasy does not, for fantasy seeks to convince by clear argument not by paradox; and the latter makes a similar claim based on the non-logical activity of fairy story that fantasy by his definition does not engage in. The games theory base of each explication rules out activities of magic or nonsensical logic, but as we shall discover there are more pressing reasons to keep this particular genre at bay.

Irwin avowedly follows Huizinga in his study of control and clearly isolates 'the problem of fantasy', which is that on the one hand fantasy attempts to isolate itself from the actual so that it can remain neutral, while on the other hand it necessarily comments upon that actual. However, both he and Rabkin avoid the implications of the 'problem' that earlier writers, such as Gerber in particular, point out. One of the few recent writers to attempt to examine this problem while developing a specific theory of fantasy is C. Manlove in *Modern Fantasy* (1975), and although the significance of this book lies in a rather different area I shall present much of its technical argument here as a means of counterpointing, along with Gerber's study, the prevailing discussion of fantasy as a game. What the following study aims to do is build up a composite picture of fantasy techniques from a variety of sources. An interesting development is the extraordinary degree of consistency in matters of technique and tactics that emerges. But more important, the emphasis on control by theorists of game turns them to a detailed study of rhetorical strategy and reader response. Here despite the agreement on technique, we find differing attitudes to strategy and, when taken further than these studies go, to a radical separation in rhetorical stance.

Definition by Technique: verisimilitude, isolation, rationalism

By far the most important technique is consistency in the verisimilitude of the alternate world. This is essential for the illusion of familiarity to be maintained. Tolkien calls for an 'inner consistency of reality' (TO: 45), Gerber for the 'consistent working out' of the fundamental hypothesis of the alternate world (GE: 82) and both place this hand in hand with Manlove's 'verisimilitude' (M1: 23):

> As long as the nature of the country ... conforms to our notion of what a country in those parts of the world would be like, its existence can be accepted by the reader as a matter of course ... (GE: 86)

Verisimilitude is achieved in a variety of ways. Gerber comments that no matter how abstract, the fantasy utopia is 'worked out concretely in suggestive detail', and the reader is made to feel what it would be like actually to live in such a utopia (GE: 82). To control this 'considerable quantity of detail' (GE: 82) the writer needs an ability to 'visualise', to represent elemental and repetitive landscapes (M1: 195) so that the reader's response may be directed correctly to the proposed world. The use of detail and control over visualisation are the main characteristics of an illusion that allows 'circumstantial realism' to pervade images, descriptions, events and characterisations (I: 70). The familiarity of the alternate world needs 'to be supplemented by a general air of realism: by an attention to amass details that may have nothing to do with the invention itself' (GE: 100).

Connected to realism are implications about the use of language in fantasy. Tolkien comments that the language of fantasy is made possible by the power of separating word from object which allows one to control significance (TO: 24). A corollary of this control is both to the opposite assumption presumably by the reader, that the image exactly denotes the referent, and to the implications of idolatry within the perfection of such a relation (M1: 111). Elsewhere Manlove notes that fantasy uses simile rather than metaphor because simile 'leaves the terms discrete' (M1: 195) or precise. Whether or not one agrees with the linguistic theory the effect is significant: fantasy writing is not to be left open to much interpretation. Another feature emphasising the enclosed characteristics of the isolated world is the use of jargon which makes the reader feel as if part of an elected group whose members all use the same language. Scientific language with its impression of objectivity is of considerable use to the fantasist not only in futuristic utopias but in inverting any world which needs convincing detail. By contrast the use of neologism to maintain an enclosed world outside the actual also ends by familiarising the reader, who takes on the privileged position of someone who recognises the significance of a secret language (I: 80, M1: 157).

However, there will always be a point at which easy familiarisation is no longer possible, when the conventions of realistic representation are no longer adequate. A central device for coping with this problem is the isolation of the alternate world, usually by enclosing it within a self-referential structure like an island or a country home, or a set of narrative tautologies. This done, the reader is deprived of any choice of an alternative to the proposed world by removing extraneous standards for assessment; indeed, choice itself is removed because it is made unnecessary. The alternate world is further isolated by an insistent use of rationalist logic. To maintain consistency of verisimilitude, and the enclosure of the proffered world, experimentation and distortion are absent; thought is in consecutive prose; the narrative is 'addressed to the reason' and must not incorporate anything 'whose essence ... cannot be rendered objectively' (I: 80, 74). Within the realistic, enclosed world there is no room for ambiguity (I: 72). The good and the bad must be made definite and clear (CR1: 45, GE: 70); the progression of thought must be from point to point. Gerber refers to that activity of logical thought which not only excludes the imaginative but is more persuasive and controlling than argument or discussion (GE: 81). Irwin observes that 'seldom does a fantasist attempt any means other than cohesive sequential narration to unify his action' (I: 73), because 'external realism, order, and clarity are imperative' (73). Elsewhere, Todorov suggests that sequentiality is necessary to the feeling of inevitability that the fantastic engenders.

But more important than this, rationalist logic allows for the exclusion of any distractions from the proposed alternate world. Irwin notes that the most effective logic is that from an unstated proposition. Because it is unstated it cannot be argued against, although Irwin suggests that it should be 'easily formulated' (I: 59). Connected with this are the denial or omission of assumptions known to be contradictory to the alternate world (I: 62); and the additional technique of positing answers that admit of no reversal (I: 63).

If all these techniques are effective they go some way to providing the author with substantial control over the writing and over the reader's response. It is this element of control that the theorists are keen to deal with in terms of strategy. Their approaches to strategy initially separate around questions of narrative technique. Both Gerber and Irwin note the authenticity derived from a first person narrative. However, Todorov extends this by saying that while the first person is authoritative it can be questioned because it is subjective. In contrast, a third person narrator can present the alternate world as actual, a *fait accompli*, without question: the classic mode of realist narrative. The effects of the two kinds of narration are reflected in two primary kinds of narrative beginnings: in the first the alternate world is simply imposed, and in the second the reader is sequentially persuaded of the world's authenticity, which two devices Gerber calls assertive and evasive respectively (GE: 100). Yet while the theorists again agree on the possible techniques, they begin to disagree on the underlying rhetorical strategies.

Gerber, suspicious of the author's control, argues that whether assertive or evasive the techniques amount to the same thing. Whether the hypothetical world is concretely enacted (assertive) or explained (evasive), the procedure is still a sequential movement from hypothesis to description of hypothetical state (GE: 86). Toward the end of his argument Gerber does suggest that with the reader's increasing knowledge the author's control may weaken. However, Irwin states that the reader's credence does not 'require sequential manoeuvre', and the alternate world must be imposed upon that credibility promptly and arbitrarily (I: 65). For a rhetorician, narrative imposition appears a crude device. Just as with forcible persuasion, it often estranges. But for Irwin initial estrangement is important because he wishes to stress the reader's choice; it is used to remind the reader that this is after all only an alternative, although it is interesting to note that it is always offered as the only alternative (I: 165).

The template for Irwin's discussion of the techniques of fantasy is Kafka's *Metamorphosis* which begins abruptly with:

> As Gregor Samsa awoke one morning from uneasy dreams he found himself transformed in his bed into a gigantic insect.[19]

This kind of assertive narrative opening is exactly what Irwin likes since distances the alternate world from the actual in no uncertain terms. Yet as the story moves forward Kafka necessarily uses less startling tactics as he solders the links between Gregor's world and our own that provide comment on contemporary life. Once into the fantasy world a more evasive rhetoric takes over. But it needs to be said that many if not most of Irwin's examples of fantasies including Chesterton's Father Brown stories, *Dorian Gray, The Once and Future King, Orlando, Nineteen Eighty Four* and *The Lord of the Rings* are sequential in persuasion and evasive rather than assertive from the start. They do attempt to lead the reader into the alternate world and provide acceptable reasons for its existence.

Nineteen Eighty-Four begins with 'a bright cold day in April' and the 'clocks were striking thirteen': thirteen itself striking a far less discordant note now than in 1949. And the narrative proceeds with the all too familiar details of 'boiled cabbage', broken down lifts and varicose ulcers, counterpointing the gradually increasing mentions of 'Big Brother', 'Hate Week', and pervasive monitoring technology. *The Lord of the Rings* is introducing a different kind of alternate world, one for which Tolkien devises a different approach. The largest problem is to familiarise the reader with the non-human beings like dwarves, hobbits, elves and so on. He does this with a 'prologue' written in a pseudo-historical discourse, with references to 'the reader' and to previous 'publications'. The vocabulary is dotted with 'in fact' s and 'however' s, with mighty periodic sentences, notes and footnotes. The arm's length introduction over, the narrative begins in a completely different voice describing the celebration of Bilbo's 'eleventy-first birthday', and the reader is transported immediately into the familiar conventions of English village life. Only gradually, in what is a very long book, do these original inhabitants of the narrative leave their homeland to go to less familiar places, and as they do so there is time to introduce the strange slowly, to surround wildly impossible creatures with the details of domesticity.

What is significant here is that Irwin is not suspicious of the author's control. That control is perceived simply as an element of the game. However, the positive aspect of assertive force as estrangement is undermined by the insistence on the fact that the fantasy world is always quite obviously not to do with the actual. If this is so, then the confusion that the estrangement stops should not arise in the first place. The question is raised why the critic should be so worried about the means to acceptance of the alternate world, if it is so obviously fictive. It is a juncture in the criticism masking theoretical unease. Whether assertive, estranging and game-playing or evasive and manipulative, the author's control leads to a similarity in endings. Rabkin claims satisfaction and fulfilment as the end of fantasy (R: 57); Todorov comments that endings are the goals of the fantastic and that no fantastic work can be re-read as fantastic; and Irwin sees the narrative world moving toward an inevitable conclusion (I: 72). Once inside the alternate world assertive techniques give way quickly to the evasive, and all evasive techniques ultimately aim at an assertive effect.

Authority is unquestionably at the centre of games theories of fantasy. Irwin even claims that the evidence of the senses to which the details of verisimilitude address themselves, are in the end less important than the reliance on the world of authority (I: 62). He goes on to suggest a possible evaluative distinction: that this authority expresses itself in both arbitrary and inevitable ways, both of which have an explicit separation from the actual that encourages intellectual interplay but with rather different strategies in mind (I: 65). Gerber is again more suspicious of the division. While in agreement that 'plain' fantasy may be arbitrary or inevitable (GE: 89), he recognises that the inevitable alternate proposed is always arbitrary in the sense that it is tied to the subjective decision of the author. The truly random arbitrariness Irwin refers to cannot be imposed because the random eludes the limitations necessary to authority. As a result, realistic fantasy or fantasy that employs the techniques of realism to persuade of the validity of its world, can only propose subject-centred authority which superimposes the arbitrary on the inevitable, denying any evaluative difference.

Rabkin's insistence on the fantasist's control over the rules all the time (R: 218) backs this up. He ties fantasy even more firmly to the authoritative and subject-centred by stating that in each case 'the fantastic involves a diametric reversal of the ground rules' (42). By specifically defining the type of inevitability he hopes to defuse the concept of imposed authority by showing that the reader will always be able to recognise it. But the concept of 'diametric' reversal is too vague for this to be effective. For example, Rabkin leaves it unclear how one diametrically reverse an ethic or a belief (180). Further, in attempting to validate authority he moves into another Huizingian tautology: 'we needn't fear that might makes right, for the highest might, as in the medieval trials by combat resides always with the man of right' (67). In other words, authority confers its own right. We need not fear that might makes right, because might does make right. Irwin softens the observation noting that the rhetoric of fantasy always comes down to questions of 'potential advantage and disadvantage' (I: 63).

All of these theorists discuss the ethos of the narrative voice, and are again in remarkable concurrence on the necessary techniques. When the rhetor, or narrative voice, defines its authority the audience must either accept it (GE: 84) or absolutely believe it (M1: 160). As Manlove observes, the rhetor denies free choice, free will or questioning. The way Irwin phrases the identical interaction is to say that to carry off denial of choice successfully there must be 'favourable responses of the like-minded' (I: 25), from an audience willing to play with the conventions of the alternate world. That willingness or acceptance is based on an established 'community' between rhetor and audience that familiarises and involves the latter by reasserting the assumptions of their world (I: 25–27, GE: 45). The rhetor has to conform to the reader's prejudices if their acceptance is to be gained (GE: 86). The reader's desire for fulfilment must be satisfied so that she or he is less likely to question the alternative. The audience above all must not interact with the rhetor (I: 28) in a way likely to change the alternate world or challenge the rhetor's control.

Since the rhetor cannot be modelled entirely on the audience's assumptions if she or he wishes to exert a private control and persuade of this alternate world, a number of rhetorical techniques are required which without exception create an ethos based on evasion, omission and deception. Irwin happily notes the use of omission of reference to the norms of the actual world, as a basic device for imposing the alternate. He also mentions the technique of speaking about these norms in a brisk, disadvantageous way in order to dismiss them. The sceptical Gerber is more acute on evasion which centres on the ability to lead the reader into uncertainty so that the alternate cannot be questioned. To achieve this the rhetor may stress the possible to obscure the impossibility of the main issue. A large number of clear details may be used to cover up one distortion (GE), or possibility of comparison may be subverted by neglecting to explain reasons for the new norms being suggested (M1). Gerber also notes the use of multiple argument or spurious analogies that allow one to evade the implications of the central argument.

The logic of fantasy, as the logic of games, is sophistical. It depends upon the distortion of a means of ordering which neglects to examine its own assumptions because they are either evaded, omitted or hidden. And the radical ambiguity in the central narrative technique which on the one hand attempts totally to convince of its reality and on the other attempts to draw attention to its fictiveness, lies parallel to the ambiguity of a sophistical logic that tries to appear neutral while persuading to a specific end. While fantasy like game has rhetorical strategies directed toward success or reward, according to Irwin and Rabkin it is apparently without any of the ambivalent implications of such persuasion. That rhetorical strategies directed toward might or advantage could just involve a negative stance does not occur, or if it does it poses no obstacle: The effect of authority in fantasy is engaging in intellectual interplay (I: 28). To those theorists suspicious of authority like Gerber and Manlove, another effect of those conventions is uncritical escape (M1: 159), and the more complete the escape the more potential for complete domination.

Irwin himself defines fantasy as 'a story based on and controlled by an overt violation of what is generally accepted as possibility' (I: 4). Fantasy plays the game of the impossible by violating the conventions of this world. It must be not only outside reality but also 'in knowing contravention of "reality"' (8). To be so it must employ the control of logic and rhetoric (9) to transform 'the condition contrary to fact into "fact" itself' (4). This mode is a knowing intellectual conspiracy which, because of its conscious nature, is held to lie outside the moral and ethical in the epistemological.

From such a beginning it is evident that the burden of the definition lies with the reader's response, and Irwin spends considerable energy discussing the reactions of the reader. She or he must 'willfully and speculatively' accept the new system of facts (I: 66). Only naive readers identify with the characters; the real reader must respond critically even while accepting the construct she or he is faced with (75). Finally, the theorist proposes an extended definition which incorporates techniques into the game between the writer and reader:

> The material must be cast into a single, continuous narrative of the impossible that persuades the reader, given his willingness to be persuaded, to grant it his credence in a spirit of intellectual play. Fantasy directs the reader to accept a paradox: temporary assent to the construct without abandonment of the convention it opposes. (89)

Exactly what the attraction of such writing is, Irwin divides between writer, reader and text. The writer can have a direct and simple control of the reader's response (184), which can be exercised possibly toward a genuine alteration of understanding (183) but definitely toward a criticism of the existing norms (96). The rhetoric must not be concealed but invite recognition/participation. It will be rationalistic, manipulative and playful (184), creating a closed system (190), but presumably considering Irwin's insistence on evasive logic, always with the perspective of an active reader in mind. For the reader the mode provides contemplation or diversion. But diversion or entertainment is strictly toward utility; it is a means of 'keeping a clear perspective' (197) on life.

Other writers take up the twin elements of contemplation and entertainment. E. S. Rabkin, for example, assumes the concept of the game and defines fantasy as dependent upon the reader participating 'sympathetically in the ground rules of a narrative world' (R: 4) which are then directly reversed. Entertainment in this theory, assumes the form of escape, but it is escape literature with a serious purpose. The concept of contemplation within escape becomes the confirmation of expectation, the knowledge of order and fulfilment of prophecy as consolation. Rabkin's thesis proposes that fantasy is a mode which foregrounds knowledge. The knowledge is specifically that of mankind and of related studies that reflect mankind's way of looking at the world. Physics and mathematics as well as psychology, sociology, biology are placed in the field. Because the concept of a human being in control of the world is central to Rabkin, the emphasis in the game shifts onto the player. The player's intelligence, like that of the great detectives in fiction, is always right.

Rhetorical Implications: the attempt at neutrality

These attempts to anchor the mode in an epistemological challenge to the actual separate when the position of the reader is considered into attitudes to fantasy as intellectual interplay and uncritical escape, and the difference between authority as game play or enforced power. All the theorists are aware of the importance of the reader but divide between the confidence or scepticism about the ability to recognise the techniques and tactics. One of the most interesting aspects of the approaches is a consistent identity of terms, used with rather different evaluative directions. Both sides note the control over word-object referentiality, both use the image of narcissus to describe the fantasist, and both agree that the stance is one of control demanding acceptance of subjective truth, centering their contradictions around the ambiguity of the terms 'imposition', 'authority' and 'inevitability'. Yet the implications arising from each approach indicate a fundamental difference in attitude to rhetoric and to the rhetorical stance of fantasy.

To turn first to the critics specifically interested in fantasy and the central concept of control: E. S. Rabkin focuses the movement of fantasy on desire to seek in the mode a flight from the intolerable (R: 194) that pursues specific values. It is structured so that 'people agree to assign known values to allowable actions' (210) and continual reassessment becomes unnecessary. In order to make such an attempt possible the rhetoric of fantasy circles around a controlling intelligence. As previously noted, Rabkin assures us that we have no need to fear the manipulation of such a rhetor because control is always essentially correct, might does make right (61): underlining the point that its rhetorical stance is oriented toward success. Yet above all, while fantasy always offers the escape of a tamed world, at the same time 'A real Fantasy uses the fantastic so essentially and so constantly that one never escapes its grip into the security of a fully tamed world for more than a moment' (218); it is never really an escape.

The conflict between fantasy as a temporary structure yet oriented toward success and gaining specific ends, depends for its resolution primarily on the reader's response. While Rabkin recognises this, he does not account for the situations in which the reader fails to criticise and the rhetoric becomes long term. Irwin discusses the reader's involvement in depth and part of his definition underlines the necessity for critical response even while accepting the impossible construct (I: 78). Behind this lies the general principle of 'distance' in fantasy, which turns it into a 'demonstrational narrative dominated by intellectual persuasion' (76). The reader has a 'continually renewed awareness that he is engaged with the impossible as a factitious reality' (76). Criticism of the actual world is the expected completion to fantasy even though the reader's 'reflective activities' may not be regular or complete. Yet despite all the interplay and critical activity, it is implied that there is never any fundamental criticism of the actual world because the alternate depends upon the existence of the actual to make its points.

In realising its relationship with its reader Irwin states that fantasy, unlike other literatures, is predominantly 'rhetorical' rather than artistic. Being so, it is oriented toward success: its rhetoric is purposive (I: 8). He claims that in this it is the same with all other persuasion. All rhetoric is directed toward rewards and its mode is 'narrative sophistry' (9). The possibility of a different kind of rhetorical stance directed toward quality and value is ignored. While the details of the creation of an alternate world are specific to fantasy, the techniques, the tactics, the definition and logic are in common with all other persuasive literature. Just so the reader's participation is the same, only differing in degree. The critic differentiates between fantasy and propaganda by noting,

> I do not propose to discuss this kind of stimulus and response fully, because its operation in a fantasy seems to me no different from what is found in any roman à thèse. The rhetorical tactics, quite separate from those that make the fantasy-illusion intellectually acceptable, are likewise the same ... The persuasiveness by which a fantasist attempts to

establish the possiblity of his factitious narrative is addressed to the intellect; the persuasiveness of the propagandist may work through the intellect, but its aim is the affections. (78)

And he relies on the concept of intellectual information and participation as a guarantee of impartiality. Irwin, in contrast to Rabkin, is aware that the reader may fail to recognise the criticism, but insists that there is a responsibility to do so, and further, he says,

no one capable of playful belief, as a certain Irish bishop was not when he doubted the veracity of *Gulliver's Travels*, confuses it with the centre from which it departs. (66)

The readers who are gulled are never considered. We know that certain writing is playful because of literary expectations, the authority of conventions, 'divine beings, sages and savants, institutions, traditions, and the heritage of common experience'. Yet he goes on casually to note, 'that [this authority] ... can be fallible is a familiar argument of skeptics and I need not stop to discuss it here' (62). The refusal to pursue the one thing that justifies 'playfulness', the grounds of the culture or ideology providing the authority/conventions, is not considered; the implications of the discourse cannot be followed through. Yet, at this further critical disjuncture, the theorist suggests that even if the reader fails to recognise the playful, the effect of the rhetoric is only short term so any possible failure to criticise has an inbuilt safety net.

At the base of the rhetorical stance in the literature of fantasy we find not only techniques and tactics specifically defined as sophisticated, but also the assertion that it is clearly directed toward success and that in this it is identical with all other rhetoric. A corollary is that fantasy rhetoric can be used as a means of controlling the external world, and to do so it posits specific facts and standards to prove its control and in doing so it creates its own theories of knowledge. Each critic has insisted on the truth of the fantasist within the self-created world. The fantasist's power has been allied with a primary aim of fantasy stated by Tolkien: to free people from the domination of observed fact (TO: 95), which has been reiterated through their individual perspectives by later critics (I: 9, R: 49). Significantly Irwin claims that it is because of this contravention of fact that fantasy is 'noncontroversial as to value' (I: 59). The split between fact and value is deeply rooted in the stance. As an almost inevitable consequence of attempting absolute control, they attack fact on its own grounds. They cannot deny its existence because the control they depend upon generates the idea of 'fact' as discrete information in the first place. The claim that they wish to be rid of its dominance is difficult to accept, and even if it were not, the opposition of one control to another is ultimately self-defeating.

Further, each theorist assumes that the reader will naturally interact critically because fantasy proposes a definite alternative. It is clear and obvious that it is a game. The point is that they appear to want it both ways. They want fantasy both to criticise and to convince. The author produces a work that is then read by the reader, yielding a consistent critical response but one which is dictated by the author. To do so it claims its own truth, its own facts and its own absolute word-object relationships. Implied in this is a control over the writing and the words which is paradoxical. The techniques of the rhetoric effect a total control so that there need be no ambiguity, yet precisely because of this lack of ambiguity and access to absolute understanding, the rhetoric itself is not necessary. It is a rhetorical stance that denies that its rhetoric is necessary. In the end it claims a severance from morality as an activity and ties itself to definite standards which must be taken as axiomatic. Its final aim is neutrality.

At this point it is helpful to turn to W. Brandt's *Rhetoric of Argumentation*. In this careful exercise attempting to justify intellectual persuasion in any area, Brandt knows that he has to discuss the negative structure and effects of argumentative strategy. The first point to be acknowledged is his dismissal of imaginative literature on the basis of it being aimed toward experience rather than judgment, which is incidentally in accord with the dismissal by the literary critics of fantasy, of a positive rhetoric which combines fact into value. But while on one hand Irwin says that fantasy is 'the embodiment of a value judgment that the reader will, I hope, accept' (I: 78), on the other Brandt points out that while all argumentation is persuasion to assent, 'This is not to say that any argument that wins assent is a good argument'[20].

Having spent much of his time providing a sound basis for argumentation, Brandt turns in the latter chapters to defective and reportorial rhetoric. Defective rhetoric fails to convince an audience that is both sympathetic, critical and well-learned in the art of rhetoric (201). That it fails is due to the use of a selection of techniques and tactics which neatly circumscribe those of fantasy. Brandt notes the adoption of a reader's prejudices in order to convince, and predicts the inevitable failure on grounds similar to those given, in the preceding discussion, by fantasists themselves. He criticises the use of absolute definitions of standards of purity, as high-handed. He focusses on the use of the narrator not just as a prerequisite ethos to be trusted or not, but as a means to persuasion; the narrator's voice, in attempting 'truth', is reduced to jargon, various 'dodges', and the use of non-existent or pseudo-logic. Brandt's concluding discussion of 'Reportorial Writing', which is not merely defective but in which no real argument takes place, says, 'the essence of the reportorial ethos is that the writer present himself as what he cannot possibly be – an impartial observer' (257). All these aspects are considered by the theorists to be an advantage to the fantasist. Yet because of the tautological enclosure of the critical rhetoric about fantasy, it is apparently impossible to see the shortcomings of the mode and it remains surrounded by ambivalence.

One of the clearest indexes to the split between those confident and those sceptical of reader sophistication is the commentary on fantasy's relationship with other genres. For example, at the level of technique the isolation of the alternate world leads the critics to quite different conclusions. Gerber notes that when the gap between fantasy and the actual world is closed, when the realism necessary to persuasion becomes complete, literary fantasy simply becomes the novel. By contrast Rabkin, Irwin and Tolkien, all suggest that the total fantasy, the complete persuasion, is necessary to maintain the power of fantasy. For them it is the completeness of the alternate world, dependent upon concealment of the artifice, that ensures that the fantasy is not about the actual world and therefore in contrast to it. On the other hand, directly relevant to the radical ambivalence of the stance, Irwin and Rabkin are keen to separate the magical or the nonsensical from fantasy precisely because they have a vested interest in making sure that the reader is at all times aware of the external world, for it is this that ensures the neutrality of the alternative.

It is interesting to note that these critics of the late 70s reverse many of the earlier definitions of fantasy by their insistence on the consciousness of the real. They push fantasy back toward pastoral by stressing the need for it to criticise its own norm. Irwin states that 'until the reader has used the story for some kind of critique of what it opposes, the experience that the fantasy enables is incomplete' (I: 76). He recovers the constructive innocence of pastoral for fantasy. It becomes an artificial device for presenting desirable patterns of purity, which is a moral simplification but not an abuse of the reader because the alternative world recognises its own fictionality (125).

At the same time they invert the definitions derived from satire and utopia. Colin Manlove reiterates Gerber's idea of paradise or of utopia as 'an enclosure, a protected place' (M1: 119). Such a place is encircling and complete; it satisfies the need for a haven and a retreat. Manlove also suggests not only that the basic activity of fantasy is to provide the retreat, but also that it will always fail. To avoid this failure, Irwin transforms the concept, by saying that utopias are concerned with the presentation of 'impossible' worlds which he connects to the desire to regain the euphoria of childhood in play. For him the construction of these worlds is not a simple gratification of a wish but an objective discipline demanding a conscious economy of energy and quiescence. In direct contrast, E. S. Rabkin suggests that utopias are unlike fantasies in that they extrapolate from norms rather than reversing them, but that satire is fundamentally fantastic because it always reverses norms (R: 146). In other words utopias are not impossible but fantasies are, and utopias are not primarily satiric.

The outlook inverts the division between utopia and fantasy made by Elliott and Gerber, which has utopia as a genre that reverses norms and fantasy as one which attempts an enclosed consistent world. The point is that Rabkin and Irwin depend upon a faith that the fictiveness of fantasy will always be perceived for the game that it is. They would not deny that fantasy attempts its enclosed world, but they take for granted Huizinga's suggestion that the activity is not taken to be real, only fictional. In relation to playful fictiveness, Irwin stresses the relation between fantasy and nonsense. Both genres are non-earnest outside the moral, logical, biological and ethical. They pose absolute rules and control their worlds through a logic of predominantly associative figurations leading to an enclosed world based on axiomatic assumptions, a logic primarily rational and analytical. But whereas nonsense attempts to sever all connections with the actual, fantasy keeps the actual always in view.

To summarise on games: the definition of fantasy rhetoric even to the separation of poetic from rhetoric, and known fact or standard from affective value and emotion, is directly parallel to the stance of negative rhetoric in the post-Renaissance epistemology (H1). Beyond this the claim that this rhetoric is the only rhetoric and that it may approach neutrality, coincides with even more basic definitions of negative rhetorics outlined in Plato's *Gorgias* . The focus is on control as desirable and necessary, that to effect it the rhetoric must be sophistical and short term, and that in being so it will achieve impartiality. Impartiality is simply an extension of sophistry. Sophistical rhetoric attempts to appear superficially neutral; yet recognising the superficiality for what it is, is intended to lead to an apparently profound neutrality, or impartiality.

Fundamental to this group of critics is that neutral rhetoric is a game. Game allows for the creation of an enclosed world which denies the possibility of effective negative rhetoric in the actual, and denies the possibility of an alternate positive rhetoric because it is held to be unnecessary. The problem is that if one admits the possibility of positive rhetoric then one must also accept the possibility that without it rhetoric may be negative and effective. To achieve the neutrality of the latter, the existence of the former must be denied. Not surprisingly the writing of these critics often manifests the elements which they find in fantasy. They present a tautological situation in criticism which is parallel to that in fantasy itself. The problems and confusion arising from a different attitude to the power of the author, the effect of the writing and the response of the reader cannot be fully recognised because rhetoric has been defined in such a way as to deny that these problems exist, or if they exist as situations, to deny that they are problematic.

In each case the critic insists that the reader recognises the game. The game is indicated by the creation of worlds totally alternate, separate from the actual in order to remain impartial, at the same time as instigating the most complete 'play' of criticism or entertainment. Yet in each case that alternate world is derived from the actual, is never completely separate and the derivation is held to be necessary for the persuasion of the reader. This particular contradiction underlies a problem that many readers have with fantasy, which for the critics is not a problem but a belated safety-net: the high failure rate and short term effectiveness of the mode. Fantasies do indeed appear to be abnormally time-bound; they date easily. Irwin discusses the short-term effectiveness and finds it a positive 'function of its utility' (I: 197). Colin Manlove suggests that fantasies fail because they cannot be true to their own internal laws; they want the alternative world yet they always have to connect it to the actual to prove it (M1: vii). The idea is reiterated in the statement that fantasies conform to their reader's prejudices in order to convince of their own worlds (R: 109). By tying themselves to prejudices they tie themselves to the cliches of the time in which they are written.

These problems arise from the attempts at internal consistency in the fantasy world, but they also apply to its overall strategy. That initial assumption or 'fact' which is denied in order to assert the main assumption of the fantasy world, is itself time-bound. The acceptance of the alternate world is intrinsically bound to the denial of the actual, and if the basis in the actual is no longer pertinent the validity of the alternative is undercut. However, the logical basis of its failure apart, the question remains why should critics of fantasy be concerned to consider it acceptable on the grounds that it ensures a short term effect. If the escape, entertainment, consolation is harmless, why should it not be long term? The internal contradictions within the criticism indicate the prevailing tautology of its attitude.

With one or two exceptions the critics who attempt to unpeel this tautology are not primarily concerned with fantasy. For example it is the critics of genre theory or of allegory who seem to be aware of the negative implications. They too look to the reader to assess the stance, but recognise that the naive reading which results from a lack of understanding of rhetoric is not to be taken as the reader's one-sided responsibility: sophistical logic may be dangerous. Further, they recognise that the propensity of readers to want to satisfy their desires by reading in this way is not a matter of unconcern for the writer, who has a responsibility actively to engage the reader, or to be aware of the implications of not doing so. The two approaches to the reader, either confident or sceptical, are set off most strongly in the political sphere to which the sceptics consistently refer. In spite of statements to the contrary, Irwin's rhetoric is one of dismissal, evasion and slow neglect of initial assumptions. The rhetoric is challenged by Wayne Booth's claim that the inability to re-examine assumptions is a form of intellectual imperialism[21]. Rabkin's comment that the fantasy stance answers the needs of the contemporary world is countered by Kermode's warning that people are predisposed to accept prevailing ideas. Hence fantasy does not resolve a need; it neither prevents nor cures, but palliates an effect. Among the fantasy theorists Manlove comes closest to the mark when he notes that the basis of fantasy is entirely in its creator, and that in demanding absolute belief the creator is in the position of a benign determinist (M1: 259).

4 THEORIES OF FANTASY AS DESIRE

The attempts by theorists to place fantasy within the neutrality of a game are concurrent with the attempts to claim purity for fantasy in the expression of desire. The critic who transforms, albeit implicitly rather than explicitly, the predominantly Christian background to desire in writers such as Tolkien or Auden, into post-Freudian language and terrain, is Todorov. Indeed both Irwin and Rabkin, although not Manlove, make explicit reference to Todorov's *Introduction à la littérature fantastique*, and their work is in part a response to it.

Definition by mode: supernatural/marvellous

Todorov's work begins as a formal study of genre: he proposes three levels of activity: verbal, syntactic and semantic, and the practical application of this division makes up the substance of the book. Fantasy is defined at the outset as the time of uncertainty between the imaginary and the real. The uncertainty is a response of the reader, a hesitation felt by someone only knowing the laws of nature yet faced with an apparently supernatural event. As such it is a 'way' of reading, in which the hesitation is based on the question of whether the unreal is actually there in which case it is uncanny, or whether it is clearly beyond the actual world in which case it is marvellous. It is not a matter of the division between appearance and illusion, which is a question of perception, but a matter of existence. The philosophical implications of an outlook that can distinguish between perception of existence and existence itself arrives later in Todorov's discussion.

But it is exactly this hesitation which is enacted in the 'hover' of fantasy writings in general, over the actual and the alternative world. Todorov suggests that when one shifts toward the alternative one moves into the marvellous, and when one shifts toward the actual one moves into the uncanny. And the two sides of the marvellous and the uncanny or uncanny are directly parallel to the studies which have been carried out within British literary criticism, both of magic and of nonsense or the grotesque. The former in each study is to do with powers beyond the human, beyond nature, proposing an alternative world; while the latter in each study addresses itself to distortions of the actual or what is held to be rationally explicable. Todorov puts it this way, that if someone in the known actual world perceives an inexplicable event:

> Celui qui perçoit l'événement doit opter pour l'une des deux solutions possibles: ou bien il s'agit d'une illusion des sens, d'un produit de l'imagination et les lois du monde restent alors ce qu'elles sont; ou bien l'événement a véritablement eu lieu, il est partie intégrante de la réalité, mais alors cette réalité est régie par des lois inconnues de nous. (T: 29)

In the course of describing the *fantastique merveilleux* and the *fantastique étrange* , Todorov takes a brief look at many of the associated subgenres particularly nonsense. The focus of the definition of the fantastic is upon whether or not there is a rational explanation for the events being recounted, and the basis for this explanation is within the reader-character identification. It is important to note that Todorov defines the fantastic in this narrow manner, and also that he restricts it chronologically to the early nineteenth century. The failure to recognise this narrowness has caused much confusion and no little antagonism in critics who have chosen to read the definition in broader and less relevant terms, applying it without question to twentieth-century literature. But the failure to recognise is itself indicative of a curious break in Todorov's thinking that while the definition is specifically tied to a chronological period, Todorov writes about it while trying to explicate theoretical concerns of mid-twentieth century literature. The definition yields to a flopping back on itself that calls a number of its ideas into question.

The study begins by presenting the different ways in which fantastic readings tend to identify with the main character in the plot. The focus is clearly upon the events represented by the writing rather than the text itself. To distinguish the fantastic reading Todorov devotes some time to two other ways of reading: the poetic which is non-representational in contrast to fiction which is representational and referential; and the allegorical which is figurative in contrast to the literal. The distinction is primarily between that which attempts an evocation of actual events: fiction through representation, or the literal through 'non-figurative' language; and that which rejects such an evocation: the poetic, through figurative language, and allegory through the isolation of the figurative. The first set of oppositions, fictional to poetic, locates itself on the grounds of referentiality; the second set of the literal to allegory, locates itself within the grounds of rhetorical figures.

The critic notes that 'le caractère représentatif commande une partie de la littérature, qu'il est commode de désigner par le terme de *fiction*, cependendant que la poésie refuse cette aptitude' (64). Speaking of fiction one uses referential terms such as 'personnages, action, atmosphere, cadre', while speaking of the poetic one uses terms such as those 'de rimes, de rythme, de figures rhétorique' (64). The literal and the allegorical are opposed in terms of their use of the 'sens figuré'. Here the literal is that which conveys the actual while the allegorical is 'une proposition a double sens [figurative and actual], mais dont le sens propre (ou littéral) s'est entièrement effacé' (67). However, Todorov complicates the issue by refering to poetic figuration as 'literal'. Here he does not mean literal in the sense of non-figuration, but literal as non-referential, in other words, the words themselves as marks on a page somehow totally separate from the world. In an attempt to clarify this overlap of word use, I refer to the poetic literal as symbolic, and the non-figurative literal as proper.

In the fantastic, fiction is dominant, the representational and referential is stressed, and this stress can be easily be taken to its extreme in magic. For example, the magical constructs an alternative world which, by means of its detailed representational points of contact attempts to claim actual existence, even though the reader accepts that it is not natural. Just so, the fantastic never discards the literal as allegory does in its use of figures which are completely separated from the actual. Because the fantastic always retains some hold on the literal, it is easy to move toward the grotesque which operates by sustaining the literal through extreme twists and perversions. And the theorist goes on to describe nonsense as lying outside the fantastic because of its ability to ignore the literal, to be aware of it yet disregard it. In this nonsense may be read as the reverse face or interior, the back of a piece of the knitting of allegory, neither having much to do with the process of the fantastic although both are often con/fused with it.

The concentration upon the reader's identification with the character and upon the events of the plot, means that within this definition the supernatural is excluded from both symbolic and figurative readings. An event exists as the case either actually in nature and is literal or proper, or actually supernatural and is referential and representational or fictional. One of the many problems here is that a distinction between the symbolic and the figurative, or between the fictional and the proper which parallel them, is a distinction that depends upon historical and ideological perspective. I am not sure that it makes sense to propose that any one reader can maintain both ways of reading. The two distinctions are predicated on a difference between the actual and the referential: existence and the perception of existence. Todorov at no point gives a clear approach as to how this difference is to be recognised, approached or experienced. If allegory is defined as a term which isolates the figurative from the actual and poetic as language which rejects referentiality, how is a distinction to be made? Indeed the word 'figurative' is used for both, while the word 'literal' as already noted sets the one against the other. More important for the fantastic, if both literal or proper, and fictional readings are to be possible, one can maintain the concept of literal non-figuration only through a referential, hence fictional outlook. If a word is to be non-figurative it must exactly evoke some thing or event in the actual world, an activity difficult to distinguish from referentiality. At the same time, the representations of fiction in the fantastic are only validated by the possibility of the literal; were they merely referential they could never evoke the uncanny. In other words the very possibility of fiction calls the literal into question and *vice versa* at the same time as each is needed to generate the other. But this proposition is an important aspect of Todorov's definition, for he is discussing a genre in apolitical and neutral terms. If the fictional and the literal or proper can be separated, history is ignored and the reader is placed in a position where she or he is expected accurately to judge an historical period without respect to history.

To maintain the hesitation of the fantastic the writer makes use of a number of strategies. To insist upon the existence of the marvellous or the uncanny natural, the writer needs to employ a language that is accepted as representational: either the literal is in absolute direct reference to an actual natural world or the figures are absolute extensions of the natural into the supernatural. In terms of narrative structure the most fruitful device is that of the first person narrator, for this narrator can insist upon the 'truth' of statements in the sense of an 'exigence de validité' at the same time because the narrator is also a character whose statements can be questioned. Hence hesitation about and identification with the character can be effected. Thirdly, the syntax of the story should move toward a culmination where the reader is faced directly with the separation between real and unreal. This syntax demands a strong sense of the temporal that is irreversible and conventional, generating a response of inevitability rather than gradation. The result is that fantastic literature usually can only be read once as such. A second reading will be non-fantastic because the reader will have made a choice either toward the natural or the supernatural at the culmination of the story in the previous reading. This presumes that the fantastic is a temporary experience in reading that is rarely if ever total or pure, that seldom maintains the necessary hesitation up to the conclusion of the story.

Part of the problem with Todorov's theory is that the potential dangers in this kind of writing are dismissed because the historical period to which it belonged has passed, indeed the moment the reading has taken place its context has irrevocably been changed. The implication is that the fantastic needs an ideology that accepts the representative function of language as literal reference, but is aware of its fictional capabilities. Just so the reader is expected to believe the narrator implicitly yet to question the character, and to follow the hesitation in a story yet make a definite choice about the events. The procedure is parallel to the analogies of the laws of thermodynamics – which I mention here because they figure with increasing prominence in the language of fantasy theory. Not only is there the general tendency of entropy to increase inevitably, thus increasing disorder, but also all energy tends to the condition of lowest entropy or high predictability. Now Todorov suggests that because we have moved into an age which rejects the absolute referentiality of language, the fantastic can no longer occur. The writers of the time may have structured their writing or language to generate hesitation, but since the fantastic is primarily a way of reading and since readers no longer accept its basis of representation, it is virtually impossible that it will occur. By analogy, entropy is total when we read fantastic writing today.

However, Todorov seems to claim some kind of superprescient ability to say how things were read 150 years ago; there is little attempt to recognise that these suggestions are a late twentieth-century reading of an early nineteenth-century situation. For all the disclaimers to absolute knowledge, the implication is that we can read absolutely, that there is no historical change or context to reading. This is important because although hidden, this lack of historical context and change forms the authority for the theory and its claims to neutrality because of just such absolute reference. But further, it indicates the danger of the kind of writing being discussed, because belief in such reference puts the reader under the authority of the writer, denies the very choice that is supposed to exist.

Because of the concentration on character, event and reference, Todorov moves on to stress the thematic and semantic aspects that also define the fantastic. He begins with a summary of his book and distinguishes three parts of the genre. The first creates fear, horror and curiosity, and is held to be pragmatic because it is in relation to the audience; but the critic does not pursue this, saying that it is too psychological. The second is the syntactic relation between signs, which creates a narrative of suspense and which recapitulates the initial presentation of reader, writer and text interaction that I have just discussed. The third is the relation to referents, or the semantic content of the genre, which depends upon the tautological creation of a fantastic universe, out of language and with no connection to external reality. Within the semantic are two sets of themes: Those of 'I' which concentrate on the perceptions of the one who speaks, and those of 'you' which focus on the relationship with the one whom the character addresses. Todorov differentiates between the two saying that the themes of 'I' become 'les "thèmes du regard", de par l'importance que la vue et la perception en général y prenaient, on devrait parler ici plutôt des "thèmes du *discours*": le langage étant, en effet, la forme par excellence, et l'agent structurant, de la relation de l'homme avec autrui' (146).

Themes of 'I' are often metamorphoses, and are picked out by their pan-determinism which derives from the supernatural as a direct cause, and pan-signification in which there is a total correspondence between semantic meaning and the world as its exists. The result of these features is that the subject/object division at the heart of the rational is lifted, time and space are transformed, personality is multiplied. The total correspondence between meaning and world that makes this possible cannot normally happen within western readings because of the physical and mental split, but the fantastic transgresses this split. Transgression is a key concept here because the subject/object division, the ideas of time, space and the individual, are first necessary to the fantastic so that it may then deny them – although this dependence is hidden by the strategy of the genre. While the fantastic is compared to the implied purity of the states of madness, childhood, drug addiction and mysticism in its ability to fuse meaning with world, it is not made clear that unlike those states it manipulates and consciously plays with the correspondence. Indeed it is stated that in the themes of 'I' the narrator/character is a passive observer of these transgressions. In contrast the themes of 'you' concentrate on cruelty and death, life and love. They focus on the relationship of human beings with desire and the unconscious. The narrator/character is involved in the actual and because of this activity the fusion of matter and spirit is questioned, often leading to conflict between the self and the external. Themes of 'you' are based on neurosis, the sexual and the unconscious. They comprehend the conscious non-sexual themes of 'I' but are incompatible with their expression.

The semantic context of the fantastic presents a tautological world dependent upon the physical/mental split which it either transgresses, or questions and ends in conflict with. When it transgresses it is passive, non-sexual and conscious, and when it questions it is active, sexual and unconscious. It is based in repressed or enacted neurosis, repressed or expressed conflict between the self and the external world that either maintains or explores the subject/object divide, which is generated at root by the representational action of the language employed. It is significant that the fantastic is presented either as passive and conscious or active and unconscious, for these are the conjunctions that allow Todorov to maintain the purity of the genre. Conscious action is passive, exerted upon the reader/writer; it is only unconscious action that is active and engaging; and by definition if it is unconscious the self cannot control it, so the reader/writer is again absolved from any of its implications. In the first case desire is repressed and in the second it is unconsciously enacted. This also provides an insight into Todorov's major exclusion: the practical effects of fear, horror and curiosity that the fantastic has upon the reader. He says that he will not discuss them because they are too psychological and possibly correctly, demurs from comment because of his own ignorance. But he cannot then dismiss the negative aspects by saying they don't exist for they may exist within the realm which he says he will not explore.

Todorov concludes that the supernatural was a way of discussing taboo topics without being censored either legally or personally, and that this is not needed now first because of psychoanalysis, and second because language is no longer held to have a representative function. However one is left with yet another question: is psychoanalysis simply encoding and perpetuating the problems of taboo activity within representative language? If so, and Todorov himself certainly suggests that psychoanalytic literature does so (168–9), then language and its attendant problems are still effective and not neutral. I would suggest that the subtle and detailed exposition provided by Todorov shows all the marks of belonging to such a discourse and is a clear indication that these attitudes do indeed persist.

Definition by mode: realism/science fiction

Todorov's fantastic, limited as it is to a specific literary historical period, has implications for the entire field of writings within fantasy. Christine Brooke-Rose in *A Rhetoric of the Unreal* is, as her title indicates, more willing to consider the inclusive situation of rhetorical stance and to study the effects upon the reader within a fantastic text. She is more conscious of the break in Todorov's writing, or has more care to discuss it. Primarily, this book of criticism tries to come to terms with what the writer calls the 'meaningless situation' of the modern world, which is parallel both to the void of endless interpretation and to the concept of entropy as an absolute zero of equilibrated energy (BR: 6–7): the running down of action into complete certainty. It is the sense of the endless repetitions of 'banana' becoming a nonsense word, depriving one by analogy of any interaction with the world through language. This meaninglessness makes the real 'unbearable' so that people escape into 'familiar reality' which is given significance by wish-fulfilment – and this itself has its own problem in its dependence upon faith in an end, in an apocalyptic backdrop. To avoid the dangerous consolations of escape, there must be another strategy to counter the meaninglessness of the world and this, she suggests after Rosset, is *allégresse* which describes the recognition of the real 'in privileged but painful moments' (50).

The process of the book is to examine the experience of *allégresse* by presenting a series of readings. The writer explicitly locates the archetype for this activity in psychoanalysis 'which is based on transfer, that is, love, or "the acting out of the reality of the unconscious"' (BR: 47), and in doing so again shows herself willing to take on the most difficult area of genre study: the individual activity of each textual interaction. But from the start there is an involution of direction in the analogies that ambitiously claim these heights. There is a curious tendency to perceive the Derridean text as without value and hence to oppose it to authority. In doing so the interaction of the Derridean text, which generates value, is lost on this writer although subsequent parts of the book examine a similar activity in Bakhtin's dialogism. And there is the odd attempt to 'justify' the focus on the reader with lists of the names of writers that authorise the deferral of authority. Indeed the reader appears to gain in authority as the writer loses it. Reading as psychoanalytic transfer, I would suggest, is a love that exchanges authority but goes no further. *Allégresse* succeeds only in pain, which is simply the other face of authority. On one level the book is a set of procedures for reading which attempts to locate points at which the reader encounters resistance; and its definition of genre as the way this resistance occurs is admirable, far-reaching and stimulating. However, when this activity is knitted into the circles of pain-pleasure, love as transfer and power as authority, the study perversely limits itself at the same time as it unwittingly presents the dangers of its topic.

Brooke-Rose's study of genre begins with a critique of Todorov's *Introduction*, which she finds wanting partly because Todorov's concept of the fantastic only describes an element in literature rather than a genre (BR: 63), but also because it never deals with adequately with the function of ambiguity. After all, if ambiguity is the only thing that distinguishes the fantastic from the marvellous and the uncanny, then how does one read other ambiguous texts (65)? She notes that the structure of two contradictory readings which maintain the ambiguity of fantasy is a development from medieval allegory and could also be said to be present in all modern texts (66). Far more important is the distinction that can be made between the ambiguity of the fantastic in relation to the marvellous which tends toward realism. The fantastic sees the world as unnamable and indescribable, whereas realism, particularly in science fiction, seeks to denominate and describe the world.

What follows is a thorough study of the rhetoric of realism and the strategies of imitation and iconographics that sustain it. The list of component strategies runs as follows: appeal to memory, which ensures a general coherence in the structure of plot; apparent psychological motivation of characters; the use of parallel stories, where one story is hitched to a 'megastory' which doubles and illuminates; systematic motivation of proper names; semiological compensation whereby a reader unaware of cultural code A can get at it by way of code B; authorial knowledge circulated through substitutes; redundancy and foreseeability of content; a narrative alibi in for example the narrator; demodalisation, or the use of merely assertive discourse to achieve a sense of transparency; the defocalisation of the hero who must be distinct but not too much so; a reduction of ambiguity; a reduction of the being/seeing opposition; accelerated semanticism, or rapid explanation of mystery; cyclothymic narrative rhythm because of the need to exhaustively present 'good' and 'bad' phases; and, exhaustiveness of description. The list is significant not only because it coincides with a number of strategies that both Brooke-Rose and Todorov set aside for the fantastic, but also because it virtually duplicates the elements picked out by the theorists of fantasy as a game.

Brooke-Rose summarises the list into 'the (pedagogic) plethora of information to be circulated, and the (pedagogic) need for clarity and readability' (BR: 91), which two aims are held to be contradictory because the former concentrates on the introduction of new information while the latter depends upon familiar recognition. And here the critic notes that in realism each term is subjected to the 'biased' sense of ideology, which enervates and reduces it to fixed definitions that simply become part of the habitual background to the reader and cease to engage, eventually atrophying into complete 'unreadability' (97), and that it is the balance of these two elements that determines the fantastic reading. The key to the fantastic is how the reader is coded: if a reader is overdetermined the writing is 'too clear', yet if the reader is underdetermined the text is too obscure to participate in. A balance between the two must be struck to ensure 'pleasure and mystery' (112), to ensure the active 'co-operation' (116) of the dialogical texts. One of the joys of this book is to participate in the wide subtlety of such a balance as Brooke-Rose presents her reading of a number of different texts. But although she does note that much of the coding is a result of historical position, she does not pursue this aspect and restricts her presentation mainly to the structural.

Within this scheme pure fantasy is the sustained ambiguity that results from a permanent gap in information. This gap is normally filled in realistic texts either by external, cultural factors of the macro text, or by internal 'textual' features of the micro text. For the gap to be sustained there must be mutually exclusive systems of the fabula and the *sjuzet* , which are terms that Brooke-Rose uses roughly parallel to the story and the plot or discourse (BR: 227). However, she retains the term *sjuzet* because the word 'plot' does not carry the full significance of a rhetoric or 'organisation', of discourse 'such as viewpoint changes, temporal changes, dialogue, irony and so forth' (29–30). In the marvellous, there is enormous thematic and ideological repetition which generates a sense of a dense *sjuzet* and a diffuse fabula. However the repetitive elements render the *sjuzet* superficial, easy to accept. In contrast the fantastic often has an apparently simple *sjuzet* that is made baffling by other means. James's *The Turn of the Screw* is given as an example of the pure fantastic which is effected by the use of two mutually exclusive fabulae that never marry with the discourse (229). The ambiguity of this text is based on neurosis and it is in the psychoanalytical state of neurosis that the critic locates the source of fear, horror and desire that the fantastic generates:

> The structure of a neurosis involves the attempt (often irresistible) to drag the 'other' down into itself, into the neurosis, the other being here the reader. This structure is successful, ... which is why I called the governess's state (her language) 'contagious'. (156)

Another cluster of significant analogies: neurosis, ambiguity and contagion.

The critic concludes by saying that the fantastic is rooted in realism partly through the need to be plausible and partly through the contrasts it tries to set up between the natural and the supernatural (234). The marvellous errs too much on the side of plausible, and devolves not into realism but into bathetic allegory. Here the critic discusses *The Lord of the Rings* which she describes as a 'marvellous' text because it provides a 'wholly invented and wholly unfamiliar ... megatext' or alternate world. The infusion of realistic devices into this alternate world can never convert it into a realistic narrative because of its unfamiliarity; instead the realistic devices encourage the reader to project the 'megatextual habits' (254), of searching for analogies between the actual and alternative world, turning the text into allegory. This 'flattens' the writing, leaving the marvellous and the readlistic 'bathetically juxtaposed' in a naive allegory.

In contrast the uncanny resolves the unnatural into the natural not by providing a parallel alternative world but by stressing the differences in perception. Brooke-Rose uses Robbe-Grillet's work to illustrate that the uncanny also errs too much on the side of realism in that it excludes the supernatural. Robbe-Grillet's writing concentrates on the bizarre and the horrific 'which opens out onto all narratives with strange or unusual events' (310). The ambiguity of the uncanny derives from doubt, bizarre shifts in perspective and time, transgressing narrative levels. There is never the fundamental ambiguity of the fantastic which avoids combining the supernatural and the natural into a natural resolution. A major part of her study is a detailed analysis of how Henry James's *The Turn of the Screw* maintains that perfect ambiguity of natural and supernatural, neither turning to an alternative marvellous world nor resolving the ambiguity of the text into explanations of perspective and rationality.

She concludes that contemporary literature needs to move along the lines of fantasy into the 'stylization' of dialogism, into the continual interaction of reader, writer and text that lies between the twin poles of parody and imitation or realism, that dominate twentieth century American literature (370). Here Brooke-Rose has in mind not the ambiguities of say Pynchon's novels which attempt to maintain a hover through their exploitation of parody, but the more 'mysterious' ambiguities of Brautigan or Barthelme. The former exaggerates features so that they become complicit in their parodised original; the latter stylise by concentrating on the detail, amplifying by reducing to bare elements of writing. Only in stylisation, it is implied, can the 'idiocy' of the world be recognised (388), and its reality be set in opposition to meaninglessness through *allégresse*. In this she is echoing two fundamental tenets of the theorists of fantasy as a game. But whereas their stress on these realistic or naturalistic elements arose from the need to comment on the world, for the theorists of fantasy as desire these are the very elements necessary to maintain the hesitation that makes comment on the world unnecessary. For theorists of game the double bind arises from the insistence that fantasy comments upon the actual world, yet to remain neutral it must be isolated from it; the bind for theorists of fantasy as desire is that for fantasy to remain pure it must maintain its ambiguity yet paradoxically remain part of the external world that it dismisses. The way that ambiguity is defined devolves it to ambivalence leaving the reader most vulnerable, most open to danger.

The main drawback to this scheme is the insistence on the purity of fantasy, the state of permanent information-gap ambiguity that should never touch upon the external world yet manages to perceive glimpses of the real in the painfulness, desire or fear of neurotic experience. There is, in effect, no significant difference between information and readability. Information is based on a concept of quantifiable knowledge that finds its source in exactly the same presuppositions of the familiar structure of the readable: both are intrinsically tied to the current perceptions of the world and determined by the same historical moments (H1: 76). The fantastic may be generated from a temporary incompatibility between the two, but this is not an actual difference. It is an ambivalence resulting from insufficient ground rather than any radical ambiguity. That ambivalence may appear to be pure because it manages to evade engaging with anything outwith itself by defining as complete the world it is prepared to see; but its process of innocent isolation is an immediate indication of the evasion of its stance.

The fantastic is indeed continually hovering over the question of information and description, of the information-gap and readability, Todorov is acute in saying that the question is rather whether it relates to the natural or the supernatural world than if it can perceive the 'real'. But in this hovering state of realised desire there is no safe neutrality or purity. It is at precisely this moment that the reader is most vulnerable, most in danger of the imposition of authority. The process of neurosis does not generate fear from ambiguity itself, but from the enforced ambivalence of the contagious state. It is the quality of imposition, of being rendered inactive, that lies at the centre of the fantastic and makes it most dangerous unless it is placed firmly within an historical context. Brooke-Rose ends by claiming that her writing does not seek something 'outside', nor does it seek an end or alternative; yet at the same time she recognises 'power' that operates outside language and her whole discussion has been set toward the possibility of recognising the 'real' through language and literature.

Essential to the purity of fantasy as desire is the activity of hesitation which means that no active choice is taken, and hence there is no participation in the world. The contagion of neurotic desire so clearly delineated by Brooke-Rose is pure because of its maintained ambiguity. It is plausible because it is related to the world, yet it never touches the actual; it sets up a contrast between the natural and the unnatural to create hesitation, but it never decides between them. For Todorov this activity is either conscious and passive, a wish-fulfilment that enacts a repressed neurosis that has much in common with the isolated world of the game; or it is unconscious and engaged in expressing the neurosis in the isolated activity of its desire. As Todorov notes, the latter activity comprehends the former, and the stress on the concept of desire in

Brooke-Rose and others is a broad comment on the short-comings of the theories of game. The theory of fantasy as desire deals with the impossibility of neutrality through isolation, by creating the category of the purity of activity. There is no spatial and temporal isolation but a posited isolation of will.

The fantastic is rooted in 'realism', in the representative function of language about which it is continually ambiguous – an ambiguity which maintains its purity. But the conditions for ambiguity presuppose assumptions that negate its validity. The hesitation created by the supposed opposition of figural and referential and the ambiguity set up by the apparent information gap between new information and readability, are called into question by the non-oppositional, self-sustaining circles of support that wish-fulfilment and desire in effect provide for each other, and each circle is itself dependent upon the very realism or representational language they are led to deny. Just so, desire is not some kind of non-authorial inner spring of essence that guarantees purity because it lies outside the world or history. Desire is man-made, ideological activity that involves choice. To define desire as neurosis to make it safe, or to say that it is a past issue, is to evade the problem. Desire can only be pure if it is non-representational, yet it is intrinsically dependent upon the representative.

Definition by mode: Freud and neurosis

A work that haltingly but effectively studies both the claims of and the drawbacks to fantasy as desire is Leo Bersani's *A Future for Astyanax* (1976). Bersani begins the study by outlining the claim that desire makes to 'going beyond the limits of a centred, socially defined, time-bound self' (BE: ix), and proceeds to expose this as delusion. The process of the writing is sideways, for Bersani is also interested in positing a different form of desire than that derived from the Sadean libertinism that generates I/thou sado-masochistic circles of power. Bersani is concerned with desire that would not be caught within forms of authority, but because he is never quite clear about the activity of this alternative desire there is considerable contradiction and negation in the writing.

Many of the strands that occupy Todorov and Brooke-Rose occur in Bersani's work, although his is specifically about desire, and only generally about fantasy. He says that the writing will explore the Freud of *Beyond the Pleasure Principle* , and take him into the fields of sexual identity and neurosis where desire is explicitly concerned with the realisation of secure self-definition. These fields are to be extended to literature as a sublimating activity, as a sensual thing: literature as desire as fantasy:

> Desire is a hallucinated satisfaction in the absence of the source of satisfaction. In other words, it is an appetite of the imagination. Indeed, the infant is already an artist of sorts in the sense that he invents and is excited by imaginary equivalent of remembered satisfactions. The activity of desiring is inseparable from the activity of fantasising. There is no scene of desire which is not an elaboration, a kind of visual interpretation, of other scenes. (BE: 10)

However, there are two types of desire working here. Freud's pleasure principle concentrates on the avoidance of pain, realising the principle of constancy in neurosis, and ultimately functioning as wish-fulfilment. In contrast, beyond the pleasure principle is 'repetition compulsion' which uses traumatic neurosis to engage in increased apprehension, which lessens fright and hence is helpful in learning how to survive. Freud uses a fascinating analogy to illustrate the difference, that of the fertilisation of an egg that leads to life,

> the introduction of new stimulus-masses. This is in close agreement with the hypothesis that the life-process of an individual leads, from internal causes, to the equalising of chemical tensions: i.e., to death, while union with individually different living substance increases these tensions ...[22]

From this the pleasure principle is set up as conforming to the ego, to death instincts, whereas repetition compulsion is a disturber of the peace, an instinct of life.

The analogy is doubly helpful to this particular study since it situates itself at the heart of a complex of informing systems. First there is the implication that 'survival' is the key to life instincts; the more tension, the better the life: Darwinian in the extreme. Second, there is the superimposition of this upon the genetic example of the egg being fertilised, as if by implication there is some kind of implicit hereditary factor involved. And third, possibly more important, is the concept of chemical tensions either growing or equalising. Entropy once more enters the description, here specifically equating the pleasure principle of neurotic desire with null entropy, and high entropy of repetition compulsion with traumatic desire. Bersani attempts to take the study of neurotic resistance of the world actively rather than repressively. He suggests that desire becomes violent, ultimately self-destructive in its attempt to impose itself onto the world in what he calls the 'theatricalised' self. However he also suggests that desire might instead be able to shatter the self into fragments, partial and marginal, thereby bypassing authoritative definition and finding an alternative to violence.

What is interesting is that while this latter aim is also that of Brooke-Rose and Todorov both fully aware of the repressive aspects of desire as neurotic pleasure, they are not as aware of the negative side of traumatic neurosis as is Bersani. His writing redresses the balance. The study begins with a series of 'realistic' readings, which highlight various strategies for reflecting or at least partly accommodating the 'natural' and the 'inevitable' (BE: 190). In contrast to writers of realism who are interested in 'being', there are other writers who are concerned not with being but with a frenzy about the possibility of being. Writers such as Lautréamont construct their language to disperse 'fixed identities' (197). The critic's description of such specifically non-poetic language illuminates the activity of the poetic literal and figural as proposed by Todorov that I called 'symbolic':

> Lautréamont refuses to acknowledge that there has to be any recognisable similarity of nature between the two terms of a comparison, and secondly he doesn't hesitate to convert an analogy into an identity ... The second term doesn't illuminate the first term; rather it proposes that we forget it, that we almost literally jump away from it (195–6).

The strategy allows Lautréamont to explore the innumerable identities of the self in his early work, but it is noted that a shift into a 'literature of anonymously conceived maxims' provides a 'seductive alternative to a self victimized by its own potential for metamorphoses' (228–9). Lautréamont is caught up into fantasy as a game and in the end isolated within its neutral world.

When Bersani moves on to Rimbaud, the further degree of fantasy which moves toward coercion, wish-fulfilment and finally death, emerges. The proposition is that to write anything at all involves one in fantasy and desire with their attendant problems:

Fantasy is central to desire ... Desire makes fiction of reality ... The poet would coerce the world into becoming an excited version of his desires. The self would *be* the objects which occupy consciousness. In a sense, then, the total invasion of the world by interpretive fantasy, is equivalent to the elimination of the difference between the world and fantasy. The world becomes what the self desires, and, at the extreme, the triumph of desiring fantasy is a denial of the role of fantasy in desire. Desire, instead of merely characterizing the self, would accurately describe the world (BE: 235–6).

This denial of the process of fantasy and the activity of imposing desire, is directly relevant to the aim of negative rhetorical stances to deny that they employ persuasion, to deny their own rhetoric and thereby achieve neutrality, purity, absolute truth (H: 14–20). If this poetic project is successful the writer either becomes entirely isolated within the desired world and is perceived by society as mad or insane, or else if society rejects the desired world completely, death is inevitable: to systematically and purposively neglect is to treat as criminal. Once this concept of desire is put into play the only opposition to it is 'continuous self-negation', '*living* suicide' (254) which in terms of social application or recognition of the world is an absurd repetition of 'no'.

As we shall see, Bersani attempts to relate this directly to the implications of *Beyond the Pleasure Principle*. However, it is unclear exactly how the relation may be made to Freud's discussion of the pleasure principle which is specifically linked to wish-fulfilment and the activity of repetition-compulsion in neurosis that lies beyond it. The pleasure principle itself is held to move toward minimal excitation, and is part of the ego-instincts impelling toward death. In contrast, the activity of repetition-compulsion is held to be a survival technique that increases apprehension and hence lessens fright and allows for a swifter reaction to danger. Repetition-compulsion is a result of 'daemonic' life instincts, 'disturbers of the peace' (82). Possibly what Bersani has in mind is the competitive, necessary relation between the pleasure-principle and repetition-compulsion that ties each to an inescapable circle of desire as violence and repression. This is the futile end that is suggested by psychoanalytical structures of desire. But the point of his analysis in the book is that he then goes on to propose that if one moves outside this concept of desire and attempts to construct a scenic version of character, without continuity or reflective subjectivity, one can move outside individual history. This movement removes literature from being a reconstruction of one person's vision, and provides a ground for testing 'new versions of reality' (BE: 256) which activity connects a revolutionary poetic to a revolutionary society.

Bersani has an idealistic concept of drama as a medium that lacks an authorial self. By means of this naive analogy he is able to move on to writers for the theatre, and the comments on Artaud and Genet are particularly interesting. The discussion of Artaud studies the attempt to prevent dissemination of self, loss of self, by enacting 'pure presence'. But the attempt is misconceived because Artaud dismisses transcendence, locating presence in the phenomenon of the body, and in doing so loses 'the hope of *any* self-contained, "non-disseminated" presence in the universe' (BE: 272). The result is that the phenomenon of the body becomes exactly that which it was attempting to deny:

> the theatricalization of desire is always a potential suppression of all otherness. The uninhibited play of desire has a logic which leads, ultimately, to the annihilation of the world. The ideal context for triumphant desire is masturbation ... The paradoxical nature of uncompromised desire is that it is simultaneously the experience of a lack and the experience of omnipotence. (286)

In Genet, this annihilation extends to all humanity as the writer coerces the world 'into being an exciting replica of the self' (288), and turns the writing into the tyranny of pornography which forces desire upon its audience. To guard against brutality and terrorism, there must be an infusion of theatricalised art by the logical argument of criticism, which calls for compromise but also makes 'reparation' to the world for the imaginary impositions upon it. But it is at this point that the critic's alternative to psychoanalytically defined desire runs into problems of its own making.

Rhetorical implications: the attempt at purity

It is made clear that within the Freudian, psychoanalytic definition of desire, the difference between actively re-making the self and social order and totally supplanting it, is one only of degree. The danger is that in the ultimate degree fantasy is denied and desire becomes reality. Although both Brooke-Rose and

Todorov stress the need to be within fantasy actively, to maintain that moment of hesitation either side of which one falls into the realism of the natural or the marvellous, they do not pursue the logical implications of the activity which can only operate if it is isolated from reality. Todorov implies that the fantastic poses no problems because the representative activity of language is no longer accepted. But in practical, effective terms it often is, and the disregard by theorists for a common daily activity makes it all the easier for fantasy to pass unrecognised, for desire completely to supplant reality. Brooke-Rose suggests that the fantastic poses no danger because it is outwith mankind, and hence she neglects the historical context. The fantastic is held to attempt glimpses of the 'real' the 'other', yet its perception of that involves privilege and pain, by implication parts of a structure of authority that make the 'other' into a man-made realisation of desire. That this is so can only be recognised from an active awareness of the historical context. Without this context the fantastic glimpse of the real all too easily becomes spurious and self-created, desire again becomes reality.

The area of psychoanalysis which underlies each scheme and which might be able to throw this contradiction into relief is treated quite differently by each writer. Todorov, possibly wisely, refuses to get into the psychoanalytic effects on the reader, but also adds the psychoanalysis has made the fantastic unnecessary. As noted earlier, he does not explore the possibility that psychoanalysis is in effect another expression of fantasy that encodes the problems attendant upon the representational. But to be fair, he is specifically confining himself to a narrow study of the fantastic. Brooke-Rose, however, tries to take a broader view and does pick up the psychoanalytic, explicitly comparing the activity of the fantastic with that of neurosis, the exploration of resistance to desire and the means of its repression or expression. Indeed, her discussion assumes that explanation can take place within the psychoanalytical and is dependent upon the representational. In contrast to both, Bersani distances himself and tries to examine the role of psychoanalysis within the different enactions of desire.

In the first place psychoanalysis is verbal, and hence according to Bersani, rational. It stops the process of discontinuity, it keeps the activity of desire within the forceful imposition of the self upon the world. But it is that very rational logic, found in Bersani's concept of criticism, that humanises the brutality of the theatricalised self which is the violent other face of such desire. Furthermore the role of psychoanalysis in stopping discontinuity is aided by the negative activity of repetition particularly within literature, yet it is repetition that the theatricalised self sets out to prevent and in doing so becomes brutal. The problem here is that there is no mechanism for sustaining the balance he wants between realism and fantasy, between criticism and the theatricalised self, so that an alternative desire becomes possible. I would suggest that the immediate problem is the naive conception of the theatre as a medium without authority. But at root the problem lies with the concept of logic that is being proposed. Rational logic is necessary both to fantasy and to realism, to information and readability, to theatricalisation and criticism, hence to distinguish between the two on this basis is to make no distinction.

It is interesting which a later essay that Bersani chose to contribute to a book on allegory, pursues different forms of logic that allow such a distinction, yet make it not between realism and fantasy but between both realism and fantasy as against non-representational literature. Although Todorov and Brooke-Rose expose the impossibility of the isolated worlds of game, and hence the impossibility of neutrality, they make their own claim to the purity of desire. Bersani is just one commentator among many, but one to whom many subsequent theorists of fantasy have turned, who reveals the limitations and dangers of this claim. Both game and desire leave their theorists in a compromised position which is preoccupied with the relationship between writing and 'reality', or rather, between writing and the representational conventions of conveying reality. And in doing so they all evade the implications of power and authority inherent in their analogies.

5 THEORIES OF FANTASY AS POWER

Humanists: Romance

Oddly enough, considering the broad adverse criticism of his work as humanist, negative and threadbare (J: 2), Colin Manlove is one of the few theorists to recognise the danger in the claim to the purity of fantasy. The conclusion to *Modern Fantasy* acutely points out the two sides of fantasy as the isolation of worlds either to delight in contemplation or to pursue 'involvement with them to the point of an imbalance of the sensibility producing

sentimentality and escapism' (M1: 259). The stance behind this
activity is one of 'benign determinism' which attempts totally to
control the reactions of the audience, and to do so becomes
involved in negative rhetorical strategies that omit, evade or
repress. One reason that Manlove may be so much criticised is that
he does not look closely enough at the contexts of such
determinism. Indeed, when he comments upon the determinism of
medieval romance as a fore-runner to fantasy, he appears to accept
it almost as necessary. Other theorists who pursue the overt
political implications of the writing, specifically Jameson, Frye and
Jackson, also trace the roots of fantasy to medieval romance but
come to quite different conclusions.

Frye's *The Secular Scripture* devotes itself to a full study of romance
and extends its connection with fantasy considerably. The
narrative of romance is 'man's vision of his own life as a quest'
(FR2: 18); it is a verbal imitation of ritual or symbolic human
action. But here Frye carefully notes that if it comes in effective
contact with the actual world it becomes magical (58). In other
words its completion, if it is in contact with the real world, implies
an existence that is not fictional and which must be magical. To
achieve realisation it splits its terms into good and bad to relieve
moral ambiguities (50), and this results in a hierarchic structure.
There is usually a theme of entering another world 'which often
involves actual forgetfulness of the previous state' (102), and these
worlds often have their own languages which aid their enclosure
and act as charms on both character and reader (110). In romance
one loses one's freedom.

The basis of the difference between romance and the magic of
fantasy is the consciousness of the fiction. At every point Frye
stresses the need for awareness. Hence the naive reader reads
romance as real, as actual wish-fulfilment; and the sophisticated
reader reads it as convention and can use it to clarify self-identity
(FR2: 170). But here the word sophisticated, as in Elliott's
argument for the sophisticated use of a golden world in utopia, is
profoundly ambivalent. It says that the reader should read in a
certain way but implies that to do so she or he have access to
information outside the text despite the need for an enclosed world
to charm the reader. Without this information how should the text
be read? Romance needs a sense of 'otherness' of 'something
uncreated, something coming from elsewhere' (FR2: 60) or it

remains narcissistic. It is only valid when the human being is seen as creator under God's creation (157).

With these distinctions in mind Frye develops a separation between romance as genuine with a revolutionary end, and kidnapped romance which subverts the revolutionary, rationalises hierarchy, posits ascendancy over nature as technology once did and comes full circle to pastoral. But here he refers to pastoral as the 'paradisal, and radically simplified form of life' (FR2: 179) peculiar to its truncated form otherwise defined as fantasy. Kidnapped romance is equivalent to 'pure fantasy' and moves to the wish-fulfilment of either group or private ideology. Frye describes it as based on a social mythology asking for adjustment, 'designed to produce the docile and obedient citizen' (167):

> romance that expresses a social mythology of this more uncritical kind, which may be intense but is not deep, and is founded on prejudice and unexamined assumptions. (168)

As an example he gives Ballantyne's *Coral Island*, saying that while it si not a 'stupid book' it produces a 'superficial reflex response' (169), as does much of the media, education and politics. Frye recognises that these prejudices, assumptions and ideologies are as much the reader's as the writer's; they meet in the generic elements appropriate to their fulfilment.

Romance and fantasy are also separated implicitly by Manlove when he notes that in romances of earlier periods shared beliefs could be counted upon. In modern romances or fantasies the writer has to lead one in, to persuade of their reality (M1: 259). In a pre-Renaissance western world the idea of fantasy would have been absurd. Not only would the concept of a human being as creator and controller of a neutral world have been lacking but also, from an attitude which viewed the world as a series of correspondences, the privileging of just one corresponding world would be silly. Any deviation from those shared beliefs would be obvious and fictional in medieval romance, but modern fantasy has to try always to enclose its world in order to indicate deviation from the actual. Irwin also restates the difference saying that romance asks one to discard one's sense of fact while fantasy asks one into a new system of facts which one knows to be fictional but pretends to accept (I: 67). Romance becomes not a conscious asking in but a sucking into. Therefore, as with theological romance, the impossible is not countenanced. Fantasy on the other hand is consciously odd, supernatural and impossible (I: 156). The corollary is that it must impose its vision, attempt paradoxically to insist on its possibility. The emphasis neatly reverses Frye's separation between romance as conscious and fantasy or kidnapped romance as unconscious.

In *The Secular Scripture* Frye moves on to a full account of political control and repression through sentimental reactions to the fantasy in romance which he defines as kidnapped romance. The whole movement of kidnapped romance is toward 'mindless' acceptance (FR2: 167) which makes possible political repression and control. The most frightening aspect is its 'automatic' nature. In this respect D. Suvin's discussion of modern science fiction is more than appropriate. He notes that 'Myth embodies and sanctions authoritarian social norms and the basic institutions which determine the life of each member of a certain collective authority-structure'[23]. Frye suggests that this use of myth is most dangerous when serious fantasy is addressed to those who like entertainment and can be persuaded to read for pleasure. In doing so, it can achieve a submissive inculcation. Significantly, Frye's essay derives from a study of Plato's concept of the artist as fantasist and corrupting; and one might here point out that Plato had serious reservations about the ability of the child to differentiate between the fictive and the actual[24]. It may be because he is sceptical of the confident assertions of consciousness by the other theorists, that Frye places the weight of responsibility for delusion upon the author rather than the reader.

In Rosemary Jackson's *Fantasy the Literature of Subversion*, romance is again indicated as the historical basis for the fantastic and the source of its political relevance. But the historical development of the writing is only one of a number of problems that the work gets into. The main thesis is that the study of the fantastic extends the psychoanalytical into the political. The psychoanalytical basis of the fantastic not only reveals the unconscious source for social structures and norms that sustain us, but also opens up gaps in culture, realises the desires that result from lacks or absences in it. And the focus of the study will be upon fantastic writing that maintains the gap.

The book is split into three parts, the first presenting the stylistic dependence of the fantastic upon the conventions of realism; the second discussing the source activity of the writing in Freudian terms of the meeting of an originary subject with ideology in the creation of the ego; and the third scanning the historical development of fantasy in the nineteenth and twentieth centuries. The fantastic is held to be anti-realistic, based on an inversion of realism that allows it to be 'all that is not said, all that is unsayable' (J: 26). As such it problematises the categories of truth, the seen and the known (49). But at the same time when it names 'other', it betrays the ideological assumptions of its author and culture in the realistic conventions it uses, and thereby reveals relations of power. While this is what fantasy does, why it does it moves us into the realm of the psychoanalytical. Here the fantastic is shown to be representative of the relationship between subject and social ideology (61). Unconscious desires, repressed by society, can be realised in this writing, erupting into the ideological. In other words the fantastic allows for expression of the pre-ideological; it is to do with a narcissistic originary subject entering and subverting the ideological, rejecting the process of its formation in social terms.

Against this background Jackson proposes that the fantastic is a mode from which other genres emerge. To elaborate upon this Jackson uses a linguistic analogy saying that:

> the basic model fantasy could be seen as a language, or *langue*, from which its various forms, or *paroles*, derive. (J: 7)

These forms are 'associated together' by their 'particular manifestations of desire'. Within the genres that result the fantasy literature that tolerates, legalises, neutralises, is close to the marvellous. This literature is based firmly in the structures of romance, and here the examples given are Kingsley, Tolkien, Lewis, LeGuin and Richard Adams. Their writings are compensatory and conservative, and often defended for this transcendent function (J: 174). But the fantastic also generates genres that transgress, subvert, focus on the unknown and move toward endlessly unsatisfied desire as in the writing of Dinesen, de Maupassant, Gautier, Kafka and Lovecraft. Because the subject never progresses to the ego, this kind of literature makes possible radical cultural transformation.

In historical terms, there has been a displacement of the 'otherness' or the unknown from a pre-Renaissance position outside human responsibility, so that it has become progressively internalised (J: 56). As it has done so it has shifted from the marvellous to the uncanny, and Jackson concentrates on following this shift from the gothic into the modern. This of course is not a new idea. It is clearly set out in several places such as Ziolkowski's *Disenchanted Images* (1977). But with Jackson some of the problems begin to show themselves more clearly. On the one hand, the tendency in the modern genres toward metamorphosis and entropy, toward endlessly unsatisfied desire, is presented as the ultimate in the fantastic because it ceaselessly tries to struggle against the reality (J: 42, 70 and 159). Jackson links the analogies of metamorphosis (Kafka) and entropy (Pynchon) through Freud's definition of extreme desire. From within the pleasure principle where all tensions are reduced, 'This condition he termed a state of *entropy*, and the desire for undifferentiation he termed an *entropic* pull' (73). She goes on to state that modern fantasies make this desire explicit in Sade's ideal of 'an absolute blurring of identities' in metamorphosis, which pulls 'towards a zero point, a condition of entropy' (73) – by which I assume her to mean 'lowest entropy'. All of which she considers subversive and transgressing, and hence positive. On the other hand, the writer is quite aware of the strength of the alternative genres of the marvellous in modern literature, but because she has chosen to concentrate on the uncanny she provides no adequate assessment of why the marvellous still operates so successfully. The imbalance is also retroactive, for the result implies that the Renaissance had little experience of the fantastic as she has defined it, whereas as we have seen there is clear evidence from the rhetorical handbooks of the period that they understood something so like this way of writing that it would be careless to ignore its activity within that history.

What is lacking in the study is a failure to take on the implications of fantastic literature that totally 'legalises', that is overtly 'romance based'. Therefore she fails to take up the intersection of fantastic desire which ceaselessly struggles against the reality principle in its endless pursuit of wish-fulfilment, with the achievement of wish-fulfilment by the desires of romance literature. Jackson herself notes that most fantasies recover desire and neutralise themselves (J: 8), but says from the start that she does not want to discuss these: the first a commendable distinction but the second an evasion that lands the ideas in trouble. It is stated that the fantasy that exposes power relations, asserts and then breaks the real. For example, MacDonald's *Lilith* or de

Maupassant's *Horla*, both break their suggested worlds first by the creation of nameless 'things' (38) that can only be suggested or indicated by language and lie outwith actual phenomena, and second on the basis that they question the referential (36). But they question the referential by 'pure signifiers', names that indicate 'nothing but their proper density and excess' (40); it becomes a 'discourse without an object' (40). Jackson is making an important distinction here between the absolute word/object relationships counted on implicitly by some earlier theorists of fantasy, and the procedure of nonsense language that results in coinages like Dostoevsky's 'bobok' or Carroll's 'boojum' and 'snark'. Because it resists signification and insists upon the literal it is also held to be metonymic rather than metaphorical. The problem here is that the whole question of the possibility of literal language in this sense, of 'pure' signifier, is not considered. And it is highly questionable that the 'neutrality' of one method of discourse can be delegated by the 'purity' of another.

As the agent of neutrality, the marvellous is clearly presented as authorial, knowledge based, omniscient, absolute, 'true', passive with respect to history and discouraging of reader participation (J: 33). But apart from saying that the marvellous displaces the 'other' outside human responsibility – which is historically questionable – and that it relates to the real by the reflection of metaphor (42) – which is philosophically questionable – there is no other distinction made between it and the fantastic. We are merely told what it does, not how it does it nor how we perceive it to do it. This need not be particularly important but for the writer's own comments that although the fantastic attempts to realise desires that refuse to acknowledge reality (70), it 'often' reconfirms institutional order (72). That she then chooses not to look at the literature that often reconfirms but at the 'more subtle' fantasy that eats away at structure, leaves her and her reader with several problems. These become most forceful in her analogies. In the attempt to fuse Freudian vocabulary about the self with Marxian concepts of history, we find not only that there has to be some kind of originary precultural man existing before the 'reality principle' (66), but also that the subject cannot exist outside ideology (178).

More important are the analogies that carry the undifferentiation of the fantastic: Sade's libertines, zero entropy and Nirvana. These analogies are held to be a 'radical form of the pleasure principle' (J: 72) and in the case of Sade's libertines this is precisely so. They are concerned with unity, with the movement toward no gender, as a zero point gained by destruction of the self by the other: total transgression that conveys the slippage of object and subject into each other through images of 'mutilation/horror/monstrosity' (82). This mutually destructive zero is gained by a reward system of I-thou payments, that does have something in common with certain interpretations of entropy as a system of energy give and take. But entropy only achieves undifferentiation by a 'running down', not a tense hover over reality and the uncanny. To call entropy the secular equivalent of God is most extraordinary. And to equate either entropy or libertinism with nirvana is pushing the power of analogy into contradiction.

Fantasy reveals itself here as having strong political potential, but of a rather different kind than Jackson overtly claims. The fantastic emerges as a private, originary narcissistic, power to persuade, to persuade of private power and of the intrusion into ideology and society of the private individual. In the pure fantastic the persuasion is destructive of the ideological by private power but supposedly leaves both powerless. The uncanny allows private power continually to exercise its own persuasion by transgressing the ideological. And the marvellous and the magical are different degrees of the insistence upon an enactment of private power in spite of the ideological. But if the subject cannot exist outside ideology then private power and ideological power are rooted in the same place, they double each other, mirror, reflect. They are caught in a vicious circle/a relationship of mutual mutilation and extremity.

Writers like F. Jameson, in an early article to which Jackson refers, set square to face the problem inherent in the marvellous. Here Jameson also proposes the basis for fantasy as romance, but he makes the crucial distinction between the differences that show up by looking at the genres of romance and fantasy, and the identity of their mode. The 'sacred magic' at the heart of romance is displaced first into providence and then into psychology, which generates fantastic readings where the sacred is held as an 'absent at the heart of the secular world' (JA1: 145). Both convey deep-rooted ideologies that draw boundaries around social order and deter deviancy and subversion. Not only do romances convey ideologies, but they try to insist on certain ideological readings of texts. For example, it is only when one reads the text in a Marxian (or Freudian) manner that one even becomes aware of its ideological structure, because Marxism directs one to the infrastructural relations that limit the possiblities of the existence of the text (158) and sees it as an historical relationship within an evolving structure.

But where the analysis catches itself up is again in the area of ideology. Here, for Jameson, romance raises 'the aesthetic counterpart to the problem of ideology ... the ideological nature of *form*' (JA1: 161). The implication is that only romance and fantasy are so purely ideological, and similarly that only the feudal and magical institutions that generate them are ideological. In contrast, Marxism is historical and revolutionary. Of course, this is one particular way of defining ideology, but it emphasises a misleading image: evolution, with all the connotations of social advance and so on that give the impression that Marxism can operate outside it, and by analogy, that modes of writing can also do so. The political implications of such a statement are radically dangerous – something that Jameson recognises and attempts to deal with several years on in *The Political Unconscious* which we shall come to later. The ideology of wish-fulfilment or the anti–ideology of desire feed on and breed each other. For the moment, in these particular discussions of fantasy we parallel the evasive strategies of other theorists as we move from a stance of control that recognises and manipulates its conditions of power by claiming the purity of desire, back to one that says that power relations are unnecessary and that activity may be neutral.

Humanists: Hierarchy

The rhetoric of fantasy as a game is clear but limited, yet the rhetoric of desire is no escape from this limitation. Both are enmeshed in each other, their analogies move synchronically toward the images of love and death as a two-way reward system of humanist rationality. There is one critic however, who not only correlates the traditions of design and desire, but also combines the shifting nature of desire and wish-fulfilment into one study, and in doing so makes the dangers all too evident. However he does so in the name of allegory and with an approbation of hierarchical authority that runs rather counter to the spirit of the present discussion. A. Fletcher's problematic *Allegory, The Theory of a Symbolic Mode* (1964) is a remarkable work, prefacing as it does all the major writings on fantasy from Todorov onwards with an unequalled density and breath of vision if with rather less clarity. It is rarely, if ever, cited by other theorists of fantasy, presumably because according to its title it deals with allegory and not with fantasy. But the similarities not only in observed techniques and structure of the books under consideration, but also in the vocabulary and direction of the critical discourse are unavoidable.

Authority

Fletcher begins where all theorists of fantasy begin, in agreement either implicitly or explicitly with the assumption that man can exactly represent the world through language. Where he differs with recent criticism is in his awareness that representation need not be naturalistic or supernaturalistic, and in his willingness to examine the broader impulses toward authoritarian control and imposition that underlie all such representative attempts. Whereas theorists of game claim neutrality for language, and theorists of desire, purity, Fletcher claims power. The work begins with an overview of the conjunction of religious, literary and psychoanalytical phenomena that surface in the genres of utopia and satire, but quickly moves on to discuss the techniques and strategies involved on a broader generic scale. Then, following an historical discussion of the development from theological and religious authority, through the sublime to psychoanalysis, Fletcher proposes psychoanalytical analogues to literary genres in obsession and compulsion, before returning to utopia and satire under the heading of 'Value and Intention'.

From the start, Fletcher acknowledges that man is not the centre of identity, essence, perfection and fulfilled will. But he also insists that such absolutes can be approached and that in order to control, a human being must subject herself or himself to absolute control. Anarchy and totalitarianism, the arbitrary and the absolute, meet each other in the extremities of this negative stance. As he says of the agent within the stance:

> There is no such thing as satisfaction in this world; daemonic agency implies a *manie de perfection*, an impossible desire to become one with an image of unchanging purity. The agent seeks to become isolated within himself, frozen into an

eternally fixed form, an 'idea' in the Platonic sense of the term.
(FL: 65)

But not just in a 'Platonic sense', rather in the sense of Fletcher's
traditionally platonist reading.

Fletcher begins by defining the stance not as a genre but as a
'mode' that informs genre. He ties it down to the expression of
conflict between rival authorities that generates either satirical
criticism or the 'apocalyptical escape into infinite space and time'
(FL: 23) of a utopia. The techniques which anchor the mode are an
expression of the genre intent. Although different in their intention
the two genres are virtually superimposed upon themselves in their
attempts to control by fixing identity or relationships. The most
important element of the fiction or artifice is the 'agent'. These
characters, because they take on inhuman powers, he calls
daemonic. The daemonic hero is 'named', his function irrevocably
fixed and made mechanical. He moves in 'fated actions' which
show him in control of absolute power. Agents are always
specifically 'good' or 'bad'. They do not choose but, as appropriate
to figures operating under the concept of fixed eternal forms, they
conform to or deviate from rigid moral standards. Further, because
they are deprived of choice, of an active morality, they are
fundamentally ambivalent; they are free from the usual moral
restraints and only 'moral' in their power over others 'Like a
Machievellian prince' (68)[25]. They appeal both to a 'need for
unrestrained will or wish' (68) at the same time as they maintain
the 'order of things' (69).

The interdependence of the anarchic and the authoritarian is
clearly put in the definition of the hero who 'arbitrates order over
chaos by confronting a random collection of people and events,
imposing his own fate upon that random collection' (FL: 69). Just
as in most of the other theories, the central character or narrator is
either absolutely good or bad. But Fletcher clarifies other
implications of this situation. The character has a claim to absolute
control within the self-made world which is made possible by the
arbitrary nature resulting from privately imposed standards of
rigid morality that deprive other characters of choice and deny
evaluation. For symbolic and practical reasons the control is
effected by a fixing of definition and an isolation from actuality
(53). Fletcher's example here is the island of Robinson Crusoe.

Underlying the fictional elements is an attitude to words which shifts the focus of control from the character or internal rhetor to the author. In doing so it makes explicit the control and the extent of the writer's responsibility. Just as the hero is kept isolated and fixed in order to impose absolute identity, so the author attempts to keep words and things separated in order to control them completely. The approach is an inversion of the usual claim of fantasy theorists that control is effected by an absolute fusion of the words and the thing. For Fletcher, separating between the word and the thing channels the power of words into significances defined by the author. Words are deprived of their power which is then turned to use for conveying that of the author. At the same time they will always pull back toward their own power. There will be that same tension of 'wish-fulfilment' and desire in the language of the literature, as there is in the arbitrary but absolute actions of the agent.

Simultaneously the control of words is directed toward control of the reader. By separating word and thing the author can think 'analytically', can circumscribe the artifice with specific definition. The analytical is aided by an emphasis on the visual: diagrams and geometric forms help to isolate and break up images; they encourage a static dialectic of 'permanent images to convey the fixed ideas' (FL: 98). The visual is also important because the 'normal sense world' is not allowed to operate (103), hence the isolation and totality of the alternate can be maintained. Isolation of word, emblem and agent allows for three avenues of reader control. The first is through insignia for immediate militant effect; the second is through the talisman to generate power to obedience and the third is through 'astral' symbolism for power to order. The reader's reaction is supposed to be a 'calculation', a 'process of explication, a gradual unfolding ... sequential in form' (73). An audience must be 'forced' into an analytic frame of mind (107), and asked to decipher the coded message of the controlled medium. The interpretation is sharply restricted because it is always toward an absolute end.

Communication of authorial desire proceeds by repetition of similar elements to indicate to the reader that the movement of the fiction is not random. All literature functions by repetition[26], but this stance does so in a particular manner; it 'encodes' the reader's response by a symmetrical repetition and can be made more efficacious still by formulaic extension. The tactic recalls Irwin's comment that, 'inherent in fantasy is a fixity of method that, for all the variety possible within it, precludes development over the course of repeated performances' (I: x). The response to such repetition is either sleep, hypnosis and enchantment, or plan, formula and design. Fletcher's combination of enchantment/wish-fulfilment with design, as fundamentally the same in their attempts at control, is an indication of the underlying similarity to the two faces of fantasy.

Kosmos

But it is here that Fletcher begins to diverge radically from all other theorists of the writing. Always beyond the fixed word and fixed response is a counter-movement which Fletcher calls 'magical' which resides in the tension between the power of words themselves and that of human beings, which tension the author manipulates through the use of 'Kosmos'. Kosmos may be read as that cluster of language that locates the tension and directs the reader to the hierarchical order involved in its control. The author restricts not only the reader but also the word. The writings 'present an aesthetic surface which implies an authoritative, thematic, "correct" reading, and ... attempts to eliminate other possible readings' (FL: 305). Fletcher studies the structure of the hierarchy and control which kosmos makes possible by looking at two primary organisations of words: synecdoche and metonymy. He extends their scope out into the images basic to the stance, which are arranged around sequence and symmetry. Synecdoche is defined as a figure in which the part elicits the whole: Something is assumed which is not expressed and Fletcher calls this an 'inferential process' at the heart of the stance. However it establishes static relations between the whole and the part because the part determines the sense of the whole. On the other hand metonymy is a figure based on a cause and effect relationship which allows for dynamic relations between the part and the whole. Here the parts are governed by the intention of the whole.

The fixed nature of the static synecdochic relationship and the ordered or governed nature of the metonymic, are results of Fletcher's own preceding choice to view both as teleologically controlled figures. As with the nature of any figure, or of inductive and deductive directions in reasoning, synecdoche and metonymy are not inherently fixed or ordered. They become so depending upon the stance that employs them. A teleological stance, a stance directed toward specific 'ends', has a restrictive direction. Hence the terms do indeed become fixed and rigidly ordered. It is probably as well to note here alternative definitions of synecdoche as the root of metaphor which may be a series of constantly resonating images (W), or metonymy as disparate, juxtaposed and radically separated (DM2).

That the definition occurs under teleological determination is of great importance to the understanding Fletcher's idea of kosmos. On the one hand the metonymic through kosmos becomes an ordered step by step sequential analysis. It becomes the informing movement behind the image of progress, one of the two fundamental movements of the stance. Progress itself may either build an ideal journey to completion or be a satirical questioning and dissecting of the cosmos. On the other hand the synecdochic attitude of stasis also becomes the symmetrical balance behind the image of battle, debate or dialogue. Steady progression is to exact symmetry, what parataxis is to hypotaxis. Kosmos combines both the static and the ordered dynamic aspects of both figures into a systematic part and whole relationship which bodies forth hierarchical structures in the tensions between the two and which directs its effective power.

In kosmos the teleological movement directs that power toward imitative magic through synecdoche, or contagious magic through metonymy. Using the imitative power the writer, or magician, attempts to bring actual events under control by placing them in parallel with symbolic events (FL: 188). She or he tries to control not only nature but also the audience. With the contagious power the magician uses the part to gain control over the whole, and to do so must maintain isolation of the word or agent through the island or the talisman; magical identities can then be fixed and labelled onto things, can contain them within lists.

In terms of chronology Fletcher suggests that pre-seventeenth-century kosmos directed people to the single hierarchy of religion, but that following the inception of 'the sciences' in the late seventeenth century the kosmos becomes more general and is only 'hierarchic in intention', thereby multiplying into a number of authoritarian hierarchies. But through the question of scientific language Fletcher reveals a number of interesting ambiguities of his own. He centres the control possible to an author in the tension that results from the separation between word and thing. But the thesis depends upon a univocal concept of language, in which word and thing naturally fuse. He contrasts '*prose* stylistics – a scientifically neutral, unadorned prose' to poetic techniques of persuasion 'employed whenever one wants to sway an audience – sway them in any direction whatever' (FL: 129). Even naturalistic writers are spoken of in terms of being able to 'free' their characters; mimesis is a process that is not in need of interpretation; it takes language as the transparent superimposition of the word onto the world.

By contrast kosmos is the active tension which organises prose into hierarchy, propriety and power. This vision underlines the kind of neutrality of kosmos in an extraordinary manner. Kosmos is not rhetorical or persuasive, because it *lacks* power but precisely because it *has* power. Poetic is persuasion but kosmos is enforcement by order or enchantment. The neutrality described is that of a negative rhetorical stance, but rather than being a neutrality achieved because of the full responsibility of the reader, it is a neutrality achieved by depriving the reader of any responsibility at all: this audience is forced to analyse but can only do so within the boundaries and to the extent already defined for it.

Both naturalism and kosmos are representative uses of language, but whereas the former is in ignorance of its own control and power, even deluding itself about the nature of its control, kosmos is the recognised side of control. What Fletcher does is to present the results of a naturalistic representation in a world which the author recognises as material, in other words a world that has its own power, to resist the authority of human beings. Kosmos in effect is a teleologically defined set of. correspondences that Fletcher suggests is peculiarly appropriate to the construction of pre-seventeenth century writing. But having outlined its techniques and strategies with a critical vocabulary relevant to the period and examples from it, the critic then pursues the structure into its developments through to present-day psychoanalysis.

Science and psychoanalysis
The hierarchy of Fletcher's kosmic mode is connected to the change in pastoral as a literature of status difference (FL: 183)

from the seventeenth to eighteenth centuries. When pastoral ceases to manifest the power of words it separates into the sublime and the picturesque as two levels within the hierarchy of kosmos. The terror and anxiety of the sublime which is encapsulated into the picturesque, becomes conventional horror when it lacks the tension of the microscopic. Similarly the picturesque devolves into its excessive feeling of comfort and becomes superficial. They become genres that encourage wish-fulfilment as the supernatural or the marvellous respectively.

Todorov's chronology for the fantastic as a late eighteenth- and nineteenth-century genre underwrites this suggestion. Both writers also suggest, from different points of view, that psychoanalytical works will assume a primary role in the twentieth century. Fletcher's extensive concluding section on psychoanalysis as the location for a resumed power of words is restated by Todorov's suggestion that psychoanalytical works will take over the hiatus between the real and the imaginary that the fantastic filled in the last century. But whereas Todorov does not want to pursue the possible reasons for the psychoanalytical, Fletcher suggests that it has been due to the theory of the sublime introducing a new subject centred, concept of authoritarian control that resulted from the theological authority of kosmos being dismantled and that in turn made necessary the sensual, (behaviourist) authority of psychoanalysis. In between the whole concept of hierarchy collapses into a series of smaller, separate authorities, although along with Huizinga he toys with the idea that science may come to provide a new authoritarian language, not through a system of controlled correspondences but through total univocity. But because power is generated by splitting univocity and channelling the released energy, this hope is implicitly undermined – indeed Fletcher says elsewhere that the univocal enterprise of science is an attempt to reach zero. Most theorists of fantasy as game seem also to have a residual desire for the supposedly totalising effect of science, even though to be consistent they have to deny it because they need the exact comment upon the world[27]. Gerber and Auden are more sensible about the potential future of science[28].

It is important to note that it was during the eighteenth century when apparently direct control by human beings over the actual, gives way to a control over the relationship between the actual and human beings' understanding of it, that the genres providing

alternatives in terms of different phenomenal worlds became
popular and generated the gothic romance, the futuristic utopia,
the child-cult and horror stories. Before that shift, direct control
over the actual was openly questioned, the stance of fantasy writing
had no need to challenge the phenomenal world and was
manifested in naturalism itself. Alternate worlds which present
creatures and events that could not exist in the actual, are even
now only a division of the genres realising fantasy. And as noted,
once entered each of these worlds still depends upon a naturalistic
representation of the actual. de Man defined as fantastic the
illusion of being able to represent actuality. Naturalism is doubly
fantastic because it is not only an illusion about empirical
actuality, but also about the representative function of words. In
these terms a genre challenging the phenomenal world is also
doubly fantastic. While it denies accepted versions of empirical
actuality, it depends upon the representative function of words to
validate its own version. Both realise the stance of fantasy which
hides its artifice by denying that artifice exists.

   The implications of the stance are widely extended when placed
in comparison with a parallel history of rhetorical studies. The
development toward a univocal language by scientists and
philosophers in the late seventeenth century was an attempt to
express precisely the actual world. The hidden assumptions were
that man could fully know the world and through that knowledge
control it. The effect was to control the reader's or audience's
response to it by claiming precise representation of it. Among other
factors the development was made possible by the dominance of a
rational analytical logic which unfortunately tends to hide or
forget its own assumptions, turning them into unexamined axioms
and finding the need for a negative rhetoric. In effect the stance of
fantasy, which is realised in both naturalism and other literary
genres, is also realised in the language of science. Just as none of the
related genres necessarily realises a fantasy stance neither does
science. Nor does their dependence on a realistic representation of
the world, a precise expression of the actual, necessitate the stance,
although it tends them toward it in order to maintain their effect.
It is not a question of genre or epistemology alone. What is in
question is the manifestation of a belief about the place of human
beings in the world which, when it passes through the current
epistemological framework realises itself in its generation of value.

Within his discussion of psychoanalytical analogues, Fletcher differs from other commentators who focus on neurosis and speaks of the manner by which the imitative and contagious magics of both naturalism and kosmos underlie obsession and compulsion. In effect rather than simply describing the activity of neurosis which represses its mode of authoritarian control, he focuses on the expression of that same power, which Todorov allies with desire alone, and shows how it splits into obsession and compulsion, desire and wish-fulfilment. The fear generated by ambivalent neurosis in Brooke-Rose's reading of 'The Turn of the Screw' is not only contagious but also imitative; juxtaposing the two strands of natural and marvellous that she proposes even more closely. But despite being most acute about the political implications of obsession and compulsion as powerful ways of speaking within a highly authoritarian system, Fletcher seems unaware of the vicious, circular activity they describe – indeed he appears to see it as desirable.

When compulsion and obsession are translated into the realm of 'Value and Intention', or overtly recognised actions, they become satire and utopia. Whereas naturalism and kosmos have to hide their representational basis to express power, satire and utopia explicitly use representation to direct power toward comment upon the actual. It is interesting that in terms of the history of the genres Fletcher once again agrees with other theorists, this time those of game and design. He notes that from Thomas More onwards one finds the activity of utopia, generated by the 'spurious rationality' (FL: 339) of the post-Renaissance individual. Gerber also allies utopia and the Renaissance with the emergence of a humanist world and the possibility that man might be able to create a perfect world. The concept of man as creator coincides with the 'fictional activity of logical thought', and this combination gives rise to a shift from the God-given earthly paradise to the man-made utopian fantasy. Elliott suggests that it is the very control by mankind that made people distrust utopias and turn toward satire. Only when total control was discounted did utopias return, and even then, when they did, they were placed in the future. The two are differentiated between by Gerber when he describes the pre-Darwinian worlds as utopias of a perfect state, and the post-Darwinian as advances toward perfectibility. But both still take as their assumption the perfectibility of human beings.

What Fletcher does for both satire and utopia is point out their mutually dependent relationship. Simply because they prompt one to recognise the representation, does not mean that they are not complicit in it. Utopia becomes an 'anaesthetic art' leading to conformity and often to a 'totalitarian world view' (FL: 326); while satire can maintain freedom against tyranny. Yet Fletcher does not choose to emphasise that both attack and defence of the *status quo* in these ways, is dependent on that *status quo*. Instead he pursues the utopian genres into the forms of prophecy and apocalypse and extends their political implications. As he does so he comes straight up against two major contradictions that sever the supposed unity and desirability of the authoritarian impulse: not so much undermining or eroding the argument but causing great chasms or faults to run through its grounds.

The teleological impulse to Fletcher's definition of synecdoche and metonymy runs throughout the book. The daemonic agent is both compulsively fixed, fated to do certain things at the same time as operating within an obsessive structure that fixes all those around, imposes upon them. This circle of private and group authoritarianism extends from agent, trope, figure and scheme to magic, religion, psychoanalysis and satire/utopia or value/intention. It brings his theory of this symbolic mode to a full recognition of the negative stance it usually enacts. The critic is particularly acute on the issues of propaganda which other writers with their trust in neutrality or purity neglect or dismiss, and which are intimately related to their evasion of the implications of political control, particularly of populist propaganda, through fantasy writing.

Rhetorical implications: the attempt at power

Each of the theorists discussed has shown remarkable agreement as to the techniques that surface in fantasy writing, and apart from the niche chiselled out for the 'pure' fantastic which is by all accounts rare and in any event short-lived, they are also in agreement with its primary effect: to deprive the reader of activity. Where these theorists differ from Fletcher is in failing to follow-up on the implications of this deprivation. The neutrality of fantasy as a game depends upon the initial choice by the reader to accept the difference between the alternate and the actual world, even though the one depends upon the other. As noted, the paradoxical simultaneity and denial of simultaneity can only function effectively if the words are viewed as neutral tools with no powers of their own. The purity of fantasy as desire depends upon the total non-referentiality of words; they may have power but it is untouchable by human beings and of little interest. Various critics such as Jackson and Brooke-Rose have commented on genres related to the fantastic; but they are only concerned with the overt authoritarian implications of the drift toward the marvellous and do not recognise the danger in the drift toward 'naturalism'.

In contrast, because Fletcher recognises a power in words he says that the author's control over the words must be effected from the start. Both the actual and the alternate must come under the author's jurisdiction. In a lengthy but revealing quotation, he says:

> Instead of seeing a free agent on the stage, the audience would see a lively *idée fixe*, which would induce the same fixated idea in the mind of the audience. By process of identification the audience ... would itself tend to become fixed into stereotypes. This of course, is precisely the aim of political propaganda art ... The victim of propaganda is allowed no other course but to empathise with scenes that are cast in highly organised, systematized, bureaucratized molds. Since this kind of order is often the aim of the political propagandist, he needs only to get his audience interested in the surface texture of the conformist action. By involving the audience in a syllogistic action, the propagandist gets a corresponding pattern of behaviour from his audience when that audience leaves the theatre. (FL: 67–8)

Yet at the same time, because the stance is 'the art of subterfuge par excellence' (345), it is also capable of conveying revolutionary sentiments within an authoritarian state that would not otherwise tolerate them, although at risk of being compromised by that permission. Irwin makes the same claim, while denying the pressure to conformity which makes up its obverse face (60). What one has to ask is whether it is acceptable to deprive people of the ability to evaluate for themselves in any conditions whatever.

Fletcher's first and central fault only emerges in the last pages of the book where he tries to separate between value and intention as if in a hasty, rearguard attempt to defend his argument against charges of totalitarianism. Although he states early on that the reader is totally controlled by the action of kosmos and ultimately by the author, he concludes by insisting that the authority of the mode can only be effective if the reader is 'willing' to accept its grounds (FL: 359). The genres of satire and utopia indicate authorial intention, but this is completely unconnected with the value which resides in the reader alone. Here Fletcher seems unaware that the compulsive author may successfully induce the obsession of the reader, whereas at other stages in the book this successful induction is the point and direction of the argument.

This raises the second major contradiction traversing the argument: that of the definition of this mode as allegory. Why is it that virtually everything covered in this work is related to the theories of fantasy and that anything that theorists of allegory discuss in terms of post-Renaissance writing doesn't fit at all? Apart from psychoanalysis, which has not yet found an effective written analogue although in the visual arts it has been explored substantially, Fletcher cannot recognise any modern allegories. He claims that in rejecting the principle of the 'goodness' of authority, of 'might is right' (remember Huizinga) which justifies his separation between intention and value, potential allegory becomes irony (FL: 339). Furthermore we discover that at the heart of this mode lies the idea of religion as comforting, set up in opposition to tragic confrontation (345) which neatly develops Tolkien's suggestion of the Christian consolations of desire. As a game this comfort is restorative , as spiritual it is 'the mirror of an ultimate hope or, rather, an ultimate wish-fulfillment, whether for life or death' (355). The interesting thing is that when Fletcher moves on, into other profoundly radical possibilities of what he terms allegory, he says that the mode ceases to be allegory at all and 'comes instead to share in the higher order of mysterious language, which we may perhaps call mythical language' (355). The problem here is that he has earlier on stated a device that all other theorists of allegory consider central to the mode, that 'allegories of major importance have ultimately very obscure images, and these are a source of their greatness' (73) and has gone on to discuss the radicalising effect of enigma. The crux of the problem may lie in the statement that the 'allegories of major importance' that he discusses early on such as the *Divine Comedy* are not the 'truly apocalyptic' modes of his conclusion.

Apocalypse, prophecy, entropy and the radioactive envelope

Running beyond the analysis of all the critics of both fantasy and allegory but continually indicated in their explorations, are the words apocalypse, prophecy, revolution and, increasingly more often entropy. Apocalypse is Fletcher's word for the individual vision. In his conclusion he suggests that when a radical 'exchange' takes place, then the 'truly apocalyptic', visionary, stance frees one into the 'pure insight of contemplation' (FL: 355). But he also recognises that most of the time the mode provides only a mirror for this vision in 'ultimate wish-fulfillment'. The writings are 'the natural mirrors of ideology' (368). As it imposes itself upon the reader, the apocalyptic becomes the conformist utopian. The apocalyptic becomes ideology as it seeps into and pervades the unexamined assumptions of the public.

Gerber comments that a utopian fantasy is a man-made perfect world which did not exist as a possibility before the Renaissance. Such creations were considered millenarian and apocalyptic in the pre-sixteenth century rather than utopian. However a corollary is that if the alternate world is not recognised as the man-made and limited construct of utopia, it may be taken as apocalyptic. The complete fantasy world is a realisation of an ideal state that precludes recognition of its man-made origin. This places Jameson's argument, which we will soon come to, for the fusion of utopia and ideology with the apocalyptic in an ironic framework since it would reverse the trend of all his careful deconstructing. Frank Kermode notes the interpolation of the apocalyptic between a beginning and an imminent end and suggests that it is interruptions such as these that create great literature (K: 127). But when the apocalyptic vision becomes fixed, and Kermode turns to the insistent example of Hitler in World War II, it becomes negative because it deprives the public of choice. All too often revolution is a group apocalypse, only made successful or long term by the employing of negative rhetoric: In other words it deprives people of an understanding of the constructive nature of the new society on offer, hiding its grounds. Sometimes the rhetoric simply makes over the previous controls over people into a new name. Any revolution which has effected its persuasion through the stance of fantasy, in other words has persuaded people just to give up one control toward conformity for another, will have to contend albeit quite willingly with the knowledge that its changes have not been effected through active choice but through submissive acceptance to an alternative.

E.M. Forster makes an interesting distinction between apocalypse and prophecy in the essay on 'Fantasy' in *Aspects of the Novel*. Whereas apocalypse is absolute reference to an external order, prophecy and fantasy both focus on something beyond the natural mind yet within the aspirations of human beings[29]: some authority that transcends our weakness rather than supplanting it, and that for prophecy, demands humility (188). Maureen Quilligan describes the apocalyptic as a relationship based on the authority of personal vision (Q: 99). By comparison, her prophecy is tradition itself and reinforces the truth of its own tradition (99). The distinction helps one to understand the difference Auden observed between the hero in an ordinary quest tale and the hero in *The Lord of the Rings*. The ordinary hero achieves full success, his vision is apocalyptic. Tolkien's hero partially fails and is much closer to a historical and social reality and is therefore prophetic (CRI: 61). Fletcher describes Shelley's writing as prophetic because rather than being a subjective vision it works by 'reading the mind of some High Being' (FL: 278). Prophecy is one step away from the absolute subjective vision but being so, it can hold out for ever the promise of an apocalyptic world.

F. Jameson refers to the prophet as the 'charismatic' figure allowing transition within society from the traditional, in other words received from the external, order to a 'rationalized' order dependent upon means or causes arising from a specific historical interpretation (JA2: 250). Michel Foucault moves the discussion out to philosophy when he contrasts the order of reduction which locates truth in the object with the order of promise which locates truth in process[30]. He suggests that this division between the naive and the prophetic, the positivist and the eschatological, is the locus of modern thought in its attempt to make the empirical transcendental. But the prophetic stance within fantasy subsumes the division. It becomes the most effective practical means of control over people because while even the extended apocalypse usually dies with its author, prophecy provides the basis for turning the short-term subjective positivism into the long-term.

Political entropy as defined by Paul de Man is the general will coming up against the inertia of the individual, but this is a continual hazard for any political system which deprives its people of active choice. One could say that all the political systems incorporating the visions outlined above, tend toward entropy to maintain their long term effectiveness, but they have to develop techniques to slow down the process. For were the entropic condition ever reached, the state would not wither away in Jackson's version of the mystic zero: 'absolute unity of self and other' (J: 77), but become the apotheosis of all institutions, institutionalising the components of private individual and state apparatus as the final immobilised face-off of Brooke-Rose's entropic 'running down'. All political expressions based on these approaches are negative in their stance, varying only in to whom they give the control. This rhetoric of control is, as de Man says, 'a rhetoric of totalization inherent in all supplementary systems' (DM1: 181).

It may be the underlying knowledge that the escape of the fantasy world as game can only be justified by its intermittency, by its short term effects, that makes these theorists of the stance so insistent, so happy to accept the failure of the form. But their entire critical structure is aimed at achieving the long-term effect. Their tautological inquiry relieves them of that interaction by denying that it is possible. Theorists of fantasy as desire stress other elements but to the same effect. Brooke-Rose for example discusses the necessary shortness of fantasy because of its need to keep the two levels of *sjuzet* and fabula apart in order to maintain the information gap (BR: 229). The moment that gap gets filled the writing moves toward naturalism. Because there are no effective devices to encourage interaction, the simple separation of levels imposes an ambivalence upon the reader which can quickly and easily devolve into the imposition of a specific authorial 'line'. But this problem is not fully faced. Always, in the practical political sphere, negative rhetoric may be shown in action: evading, omitting, deceiving, depriving people of choice, of moral activity, of dialectical interaction with the world. And in the mid-twentieth century as Huizinga witnessed and Orwell eloquently testified, that short-term effect is getting longer and longer. As long as the short-term only gets longer and longer it will inevitably come up against entropy, in fantasy literature as much as in politics and it will be that 'metaphysical vision of kosmic entropy' (JA2: 252) outlined by F. Jameson in his discussion of the mutual exclusion, or antinomy of activity and value. But what Angus Fletcher presents is the possibility of the combination of a negative stance with the power of words, which could extend the effect into the long term.

Take a flexible lead envelope coated with radioactive solution on the inside, which is sealed off and passed safely from hand to hand. Fletcher takes this innocuous envelope, carefully opens it up and turns it inside out, smoothing the sides and pulling at the tips of the corners to refold it into the same shape but with the lead inside and the radioactivity emanating out from all its surfaces. Games and designs deprive people of choice by default. They remain unaware of the implications of control and simply hand the intitially sealed envelope from person to person, assuming that the choice comes in the acceptance or rejection of the envelope rather than in opening it in its interior, nor considering the implications of breaking the seal, and not even suspecting that it may have already been turned insideout. Fletcher's theory suggests that the stance consciously deprives people of choice. The author creates the lethal object, hands it to the audience who takes it and passes it on, each person being contaminated by its unseen radiation. The fantasy stance which attempts to control the external world by hiding its artifice in the creation of a fictional alternative, informs not only a number of literary genres, but also science, politics and all other forms of naturalism, discourses that claim to represent the world exactly.

6   THEORIES OF FANTASY AS POLITICS

Jameson: ideology and class collectivity

It is with some relief that we can turn to Jameson's book *The Political Unconscious* (1981) and watch some although not all of these implications of desire and wish-fulfilment being disentangled. One of the main differences between the earlier article referred to by Jackson, and this major collection of essays is the emergence of Frye's *Secular Scripture* to which Jameson generously and consistently refers: not that the effective politics of either writer is similar, but their understanding and awareness of specific kinds of authoritarian power structures have much in common. To recall Jameson's outline of genre described earlier:

Working from Frye's comments on the relationship between romance and utopia, he refracts the discussion of genre through a Marxist perspective that returns us to the synchronic/diachronic debate, and suggests that genre study is important because it is, 'mediatory ... , which allows the co-ordination of immanent formal analysis of the individual text with the twin diachronic perspective of the history of forms and the evolution of social life' (JA2: 105).

The nature of this 'co-ordination' is dependent on a reinterpretation of evolution. Jameson claims that evolution for Marx and Darwin is not a question of necessity, or the inexorable *form* of events (JA2: 102) in history. Rather, it is like Nietzsche's genealogy which allows one to perceive an articulated system through the diachronic perspectives of the history of forms and social life (105); isolate its elements in the present and in doing so renew one's perception of the synchronic (139), or the system we are in at the moment. In other words this genealogical evolution expands more clearly on Jameson's the earlier 'combinatoire' or permutational scheme whereby history enters genre study, as the limiting rather than causal factor. The limitations generated in history give rise to Jameson's idea of the 'ideologeme', or narrative paradigm expressing the dialogical organisation of class discourse in a mode, which are in turn important to the definition of the limitations beyond which the political unconscious operates.

Note here the use of 'dialogical'. Jameson makes an interesting distinction between the dialogical contradictions of class conflict which are usually antagonistic, and the dialogical contradiction that is more fundamental because irresolvable. It is an important distinction not only because Jameson goes on to articulate his perception of the irresolvable, but also because Bakhtin's dialogism is an authorial tether for many other commentaries on both fantasy and allegory: The two often being defined by the distinction between antagonistic and irresolvable contradiction, respectively.

But to return to the 'ideologeme' and mode: Jameson mentions that mode is 'generalised existential experience'; it is 'intentional meaning' as against fixed form and articulated systems (JA2: 107–8). And later he provides a neat diagram taken from L. Hjelmselv's *Prolegomenon to a Theory of Language* (1961) to expand mode specifically into the expression rather than content of substance or historical limitation of an ideology. What is of particular interest here is the close similarity with Robert Scholes's

genre diagrams in *Fabulation and Metafiction* (1979). Scholes too
comments upon the formal as part of the existential, but in
opposition to the ideational and essential. The pattern provides a
neat illustration of exactly the fundamental impasse Jameson is
concerned to avoid by restructuring genre. Scholes concludes that
'literary genres [formal] ... evolve in time' and 'literary modes
[essential] exist across time' (S: 107), thereby reinforcing the
diachronic/synchronic division that permits the evasion of history
by building on the essentialist view that the most important aspects
of life are to do with 'deep structures of being', that behaviour and
material context are secondary, ephemeral, almost trivial. This
impasse is one that Marx, Hegel, Benjamin, Lukacs, Althusser, and
all the others invoked in Jameson's litany are also concerned to
avoid; and it is useful to remind ourselves when reading Jameson,
that this is the primary target, not the versions of Marxism on
which he concentrates his analysis. Jameson however, suggests a
way forward from this impasse by locating the 'ideologeme' as an
historical limitation to genre, something which is neither
synchronic nor diachronic but which, secreted like a shell or
exoskeleton, continues to emit its ideological message 'long after
the extinction of its host' (151). And elsewhere he refers to genre as
'sedimented content'. These evolutionary metaphors are most
interesting in the light of the running analogy beyond
contemporary genre criticism, but become more significant in view
of Jameson's own definition of evolution.

The practical example of these secretions and sediments is
presented by Jameson in terms of fantasy:

> the primal motor force which gives any cultural artifact its
> resonance, but which must always find itself diverted to the
> service of other, ideological functions, and reinvested by what
> we have called the political unconscious. (JA2: 142)

Fantasy is the 'ideologeme' behind both romance and utopia,
studies of which complete Jameson's collection. Romance, as in the
early article, is seen as the ultimate ideological form which 'must
produce a compromise' (149). But the novel, invariably utopian in
form and initially presented as non-ideological, is then
reconsidered in a study of the ideology of process found in its form,
which is directed to securing 'the reader's consent' to the author's
desire (156). What is interesting is that in *The Political Unconscious*

Jameson appears surreptitiously to recognise that fantasy, and indeed allegory, are not simply generic 'modes' such as utopia or romance. Fantasy is defined not in opposition to reality but as 'a protonarrative structure as the vehicle for our experience of the real' (48), because the 'Real' itself – Althusser via Lacan, or Spinoza's 'absent cause' – cannot be expressed. Allegory is fantasy's counterpart as it searches for narrative in reading the text. When fantasy presents an ideologeme of individual desire and collective wish-fulfilment in genres such as romance and utopia, it may be matched by allegory which will read a 'master narrative' of desire as its interpretive form, but the implication is that for desire to be the only narrative debases interpretation just as it visits 'disrepute' upon allegory – and by corollary, on fantasy. However, Jameson does not pursue this implication, so that we are left with the impression that he jettisons the writing of material existence by concentrating solely on the fantasy text which not only infuses ideologemes of wish-fulfilment and desire in romance and utopia respectively (185), but also the agreed-upon concealments of that wish-fulfilment and desire, that Freud suggests are necessary to aesthetic creation (174). We should perhaps note here the parallels with Todorov's fantastic which is separated into the themes of 'I' which are conscious but also passive wish-fulfilment, and those of 'you' which are unconscious but active, engaging and directed toward desire.

Jameson then goes on to underline the political ambivalence of such strategies in different writers of different chronological periods during the nineteenth and twentieth centuries, stressing the dangers of the compromises and consents of fantasy ideologemes. After considerable discussion he suggests that the irreconcilable contradiction of the class conflict of these centuries is rooted in the mutual exclusion of activity and value perpetuated by the ideologeme. He notes the inevitable and generative and/or necessary connection between activity and value, citing Greimas as his authority; and comments upon the complete antinomy or aporia of their separation under capitalism (JA2: 254) which can only lead to a 'metaphysical vision of cosmic entropy' (252). Jameson's discussion of the interaction between historical 'necessity' and genre provides one of the strongest arguments for the technical stability of 'mode'. It suggests that the extraordinary agreement between the theorists about the analogies which enact fantasy – games, desire, wish-fulfilment, neurosis, obsession – result from a long term definition of the literary strategies of the stance. Yet he ends the book noting that his own critical practice is inevitably part of the dominant ideology. Hence there is no guarantee that these writings will not be analysed and read differently at another time. This is the heart of rhetorical study: not certainty but possibility.

However balefully fruitful Jameson's discussion, his final three possible solutions circle back upon themselves and leave the antinomy intact. First, he proposes a de-centring, a dialectical reversal of the ideologeme which although painful and 'fitful', for the retreat 'into this or that intellectual comfort' is perpetual (JA2: 284), would allow an approach to the 'Real'. The problem here lies in the idea of 'approach' to the Real, as if as Brooke-Rose suggests there were something human beings could do to get closer to it. Second, he addresses the dangerous ambivalence of the fantasy ideologeme and its power to manipulate its audience, and suggests that after all we need not be so afraid of this power since to manipulate in one direction implicitly indicates the direction that is being excluded and mitigates against manipulation. To deny desire one must awaken it in the first place (287). This is so, but the effective techniques and strategies of the ideologeme are toward evasion, hiding and omission. One denial of desire may simply cover for the omission of another. And even if Newton's theories of mass and force manipulated (unconsciously) against relativism only to generate it eventually, it took 200 years or so before this happened: an unacceptable length of time for the uncritical domination of any political authority.

Third, Jameson states that the positive way forward is to find a vocabulary that will fuse utopia and romance, desire and wish-fulfilment, a fusion that will conflate ideology into class collectivity. But he also states that they will only achieve this, only 'know their truth and come into their own at the end of what Marx calls prehistory' (JA2: 293). Once more one finds a quite definite, apocalyptic ending suggesting that a time will come after which the conflict between individual and collective desire will cease. Ironically what this presupposes is that value and activity will once more be divorced because activity will be necessary no longer. I think that Jameson's clear intuition of the necessary interaction between activity and value, goes astray partly because he appears to see the problem as one limited to capitalism particularly in the post-eighteenth-century period, hence presumably the citing of Greimas. However, written commentary in Western philosophy can be found for this concern in Plato and Aristotle: both of whom discuss it in terms of rhetoric emphasising that positive rhetorical stance encourages such interaction while negative stance hinders it, although different history and social conditions will allow for different material expression of each stance (H: 13-14). And it is within studies of rhetoric that the political implications of writing have been assessed ever since. Jameson's excellent analysis of the politics of fantasy remains constrained by his neglect of the much longer term analysis that has already called into question any approach to the 'Real', already discussed the effective strategies of manipulative evasion, and already discounted any apocalyptic answer.

Summary: Rhetorical implications and the necessity for doublethink

The fantasies of desire and game both generate a politics of imposed authority, not only in their attitude to language as representative but also in the concomitant belief that the material world is a place that may be controlled by a private individual. What is interesting is that such large divergences of opinion should, despite an identical naming of technique and strategies, shun each other so strongly. I would suggest that this arises from the genre expectations, not only about the writings but also the structure of genre itself, on the part of readers and critics. We cannot resolve the confusions by looking at genre alone, we have to move to the broader rhetorical concerns that lie beyond them.

Fantasy's denial of value lies close to the positivist ethic which separates fact from value by evading the evaluated process whereby facts are generated in the first place, and by treating value as a fixed standard that has always been there. Just so, many of these critics, with exception of Todorov who does not pursue the idea far and Jameson who gets but a little further, view mode and genre as if these could be fixed things, and dismiss as foolish the possibility that for example Kafka's *Metamorphosis* can be read both as grotesque/uncanny and as satire. But it is clear from critical responses to, for example, *The Lord of the Rings* as both marvellous and consolatory, or to *Nineteen Eighty-Four* as both fantastic and dystopic, that stance or the interactive meeting of reader, writer and writing in the text, is of paramount importance in speaking about both mode and genre.

When speaking of generic kinds one is usually dealing with groupings of techniques, and the intriguing aspect of this whole critical area is that identical techniques appear to define several different genres. To solve this problem, most critics of fantasy turn to a discussion of mode, which begins to look at rhetorical structure in terms of epistemology or ideology; for example one finds Jameson writing on the need to get rid of the synchronic/diachronic and replace it with Marxist production: and so far I would agree, indeed the methodology of dialectical materialism can well be seen as Western Europe's main answer to the loss of a rhetorical tradition. But unless one moves further, toward the values enacted through structure in rhetorical stance, ultimately generated by a belief, it is impossible even to begin reasonably to separate between modes.

Beyond the structure of fantasy as desire, in which the world and the not-world are ambivalently related, one has the activity of stance to push forward either the world into the uncanny/grotesque – emphasising the strangeness of natural conventions – or the not-world into the marvellous/magical – pointing to a separation from the natural – or the waver between both: the pure fantastic. Each of these activities has a common ideological structure in that they all assume the possibility of power as control by human beings over nature, and declare it pure either as wish-fulfilment, desire or ambivalence. The structure of fantasy as a game is similarly moved by stance to lead out toward the conventional world in satire and to stress the not-world in development of utopia. The common structure for game is the epistemological assumption of neutrality, of evasion of the authority in which the writing is implicitly caught.

I do not know whether it is possible to have an ambivalence between satire and utopia, a waver similar to that of the fantastic. One may place de Maupassant's *Horla* among the uncanny with their strange versions of the natural world, and Tolkien's *The Lord of the Rings* among the marvellous other-worlds, and appreciate the fundamentally ambiguous position of James's *Turn of the Screw* in the waver between natural and supernatural. Yet while one may place *Gulliver's Travels* among the satires firmly based upon criticisms of convention and Butler's *Erewhon* among those utopias which attempt to lead away from and idealise convention, it is difficult to point to an ambiguous middle way. It is tempting to suggest that such a waver is parody, or possibly 'realism'. I could suggest that it is along the axis of the waver that the fantasies of game and desire are joined; an axially rotated form of the fantastic in the manner of the physical structuring of optical isomers rather than their deduced effects, could provide the waver point for utopia and satire itself. The constant activity of waver might even be the basis of a connection between fantasy and allegory.

This aside, both modes of fantasy are rooted in the same stance: the activity of control, which is generated by an apparent belief that the external world is something over which human beings can attempt authority, and one of its most important corollaries: that language can be made exactly to represent the world. The split in opinion over whether this control should operate neutrally in game or purely in desire, both being dangerous circles of authority because they try to dismiss questions of value, is a result of the activity of stance. It is a stance that tries to hide its own stance, a negative rhetoric. It is firmly based within the rationalist humanism of the last three hundred and fifty years, and tied closely to its epistemology and ideology.

3 Theories of Allegory

i A BACKGROUND TO ALLEGORY AND REPRESENTATION

Unlike critics of fantasy, those writing about allegory rarely assume neutrality, indeed they are often overtly interested in power. They do not assume a (con)fusion of worlds, the hover of the actual over the alternative, and are usually explicitly interested in the comment of one upon the other. These aspects of reading do not define the allegorical genres in the way that the written techniques do those of fantasy, but they do go some way toward outlining a stance. The primary activity of allegory is to stimulate various forms of reading and writing, different ways of approach and interaction. It encourages study of and participation in language and literature, and in doing so indicates various relationships between human beings and the world. Allegory is not that interested in outlining specific epistemologies, it is more concerned with the relationships they indicate. Within this definition, allegory is a word which is best described by the rhetorical terms of any poetic structure. It may of course refer to fantasy and in this sense it may overlap with its activity. But such a use, albeit apparent from the following collage of criticism, is contentiously broad. It moves us too swiftly into methodology.

Critics confident of using the word allegory almost invariably now speak of the way the language and structure work, not the genre but the activity itself and this generates a wide variety of names, none of which attempt compatibility with others. But we need to deal with an additional aspect: that theorists of allegory are as eager as those of fantasy to differentiate between the two kinds of text, but do so in a very different manner. Theorists of fantasy dismiss allegory as a different kind of writing, using different techniques and strategies. But those of allegory describe fantasy mainly in terms of structure and of the reader. While critics of fantasy perceive different kinds of works as a function of strategy and therefore label different works fantastic, uncanny or marvellous; those of allegory perceive different kinds of works more often as a function of stance: allegoresis, romance, and fable may indicate the same written object/artifact but different texts, different interactions of reader, writer and writing.

Yet most of all the two areas of theory impinge upon each other through their recent parallel histories. Fantasy theory moves from the 30s work of Tolkien and Huizinga roughly to Todorov in 1967, to Rabkin, Irwin and Frye in 1976 to Brooke-Rose, Jackson and Jameson in 1981. Allegory moves from C.S. Lewis in the 30s, through Honig and Fletcher in 1959 and 1964, to de Man and Kermode in 1979 and the collections of Greenblatt and Bloomfield in 1981. It is Fletcher who appears to galvanise the two traditions by insisting on the power of words. Todorov stakes out the subsequent field of fantasy theory by attempting to divert this idea of power, and at the same time instigating much recent work on allegory as a counter-response discussing the implications of this power.

Theories from the 30s to the present day

To halt briefly in a potential history, that helps make the plausible possible, helps make relative methodology ideologically specific: In contrast to fantasy criticism where theoreticians battle to confine the name to their particular area, exhibiting a private, emotional attachment to the name entirely appropriate to the stance, with allegory theoreticians rush to find new names, to leave that word behind[1]. Because fantasy is so tied to a particular epistemology there is far more specific evidence for defining strategies; and since the function of fantasy is to hide its stance there is a tendency to fuse strategy with genre. Hence, when a difference within fantasy writing occurs, the related works can be hived off, given another name that relates to the technical or strategic. Despite the forelock to mode, there is, as we have observed, a tendency to discuss fantasy in terms of genre as kind. Fantasy theorists are to a woman or man willing to define and criticise allegory – which they do in terms of its limited one-to-one images, its didacticism, its clear connection to the real[2]. Because they are rooted in the idea of representational language they have no alternative but to assume the naively mimetic, static nature of an emblematic structure. Just so they discuss 'allegory'; which is otherwise an encouragement of reader and writer interaction, in terms of static criticism. Tolkien himself, as well as many other writers including Bersani and Frye, ally criticism with allegory as something that reminds us of the limitations of human beings. But within a representational context that limitation is the unsatisfactory, frustrating reminder of shortfall and failure, rather than the extensive reminder of the gaps that separate us from the material world.

The dependence upon a rational analytical epistemology and a representative language, the definition of criticism in primarily static terms, indicate a tendency within theories of fantasy that allows for a greater concentration on the literary history of fantasy in terms of 'named kinds' for each historical period: For example, linking the 'fantastic' specifically with the early nineteenth century. It indicates a belief in history as empirically representable – neither material, metafictional or mythopoeic but as it is[3]. Hence the current reader is excluded from the definition. The criticism is, as we saw with appraisals of Tolkien's work, constructed in much the same manner as the fantasies themselves. The result is first that as the current epistemology shifts, the critical comments date. Just as with fantasy, the stance and structure of the criticism are refracted through epistemology. They are tied by representative conventions of language so closely to the current ideology, that the refraction is perceived only slightly at first, if at all, yet later reveals itself as a source of inflexibility. And, just as within fantasy where the names of the parts of the writing are all-important, there is that enormous and overt disagreement between critics about the use of those names: for example the wrangling over uncanny *versus* grotesque or marvellous *versus* magical – as if one is right and the other is wrong. The batteries of authority used to fight for one usage over the other remind us of the 'might is right' adage of fantasy theory.

With allegory there is a far greater awareness of stance, of the separation between stance and structure and strategy[4], and of the implications of both mode and kind – probably deriving from the greater awareness of the working of the language itself and the different readings and writings instigated by allegory. It is difficult to discuss genres related to allegory mainly because of the lack of theory on the topic. The studies split roughly between pre-Renaissance and twentieth-century readings, with passing glances at the seventeenth to nineteenth centuries which are often anachronistic and foreshortened. This may have occurred because the pre-Renaissance word is part of a world about which humanism conveys little, and allegories of the medieval period pose considerable theoretical problems for an active, contemporary reading. And as indicated by theorists of fantasy, in the post-Renaissance period the word 'allegory' becomes synonymous with limited emblem, essentialist one word/one object language[5].

But this theoretical predisposition has also occurred because pre-Renaissance allegory is tied up with the history of rhetoric in a manner that has treated fantasy quite differently. The very conditions of the Renaissance and post-Renaissance implement-ation of essentialist conventions and rational logic that so encouraged the fantasy stance in literature, have reflected back upon and restricted the working of both allegory and rhetorical study as a whole. Rarely can the refractive power of epistemology and ideology be seen so clearly as in the seventeenth to eighteenth century shift in definitions of allegory and rhetoric. In both cases the power of this shift operates externally on the criticism of the ostensible aims of the topic rather than upon its stance. It does not destroy allegory or rhetoric, but simply deprives people of a way of discussing how it works. The devaluation of rhetoric and its reduction either to 'false logic' or 'mere ornament' during the late seventeenth century had enormous ramifications for allegory: ramifications that are reflected in the changing definitions in the dictionaries and handbooks of the period. Allegory moves from the earlier medieval approaches to 'misticall speech' (1604), diverse tropes (1616), dark speech (1656) and mysterious saying (1658), to 'rhetorical term' and 'extended metaphor' (1686), and 'figurative speech' where figures are simply 'ornaments' (1702)[6]. Of course by the end of the eighteenth century, Goethe and Coleridge[7] had in the understanding of many readers reinforced the idea of allegory as simply an extended metaphor and mere ornament, helping to reduce it to a mechanical device.

It is interesting that the idea of 'poetry' became important at this time, and it is used by many to compensate for the loss of an interactive methodology in allegory, and for the work / writer / reader locus in rhetoric. But poetry develops an individualistic, essentialist, originary bias alien to allegory and many earlier modes of rhetorical stance and strategy. It is a bias that contains an inherent dualism, always in danger of becoming a vicious circle, in effect the source for the two faces of fantasy. When rhetoric is hidden the two faces of fantasy emerge; when it is apparent, poetic can become active. This lack of rhetoric is at the heart of both the confusions and the aims in the debate about 'pure poetry' and neutral discourse.

The distinction provides a useful analogy for looking at the influence of Bakhtin's writing about Dostoevsky, which as we have seen filters through much recent work on fantasy. In speaking of Dostoevsky and the 'split personality', Bakhtin generates two clear readings: the first is that of wish-fulfilment and desire, ideology and anti–ideology which leads to the sado/masochistic, sanity-madness, private/party circularity; the second is the loss of the subject, the absolute loss of personality – but always originating with an idea of personality. There is at least one more possibility: the jettisoning of personality itself and the concentration on interaction.

The first reading is picked up on by several writers and the second recognised by some, the third is rarely considered by the theorists and few ever try adequately to deal with the complexities of Bakhtin's thought. Here in small compass lies a discrete story of the confusions between fantasy and allegory. The originary, essentialist readings of 'pure' poetry generate the theories of fantasy but once the materiality enters, structures of allegory become apparent. Once you realise the contents of the lead envelope with all its literally unseen potential for generation and destruction, then your choices are of a different quality, your responsibilities change.

But early theories of allegory are quite problematic. Many even fairly recent contributions, are infected with a deep prejudice about its mechanical nature, and are most strongly seen in terms of the formal principles of genre that they try to deduce. G. M. Spivak notes that the idea that words can be a representational code leaves the separation between word and topic, about which allegory is concerned, as a mechanical operation[8]. She goes on to suggest that the Romantic concept of the symbol as having a mystical unity between word and thing, reintroduces a positive function for allegory as a device which separates between the two in a non-mechanical manner. W. Benjamin outlines the tendency for the Romantics to define allegory as of 'excessively logical character', generating the split between expression and idea analogous to that between symbol and allegory [BEN: 162]. What one then does with this separation is of the greatest importance. A. Nuttall uses the separation to propose a metaphysical definition that has allegory realising 'instantially viewed universals' or 'this-ness' (N: 106) of things, the inarticulate sensation in coherent experience. The account appears directly to address C. S. Lewis's statement, inverting the Romantic, that 'Symbolism is a mode of thought, but allegory is a mode of expression' (L: 48).

M. W. Bloomfield expands on Lewis's comment in a different manner by discussing the difference between symbol as unifying and allegory as generalising, yet carefully delineating the concrete and material operation, especially of personification allegory, saying that 'to any age which is committed to a set of organised beliefs, the more general is not necessarily the more immaterial' (B: 170). But Gay Clifford underlines the split in critical opinion by defining allegory in contrast to symbol as 'abstract and intellectual' (C: 8); and Edwin Honig's *Dark Conceit* at moments suggests that allegory can be perceived as a device that constructs a rational picture of the world.

2 ALLEGORY AS GENRE AND/OR MODE

Relationships with genre: fairy tale, fable, parable, apologue, emblem, levels, menippea

The division in understanding of the term is not new[9] but has recently led to a number of attempts to find another 'word' for allegory. Many of these initial definitions have been essays in generic categorising according to formal principles, in much the same way that theorists of fantasy have sought to understand the stance by turning to genres in which it is most often read, or to which it is most clearly related. M. D. Springer suggests that apologue is the modern counterpart to allegory[10], the former being implicit and the latter explicit. Todorov connects allegory with fable and fairy tale because they are all involved with morality. Yet he goes on to complicate the vocabulary, differentiating between allegory as explicit and nonsense as implicit. 'Explicit' for Todorov is not a simple overt statement of meaning but a disruption of the accepted referential impetus in communication and a direction to the literal. Richter in *Fable's End* returns to apologue, placing it with fable as rhetorical and relational in opposition to the one-to-one movement of allegory[11]. The search for new vocabulary derives from the idea that earlier allegory was rigidly didactic and imposingly hierarchical. Medieval allegory has been defined as emblematic, encoding, operating a system of 'levels'. Sontag expresses the misconception in her comments on Dante's allegory as a function of simple redundancy[12]. And it is a widespread assumption that if one can pin a 'meaning' down, as with the supposed point to point correspondence of *Animal Farm* with events in the early Soviet Union, then it is probably allegorical.

On the other hand Clifford suggests that the modern return to fable has occurred precisely because allegory is not moralistic and rigid, and yet the age needs a form for authoritative expression (C: 45). Just so, S. Sacks defines apologue as the 'fictional example of the truth of a formulable statement'[13], claiming that there is no elusive element and that apologue is as rationalistic as the 'old' form of allegory. The definitional confusion is primarily confined to the attempt to keep allegory within a formal genre. Although the scope of genre studies is broadening, it can become misleading to force a mode within it. For example an article in *Genre* attempts to define allegory, apologue and menippean satire as 'species' of one genre[14]. Unfortunately the issue is not clarified because apologue is an increasingly well-defined formal genre, menippean satire is more often viewed as either a structural or thematic mode, and as I have been suggesting and will continue to argue allegory is a rhetorical stance.

Relationships with mode: structural, ironic, symbolic, satiric

Maureen Quilligan breaks the emblematic mould at the start of *The Language of Allegory*, and suggests that genre may be structural or formal and that allegory is structural. Formal genres are 'what the author imposes on the content' and that make it into a play or a sonnet. Structural genres are concerned with 'internal, structural operations – how the reader is made to respond' (Q1: 18), and by example she cites satire or allegory. Furthermore the structural genre of allegory is only made up of the 'pure strains' of allegory which may otherwise be a modality of a formal genre. This definition reflects a widespread opinion in the more serious and extensive theories of allegory. Clifford notes that 'essentially allegory is, like irony, a mode capable of subsuming many different genres and forms' (C: 5). And Honig's writing which radically shifted the old perspective on allegory as an emblematic code, links allegory to the metaphysical impulse of 'the desire to know'. It is a metaphor of purpose which may inform any kind, may shape a set of 'symbolic types' in a way that distinguishes them from the shape suggested by pastoral or epic.

Although it does not address stance directly, Quilligan's separation between formal and structural genres is helpful in preparing the background to a distinction often made by theorists of allegory. Honig suggested that allegory gave way to pastoral and satire; Clifford says that modern allegory is closer to satire and irony; and J. MacQueen comments that allegory and satire are respectively the general and particular sides of the same meaning[15]. In Quilligan's definition all these modes can inform the formal genres of drama, sonnet or novel presumably because of their specific relationship with the reader's response. But at the same time it should be noted that formal genres also call for reader response, and I am doubtful that one text could be defined as either formal or structural with this criterion. However, what is being pointed out here is a grouping of genres according to a particular kind of open response that they generate in the reader, even though each response is different.

For example a pastoral such as *The Tempest* allows for removal from the actual, and then lets the reader choose to return to it changed or unchanged. Honig opposes allegory to irony and satire saying that the latter two offer a discrepancy between the assumptions of the actual and those in the fiction; the choice is made by perceiving the incongruity. In contrast, allegory allows for choice based upon the perception of congruity. The difference is rephrased by Kermode who suggests that while in irony the choice of interpretation by the reader, even if incongruous, is ultimately based on a known assumption, in the secrecy of allegory there is 'something irreducible' (K: 16) involved, giving the example of Henry Green's novel *Party-Going* which generates readings that assume:

that the absence of the same usual satisfactions, the disappointment of conventional expectations, connote the existence of other satisfactions, deeper and more difficult, inaccessible to those who see without perceiving and hear without understanding. (7)

The assumption cannot be pinned down and the choice can never be finalised. Paul de Man moves one step further positing irony as a referential device and allegory as a confusion of the referential (DM1).

Although there appears to be a widespread attitude that allegory does have something in common with these modes, problems arise. They are highlighted by Quilligan's own account of the differences between allegory and irony or satire as structural genres, which reverses many of the previous distinctions. In her 'pure irony' there is no pretext or reference in an actual or absolute sense . Ironic pretexts exist only in pretence, so that the reader's response can be guided to the correct interpretation of the subjective ironic term. They do not enter into a commentary or questioning of the text. Parody and satire go so far as to undermine the basis of the referent they devise and use in order to make their point. Allegory on the other hand, comments directly on an actual pretext and aims at a correct reading (Q1: 145). The example she gives is of Nabokov's *Pale Fire* which is pure parody because it 'never points to anything beyond itself'; it has no pretext. This in contrast to Swift's *The Tale of a Tub* which depends on 'the allegorical misinterpretation of the words of the Bible' (144) – the Bible providing the constant sacred pretext central to the argument. However, her attempts to define *The Tale of a Tub* as either allegory or satire, a distinction which should by her account be reasonably clear, founder and fail because there is also a 'sacred edge to the satire' that immediately calls up the Biblical pretext and blurs the distinction between it and allegory. Booth's *Rhetoric of Irony* provides an interesting extension to the distinction. Here, allegory differs from irony because it asks for further discussion whereas irony provides interpretation by rejecting one term of its image. Furthermore, overt unstable irony, one of the final categories discussed, indicates meaning beyond the work itself. In this case where rejection of a term gives way to a 'paradoxical communing'[16] beyond the actual, interpretation as irony and discussion as allegory appear to fuse. Not only is it in practice difficult to separate in Quilligan's structural manner between allegory, and irony satire or pastoral, but also there is the whole question of how far one 'structural' genre can combine with another.

3   ALLEGORY AS STANCE

The attempt to define allegory in this structural manner is an attempt to define it as a particular way of learning about the actual world. In some cases this is held to be carried out by guidance from pre-existing assumptions, in others by rejection of those assumptions, and in still others by a confusion of those assumptions. The real questions here however, unlike those in fantasy theory where the evasion, omission or hiding of assumptions are a fundamental part of the strategy and tie it inextricably with the ideology and epistemology of the age, arise not from whether there is a known assumption or not, but upon how the choice is made.

Although the theorists never seem to be able to agree on specific techniques as do theorists of fantasy, they are in surprising agreement over two basic aspects. The first is that allegory recognises the world external to human beings, the material world of which language is a part, and hence recognises the need for a discussion of relations of power when considering the use of language and literature. The second, which may be seen as a corollary, is that the reader is always aware of that materiality and of the interaction with language that texts engage us in. It is as if once you make a decision to read actively you enter the allegorical, but if you make no decision, you enter fantasy by default.

The external world

The changes in the theory of allegory since the mid-twentieth century reflect the manner in which people have responded to the material world and to relationship with it. This relationship is paralleled by the critics' attitude to language and literature and their response to it. At heart the discussion lays bare a segment of the western dilemma, a civilisation apparently caught between process and product, means and ends. The limitation to the epistemological and ideological which we can see in the pursuit of generic explanation, holds a mirror up to one of the strongest limitations of our society. In a manner similar to the varied politics of our time, theorists of allegory have tried to rescue it from simple mechanical activity by justifying its relationships of power against a background of theocentric, supposedly medieval, transcendent hierarchies, rather than its materiality. For example, Spivak separates between medieval and modern allegory mainly on the basis of changes in ideology rather than in the activity of the text. She notes that the difference 'is largely sociological, not literary, lodged in the nature of the externally given code, not in the behaviour of the discourse' (SP: 332) The same separation on the basis of hierarchy in ideology is made by most writers on allegory, and it has stylistic ramifications that produce striking fissures in their work.

Edwin Honig's *Dark Conceit* is a book of considerable significance for he not only recognised the hierarchical background of overt public authority complicit in the authority of the private individual, but also proposes the 'allegorical waver', an axis of activity out of the circular struggle of totalitarian and anarchic power toward the enigma of the material world. Honig's theory proposes that the difference between medieval and modern allegory lies in the loss of an overt authoritarian hierarchy at the time of the Renaissance which put paid to allegory for a while because a sense of overall purpose was lost, and gave rise to satire, epic and pastoral. Honig also notes that the mechanical role of allegory that arose in the post-Renaissance period was the 'sheerest kind of personification'. Allegory became moralising without art, rhetoric without imagination, symbolism without mastery and, significantly for the purposes of this study, fantasy without reality. No tension remained between the fictional and the actual and there was a correlative attempt to control within the extent of its man-made authority. In other words it comes close to a negative stance and the restricting potential of fantasy.

Honig situates the change in allegory's fate in the philosophy of Kant and the idea of the self-determination of human beings. With this outlook allegory becomes the merging of the subject-object relationship which raises it to a 'universal' (HON: 41). The desire of human beings, rather than being something that they specifically want, as it is in wish-fulfilment, is here desire from the irrational and therefore valid desire, which would ally it with Todorov's desire in themes of 'You', and with Jackson's pure fantasy. It is the subconscious surfacing beyond control into the conscious and needing allegory to communicate. For Honig allegory can account for the irrational because it does not need reference to external authority, but like Jackson's fantasy it maintains the authority of the unified subject/object from within the integrity of the text itself. Modern allegory, far from being an encoded emblematic representation, 'dispenses with the concept of allegory as something preconceived... Allegory, which is symbolic in method, is realistic in aim and in the content of its perception' (180). But more than this, allegory holds a dialectic with the irrational through the activity of the 'allegorical waver' that is essential for modern literature if it is to meet the enigma of experience lying outwith accepted rational logic.

It is here that we become aware of one necessary distinction that has to be made if we are to understand the division within the criticism of allegory. The separation is not between logic or illogic, rational or irrational, explicit or implicit, acceptance or rejection of assumptions, nor in the end between private or external hierarchies. The separation occurs between the recognition of the 'other', the *allos* in allegory, which is the sense of the external world as an 'other', outwith the control of human beings, or as something 'other' that we may control and dominate. Hence theories restricted to genre are divided because the same formal or structural generic elements may be used both to exercise control over and to establish interaction with the material. The restriction to an epistemology which places the human being at the centre of the world, as its subject, can lead both to Honig's positive or Clifford's negative role for modern allegory. The former views allegory as necessary for the irrational, for the unconscious and all those aspects lying outside mankind's scope, whereas the latter sees modern allegory as the subjective domination over the actual. These latter theories are most precise about the dangers of such domination but tend to stress the positive, or more helpful aspects of the control in justification of it; they also tend to be preventative, emphasising what goes wrong with allegory when the control is not carefully directed.

The distinction also goes some way to elaborating on the confusion and overlap with the theory of fantasy. Those critics taking 'explicit' language as an imposition rather than an overt fiction, begin to define the techniques of negative rhetoric used by fantasy. Those who take the separation from the actual as the mechanical artifice of eighteenth-century images are noting the non-real, the lack of interaction common to fantasy rather than the condition necessary before interaction can take place. And those who take the subjective vision as defining rather than limited, read its vision as a short term imposition which is as bound to fail as that of fantasy. The overlap occurs because control of the external world is the basis for negative rhetoric. In the current epistemological framework it is not surprising that its manifestations as stated in some kinds of allegorical theory should overlap with those of fantasy.

The allegorical waver moves out from between myth and philosophy, from the symbolic creation of a world and the attaching of meaning to it, to an anagogical purpose. But Honig does not develop the details of this process and as a result leaves allegory primarily as a form of knowledge, caught between the ambivalent tendencies of wisdom and the commodity of information. Subsequent theories each attempt different extensions of this 'process', and in this they are significantly different from theorists of fantasy who concentrate on techniques which reside either side of the waver or hover, and in doing so evade the implications of their central valorised, rare, pure activity. Theorists of allegory lay bare all too starkly the political dimension of the process.

Although Angus Fletcher's *Allegory: The Theory of a Symbolic Mode* has already been discussed under writers on fantasy, the publication of this book in 1964, closely followed by Todorov's *Introduction à la littérature fantastique* in 1967, was enormously influential on theories of allegory. Gay Clifford's *Transformations of Allegory* is specifically about the way allegories convey enigma and how readers respond to them, but is caught into a paradoxical contradiction by incorporating some of Fletcher's terminology. The idea of a loss of hierarchy in the modern world is taken up in this study from a different perspective. For her, early allegories like *Piers Plowman* break down coherence and order but only to reunify and make perceptible a new order or system. They are unvaryingly authoritative. Modern allegory such as *Titus Groan* of Peake's *Gormenghast* trilogy also breaks down coherence and order but leaves them fragmented, frustrating the perception of any new order or system. These new allegories are authoritarian but from a private, subjective point of view.

Far from being rigid and moralistic, Clifford suggests that modern allegory is sceptical, flexible and against social hierarchy. Yet these distinctions are, in contrast with Honig's, used to provide a basis for the thesis that modern allegory just does not work. Modern allegories 'assert personal choice and subjective evaluation against collective or cosmic systems' (C: 116). Hence they curb the writer and they impose upon the reader. Their style is too artificial for the modern individual consciousness which has turned to symbol as a more 'natural' expression (117). What the modern allegories lack are the 'transformations' that occur in the earlier writings. The definition, which is significantly allied with the possibility of a 'natural' language, brings Clifford's modern allegory in parallel with fantasy: they both provide their own subjective, alternate, artificial world which controls the reader.

Contradictions enter Clifford's work when we turn to the statement that expands on Honig's 'enigma', that the greatest allegories are:

> intransigent and elusive not simply for defensive reasons such as political caution but because they are concerned with a highly complex kind of truth, a matter of relationships and process rather than statement. (C: 53)

However, for her the function of this elusive process is to perceive coherence in enigma and to underpin the hierarchical structure that conveys its authority. The definition lies in paradoxical conjunction with her argument, parallel with Fletcher's, that myths attempt a true explanation, while allegory can only provide a fictional figuration of events and can never achieve truth (66). This desire for authority without authority is reflected in the definition given of 'transformation' which may be directed toward imprisonment and fixity or toward freedom. Yet how freedom can occur without some kind of imprisonment is never discussed, although central to the realisation of the argument.

The Reader

In a sense Honig, Fletcher and Clifford present allegory's construction primarily from the writer's point of view, although as we will note, Clifford has much to contribute about the reader's response. But the next major writers on allegory, Maureen Quilligan' in *The Language of Allegory* and Frank Kermode in *Genesis of Secrecy*, radically alter the definition by placing equal weight on the reader's participation. For Quilligan allegory splits into the simultaneous commentary of one text upon many others although ultimately upon the one Biblical pretext, and *allegoresis* which is the commentary of the reader upon the text. She severs medieval from modern allegory in terms of a succinct literary history. The central theory is that the Christian belief gave to the classical figures of paranomasia and prosopoeia the 'capacity for massive narrative extension' (Q2: 19). For her Christianity is the central defining factor, and the study is founded on the relationship between all texts and the single acknowledged or unacknowledged pre-text which is the Bible. The relationship focuses on revealing through the open admission of our limitations with language, that there is a recognised external part of the world outside our control.

The study is illuminating, but given this focus it need not be restricted to Christian literature. After all Quintillian defined allegory as the linguistic process of working against the accepted meaning of words. In this case the pretext is not the Bible but language itself. Quilligan also follows the diminution of allegory with the loss of rhetorical study, and the rise of scientific univocal language during the seventeenth century. She goes on to place the resurgence of the mode squarely in Emerson's perception that words are part of a natural world, and that both words and the world elude the dominations of human beings. Modern allegory goes hand in hand with a renewed concern for language. Whereas now allegory concentrates on the relationships holding between the gaps in meaning, and previously the emphasis had been on the separate existence of the gaps and the meanings, both medieval and modern allegory, and here she gives the examples of Langland and Melville, have a common 'concern for the polysemous slipperyness of a shared language which can easily lie, but which is the only tool for stating the truth' (221). Both convey this truth as authority or presence in their commentary on the Biblical pretext.

Both foci comment on the Biblical pretext and hence convey its authority. But Quilligan is careful to separate the horizontal process of authority, continually moving toward truth but never reaching it, from the vertical process of authority in *allegoresis* which attempts to achieve truth by imposing it. She contrasts the reading of Sterne's Tristram Shandy which invites the readers to be self-conscious, to 'reflect that the choices they have made about the text also reflect the kinds of choices they make in life' (253), with readings of Pynchon's *Gravity's Rainbow* which 'constantly invites and then exposes the reader's imposition of meaning' (277). The former reading is conscious of the pretext, and the latter is not – indeed cannot be because the writing has no pretext. Kermode also separates between imposing, institutional or carnal readings, and the spiritual which have no final form. But he shifts the emphasis more firmly onto the reader, and goes on to note that the attempts at spiritual writings in modernist texts which arose in reply to the tradition of representational realism, should not divert us from the recognition that 'all narratives are capable of darkness; the oracular is always there or thereabouts.' (K: 15). Allegories, texts of displacement, have always existed. They are not only within a Christian tradition. Furthermore, medieval and modern allegories are not substantially different for they are defined by the way the current reader reads.

Institutional readings and *allegoresis* deny the materiality of language, while allegory 'proper' and spiritual readings conflate it with otherness. Hence for Quilligan allegory is always potentially 'sacralising' and can only be read fully by cultures which believe that language is not simply an arbitrary system of signs for man's use. And it is here that the shift occurs toward the other primary definition of allegory which is concerned with the reader's response. Quilligan observes that the 'action' of any allegory is the readers learning to read the text properly' (Q1: 24). With that reading, questions of both 'certain or doubtful authority' from the Bible may be discussed. For Quilligan, the existence of God is revealed through the externality and otherness of language. Both result in people attempting to approach this otherness in reading and commentary upon reading, and it is this that moves us into the area of the reader's response.

Within the definitions stressing the hierarchical purpose of allegory, it is emphasised that the reader must be taught to read at the same time as being left free to respond. The strength of early allegory is, Clifford suggests, that despite its collective morality, undemocratic and authoritarian nature the reader is still left room to interpret. Allegory was 'an energetic form of reading, in which the reader's critical abilities are constantly brought into play by a desire to know and understand' (C: 42). Not only had the reader freedom of imagination, but was left free 'by the massiveness and enigma of the central concepts' (94). However for her modern allegories, by getting rid of hierarchy and their central enigmas, imprison the reader within a subjective vision. Just as in fantasy there can be no true questioning of authority, simply burlesque or parody of its bases. It is this extreme of imposed didactic purpose that possibly lies behind Springer's definition of apologue as a domination of mimesis in order to maximise truth; or of Richter's suggestion that the satisfaction of the reader being convinced of the 'truth of propositions'[17] is a 'consoling form'. There is an unavoidable coincidence here with the face of fantasy as wish-fulfilment. This extreme of 'allegory' which has sacrificed the external to the subjective, attempts an absolute truth, denies active assessment and consoles the reader. Once more Fletcher's authoritative definition of the stance underlines the dictatorial and 'correct' thematic readings which eliminate all alternatives.

But reading and interpretation does not, as Sontag asserts, have to be restrictive. Thematic interest does indeed provide for interpretation, and Frye, providing a complement to Honig's failure to discuss the reader comments that allegories undercut possible catharsis by creating a strong reader and writer relationship in the thematic interpretation. In 'actual allegory' the poet 'explicitly indicates the relationship of his images to examples and precepts, and so tries to indicate how a commentary on him should proceed' (FR1: 90). But reading need not be directed toward a specific end. Anagogical texts, which Frye differentiates from allegories, unite ritual and dream, external society and the individual into a text which no longer comments 'on life or reality, but contain[s] life and reality in a system of verbal relationships' (122). In the anagogic, which Honig attributes to allegory, the text attains its own intrinsic presence which evades explanation.

Kermode discusses 'oracular' texts as resistant to interpretation (K: 15). Allegory is the way in which the reader reads such texts, recognising their resistance. He too comments on their ability to 'prey upon life' (20) if they are read as in fantasy as absolute truths, specific ends. The heart of the allegorical stance is fortuitousness; it is enigmatic because life is enigmatic (63). In *The Rhetoric of Irony* Booth defines the reader's response to ironic texts as a matter of responsibility. Irony which in some forms lies so close to allegory, moves the reader to 'judge the work by the values which we have learned to employ by reading the work'[18]. The emphasis here is on the word 'reading' as an active involvement. It is not a matter, as with fantasy, of judging the alternate world in terms of its own dictated rules, but of learning how to read and through that process learning how to assess and evaluate. Quilligan rephrases this concept of active interpretation when she locates 'meaning' in the self-consciousness of the reader, but not as a finite thing rather as a relation to the enigma, to the 'sense of the sacred' in the text (Q1: 29). She goes further and claims that allegory does have a didactic function: to correct the tendency to misread. But misreading is not a matter of arriving at an incorrect significance but of failing to recognise the restrictions of language that limit reading. The correction proceeds not by designating meaning but by engaging in an active and alerting 'wordplay' (85).

The most extensive discussion of allegory as defined by a certain kind of response, is found in Paul de Man's *Allegories of Reading*. As the title suggests, allegory is a way that writing is read as well as there in de Man's book specifically as a way that reading is written (DM1: 76). Allegory narrates the impossibility of reading to a specific end or truth. It is always an ethical and didactic writing because there will always be 'structural interference of two distinct value systems' (206), those of the writer and the reader. But it is devoid of authority; it is only effective to the extent that it will 'undermine' its own logic (247) and is an 'epistemological abdication' (209).

For de Man, allegory is a denial of representational referentiality (DM1). It generates a non-authoritative statement. There is no question of its being hierarchical, so the discussion does not deal in the question of 'waver', Honig's overt speaking of the fantastic hover which depends upon the representational, the belief in language as a given thing which realises the constant unending process of desire, and which catches allegory into problems of institutional and carnal readings that tie it to the ideological alone. Here allegory is entirely a consideration of the activity of the axis of the waver out toward the material world. The definition, although lying out toward the continual regression of a one particular type of deconstructive reading, does posit the enigma of the material world lurking within its interstices. It suggests that the material exists where the literal and the referential converge (274), even though for human beings such matter is impossible to know.

4 ALLEGORY AND MATERIALITY

Techniques for Representation

In 1981, one of those felicitous doublings of ideology that quilt this stuff into substantial fabric saw the simultaneous publication of two collections of essays on allegory and related topics. They have rather different emphases – Bloomfield's *Allegory, Myth and Symbol* toward technique and Greenblatt's *Allegory and Representation* toward philosophy – and together present a diversity of approaches to the material world that underlies this field of criticism and theory in brief compass if not succinct manner. The collections underline several directions of thought established during the previous decade, indeed Quilligan and de Man take the opportunity to condense and rephrase their critical stance. The one aspect the writings do have a consensus upon is the ability of allegory to engage with an external world. Whether that world be physically exact, representable, material or transcendental differs in each case and defines the differences in/diversity of the discussion about technique. Yet curiously, there is an odd avoidance of the reader which sharpens the contrast between these collections and their predecessors. Even the two up-dated essays ignore the reader, and only one essay, Holquist's 'Politics of Representation' addresses itself directly to audience involvement. There would be no need to worry about the contrast if it were not for the radical effect it has on the kind of external world in question, the techniques involved in engaging with it, and the willingness to deal with questions of power and political action which characterised the earlier theories.

Allegory as Truth: Tendency to fantasy

In an attempt to 'discuss' the diverse views in question from earlier and later theorists, I have made a rough division among the writings based on the kind of external or *allos* they indicate. The division is imprecise and I expect disagreement, but it acts as a summary needed for clarity and once stated can provide a basis for informed discussion. So, in amongst God, unity, matter, nothing, truth and goodness, there is first a belief that allegory speaks about a specific that can be apprehended Truth. Moving on to approached rather than apprehended truth, extensions of this belief are first into the idea of truth as polysemous, that multiple layers of discourse intercomment upon each other to indicate truth. And second into truth as a product of contradiction, that if one constantly disrupts and opposes, this will indicate an external – although this ignores the problem that because contradiction and opposition need something recognisable to react against, they become complicit with that which they oppose implying that the truth or external is part of a polar opposition.

Broadly speaking, each of these three indications of *allos* considers value as an adjunct of truth. In other words when truth is approached, revealed, attained, value comes to be defined by acts which get one closer to approaching, revealing and attaining. In crude terms, the product is all, ends justify means. The fourth belief that this crude summary leads toward changes the role of value. It argues that means are important, that they are implicit in actions which others may regard as ends. Most important, it does not believe in attainable Truth. This is not to be understood as some excuse for liberal relativism or an unrigorous plurality of texts. What it is, is a rejection of the separation between ends and means, between truth and morality between fact and value. The basic assumption is not that human beings can approach, realise, attain a total vision of the world, but that the world is not to be comprehended that way. The value in being a human being is not to achieve some vision of what the world is, or reach a definition for a dominance over it, but to acknowledge that it is there.

This sounds simple, naively stone-kicking; but the kind of empiricism that it might indicate, with its skeletal attendants rationalism and analytical logic, does not take us far and is not intended. The attitude is after all, based upon a vision of the material world as a physical phenomenon that can be exactly represented in human language. It is almost absurd in these days to entertain this elementary discourse. But we do occasionally need to remind ourselves that a majority of people involved in science and technology, intimately defining the effective reins of government power, depend upon this view of the world to carry out their science and that government depends upon it for effective implementation of that science. The stances of this discourse are fundamentally ahistorical and non-material. Those claiming historicity / the historical do so on the basis of history as a set of fixed facts that can be known and represented in the same manner as the facts of the physical world, and just as the latter dominates over 'nature' so the former dominates the 'past'.

Theories of allegory that move toward the specific truth, polysemic revelation or truth by contradiction, differ in one fundamental aspect from this kind of rational, analytical empiricism: they are not sure the truth can ever be known or represented and therefore concentrate on the process by which we grow closer to knowing and representing. In many ways the procedures of modern, western science and politics or state government are similar in this respect to fantasy rather than allegory: they often ignore the process of their methodology. As long as the study of that process includes audience, writer and writing, the domination implicit in the end product of its actions can be kept in view, made overt, weighed and considered. But as the reader or audience drops out of the study, they bend imperceptibly and often contrary to stated intention, toward the imposition of power. In contrast, theories that try to acknowledge the material world without dominating are more concerned with history as an interaction between human beings and their surroundings; they consider the active interrelationship that goes on, process and product fused into one. By definition, they cannot forget the text, forget the historical moment.

Just as the concept of knowledge may be divided between wisdom, which is an activity, and information which is a set of unitary facts, the concept of purpose is divided between the values within the activity itself and the end values the process achieves. Honig refers to allegory as a metaphor of purpose not a moral lesson. But whereas Clifford takes this definition as one of 'relationship and process' that leads to a transformation, Quilligan interprets it as a basic lack of transformation, that it is not about specific values but about the ability to reveal value , specifically a value that indicates a polysemic truth. As Kermode observes, any interpretation based on the acceptance of an absolute or an end time always retains the possiblity of becoming reductive and idolatrous. And de Man simply undermines any concept of specific value by denying the referential value of allegory.

Many theorists trying to delineate the technique and strategies of the writing, begin with the word 'allegory' itself. We are told that it is made up of *allos* or 'other', and on this there is agreement. But its second part is not so easy. This could derive from the stem λεγω, – to speak, from αγορευω – public assembly or an αγορα – to speak in the marketplace[19]. Each derivation has widely differing emphases ranging from the enigmatic complex of 'to speak other', to speaking in a public assembly or speaking to the masses. The one common denominator is that one speaks, one communicates, one has some kind of audience. So from the start the word indicates first, the sense of an external world and second, an intimate relationship with an audience. But the sense of 'other' is, as I have already tried to indicate, complex. Edward Phillips defined allegory as a device 'wherein ther is concealed something that is different from the literal sense'. Yet how one chooses to understand this depends largely upon one's idea of 'literal': whether 'letter' and writing are representative, symbolic, analogous or other. Angus Fletcher thinks of allegory as something which 'subverts language itself' (FL: 2), and hovering behind this definition is the concept of a precise language, a language which has identities and relationships which can be both known and subverted by the abuses of human beings. It is a definition placing him firmly within theories of fantasy. Clifford suggests that allegories always take specific steps to ensure that *allos* cannot be 'straight-jacketed' (C: 94), but there is still a central image and idea in view. The two part movement of the definition parallels Empson's statement that it 'is not ... the normal use of allegory to make a statement which is intended to have several interpretations... The reader does not think of it as ambiguous, but as pretending to be ambiguous, perhaps to evade some censorship'[20]. Implicit in the double-edged nature of these definitions is that *allos*, the meaning or purpose or moral, exists as an identity and even that it may ultimately be reached and obtained. These definitions depend as does fantasy on the activity of the reader to understand the process of evasion and omission. It is significant that Fletcher decides upon the word αγορα as the derivation of the second part of allegory. For him it is a discourse that involves an audience of the market, one that can readily understand the speech that is being presented. His definition superimposes on that of fantasy because it is founded on the idea of a precise representative language and has a similar two-way movement to neutrality/perfection/unity and to manipulation.

Apprehended truth

Not surprisingly, Clifford's alternative allegorical worlds aim for plausibility and exactitude in the persuasion to truth. She cites the veracity of the Italian landscapes in *The Divine Comedy* as necessary not to make us feel that the landscape 'is *as* real as the Italian one, but that it is more real' (86). For this to be effected narrative movement or episodic repetition becomes an illustration of an ideal state and progress toward a transformation (28 and 29) that is amplified in her proposition of allegorical logic as 'rationally structured and ordered action... Concerned with linear movement' (35). It is suggested that the activity in progress results in an emphasis on verbs, not only in description but in the construction of images (13). Later it is claimed that the visual needs support from verbs rather than from nouns and adjectives because verbs present a metaphysical form of interaction (81). That verbs may be the primary signal for activity underlies the need for linear rational development of the narrative but verbs are only an abstract indication of activity. However, there is nothing inherently 'active' about them. They may be used to give an illusion of activity, just as any other grammatical form may convey interaction.

The result is that Clifford is left with the apparent paradox that allegory has a series of static repetitions that overall present the possibility of change (C: 28–9). The paradox mirrors the coincidence of both hierarchy and progress which her theory claims, but it is not contradictory given the partial, incomplete, structure of allegory and her concept of transformation. The partial structure is sustained by a narrative movement that allows for the restatement of the ideal in a number of situations. Alone this may be inconclusive; so, to effect the transformation of the hero and avoid 'seemingly endless' repetition, the allegory must invoke a *deus ex machina* provided by and supporting the hierarchy in question (22), for example the transformation of Piers into Christ at the end of *Piers Plowman* (30). If the hierarchy is authoritative and moving to a specific end which it does here, then the repetition of the hero's movement will appear as progress, as a linear and rational development to an end, when put under the perspective of a *deus ex machina*. The partial nature of an allegory without hierarchy would just repeat; there would be no direction in human or heroic terms. The presence of hierarchy makes possible a direction of becoming for the movement of the narrative. It becomes a progress, or at the least a total non-human transformation, a magical removal beyond our limitations.

Why it should do so is possibly easier to comprehend from her term 'digression', another technique related to repetition. In early allegories with an accepted hierarchy, the repetition is encyclopedic, it has a fictional function to remind one of artifice; it places a large number of corresponding allusions within one system, and tends like the *Divine Comedy* toward the general, eventually to the universal and absolute. In modern allegories such as those of Thomas Mann, the digression simply fragments the allegories. It reminds one of artifice but does not direct one to a universal, only to the arbitrary and dilettante. The point is that there is no concept of what lies outwith human beings unless it is conveyed by the enigma which is the absolute in the hierarchy. Therefore, getting rid of hierarchy leaves one without an external world. This is no mere rigid rhetoric as the critics defining allegory as a formal genre would have it. But again, because it confines itself to design, relation and transformation, which are all within the comprehended world of man's attempted control, it cannot account for the material in the external world which has no man-made hierarchy.

The incompletion of narrative movement is not only related to repetition and digression but also to the paratactic structure of allegory. The structure can generate a strangeness (C: 2), an invitation into a different kind of logic by the juxtaposition of narrative elements with their causal relations severed. It has been suggested that paratactic structure replaces narrative sequence with thematic repetition (R: 17), becoming the basis for the potentially open ended form of the apologue, that raises the problem of closure or of reaching an end without completion. To do so parataxis must provide an additive number of exempla that are not inductively guided by the author, yet the withdrawal of the author sometimes means that any closure is impossible (R: 99). To illustrate the point, Richter compares Pynchon's *V* with Joseph Heller's *Catch-22*, saying that Pynchon creates a chaos that confuses the reader, disallows not only completeness but closure. In contrast *Catch-22* forces the reader to read paratactically:

The sequence of 'bits', related to one another in nothing save their absurdity, forces us to find the structuring principle...to generalise a thesis about the absurdity of the world... (139)

and thus find closure.

The withdrawal of the author does lead to 'obscurity', but for differing reasons and with differing effects. Clifford suggested that in early allegories it was for the protection of the author, just as Fletcher notes the aptness of the mode for subterfuge and propaganda. In contrast to Empson who implies that authors only pretend ambiguity and cannot truly hide[21], these two critics assert that the author is capable of fully disguising himself. As a direct result, Clifford charges modern authors with irresponsibility when they hide. Their withdrawal is an attempt to absolve themselves of the consequences of their subjective vision, and place the onus upon the reader.

In the end, these relationships are founded upon each unique belief in the relationship between words and object that bodies forth the specific idea of *allos*. Clifford points out at the same time as discussing narrative movement, the 'kinetic' nature of allegorical images, contrasted with symbols which are focused in upon themselves. Allegorical images are here concerned with the process of signifying more than what is signified. Yet the underlying ambiguity in this critical approach, which most fantasy theorists manage to cover up, emerges quite clearly in this study when the writer separates between personification and personified abstractions, going on to discuss the symbolic in allegory itself which must refer back to the 'overall purpose and certainly not conflict with it' (C: 12). In discussing the work of Melville, Frye suggests that any lurking antagonism between image and the literal aspect of nature is antiallegorical. He defines the ironic and antiallegorical as 'withdrawn from explicit statement' (FR1: 94), and that in formal allegory there must be a continuous relationship between nature and the image. Both these theorists also stress the visual nature of the explicitness. The abstractions of allegory need concrete and visual imaginations to relate them clearly to the precepts (C: 8). The visual makes explicit by reinforcing 'the significance of events by association' (73); it helps the reader form a codified set of associations which are memorable, and also intensifies the moral and historical associations necessary to recognition of the hierarchy.

The opposition and complicity of allegory and symbol as devices of movement and identity respectively, is made more explicit by S. R. Levin's essay in the Bloomfield collection which reverses the definition. As the single champion, in the collection, of allegory as a writing that strains toward identity, the discussion of personification in allegory takes on considerable significance. Levin suggests that personification is structured semantically so that the verbs are 'humanised' and the nouns non-human. The possible combinations that emerge when one literalises or changes one or the other are educative, but more to the point here is the concluding discussion of Keats's 'negative capability'. Levin takes the opportunity to claim that the necessary human limitations so firmly expressed by Keats are in effect restrictively, hinderingly 'negative' and that the 'positive aspect lies in the capacity to overcome this limitation' (LE: 32), and to achieve 'pure allegorical reading – pure in being univocal' (35). However, if this occurs, we are told that allegory becomes a general aspect of the activity of metaphor with its movement toward identity and univocity, that maintains the authoritative hierarchy.

If we turn now to Honig and *Dark Conceit* for a rather different attitude toward hierarchy, we find the possibility of an allegory based on dialectical transfer. The strategy of allegorical waver, so expressive of the constant interaction between word and object and human being, is the way analogies set up correspondences so that they gain a meaning within the context of the narrative itself rather than by relating to external hierarchies. Honig defines the analogical as an indication of something other than an exact referent, but as having a fundamentally conventional reference, as the function lying at the root of allegory. The literal, with its specifically referential action, becomes opposed to analogy, in a similar manner to the way that the representative is opposed to an acknowledged, incomplete and partial representation. The allying of the literal with the referential also encourages, as in Levin, an alliance with the metaphoric and symbolic. However, allegorical waver results in the 'dialectical transfer' of the 'relatively static ideational figures' of analogy to 'more active and meaningful roles' (HON: 138) as the text is constructed during reading. The movement described contradicts the assumption that allegorical symbols move toward the abstract (Frye), that the ideological is more important than the structure of the fiction (Spivak), and that the structure is dictated by the doctrines (Clifford). If the text moves toward an iconic status, dialectical transfer should act to prevent this by insisting on the continual interaction of audience, writer and writing. But once there is an end in mind, dialectical transfer becomes fixed in a specific idea and authority.

It is interesting that Spivak, who looks upon allegory as a double structure of a 'metasemantic system of significance' corresponding to 'a system of signs present in the text itself' (SP: 348), asserts that this latter system attempts an 'iconic status', a position of static hierarchy within language itself. Further this procedure between the metasemantic and the sign is spatial and visual; it controls the iconic. Even Todorov whose idea of 'explicit' movement refers rather more subtly to the overt artificiality of the relationship between the figural and proper meaning, still emphasises that the movement must be toward a particular significance. *Le Nez* by Gogol is ruled anti-allegorical because its meaning is not exact.

For the most part Honig's concept of allegory is close to Clifford's. The primary devices it employs are allusion which is dependent on tradition, anthropomorphism which substitutes a natural landscape for the activity of the mind, and, preparing for Clifford's separation: personification which yields ambivalence and nomenclature or the personification of abstractions in metonymy (C: 116). Yet where Honig presents a non-authoritarian hierarchy explicitly different from Clifford's or Fletcher's is in his discussion of narrative. While narrative movement is held to be episodic and repetitive, the action is primarily dialectical rather than rational and he stresses that rational analysis is not sufficient to cope with the irrational forces allegory conveys. If movement is confined to the linearly rational, repetition becomes progress; but once involved in the dialectical interaction with analogy, the repetition becomes a continual process toward *allos*. *Allos* here is still hierarchical, but there is no question of ever being able to attain/obtain it. Yet the repetition involved is not 'endless' for it comes to rest in enigma. It is with the enigmatic that Honig prepares the way for the possibilities of both polysemy and conflict/contradiction within other emerging theories of allegory.

Polysemous truth

Honig of course pre-dates Clifford by fifteen years, and undoubtedly provides a context for some of what she suggests about allegory's approach to truth. His writing also opened up the field of allegory for two other related concepts of *allos*: polysemous truth and truth in opposition. To begin with the former we need to turn to Quilligan's understanding of *allos*: Here *allos* is not a naming of other meanings but the process of naming many things with one word, or moving toward an understanding of unity by the correspondence of many. It is not based on identity or difference but upon a dialectic of simultaneous commentary. Ultimately, within this theory, allegory redeems language from human beings because it protects it from their activity (Q1: 79).

Quilligan splits apart Honig's opposition between the referential/literal and analogical, opposing the referential to the literal as representation to the process of interaction. Here the literal becomes a metonymic interruption of ideological expectation, acting against the metaphorical substitution of referent, in sharp contrast to the static metonymy of Honig's personified abstractions. Yet Quilligan also differentiates between typology or abstraction, and personification. In her study typology comes directly from the examples in the Bible (Q1: 115), whereas personification is indirect: It is a 'reification of language' that searches for things in words (115-6). Personification acts like a pun which 'mimics' or presents an artificial version of the life of the mind (42), and alerts the reader to the fictive device. For the critic, it becomes a question of the action between the image and the Bible, the text and pretext. Furthermore, typology and personification indicate differing attitudes to the presentation of a pretext that are both dependent on ideological assumptions.

Several essays in the Bloomfield collection, to which Quilligan contributed, echo this concern with metonymy as interruption and metaphor as substitution of identity and indicate the change in emphasis Quilligan herself seems to develop in her contribution. After distinguishing between metonymy as contiguity and association, as against metaphor as similarity and substitution, H. W. Boucher looks carefully at the role of metonymy in both typology and allegory. He concludes that in the former it is simply 'replacement' of one name by another, while in the latter it functions by *alieniloqum* 'speaking other', which includes irony. What is interesting, although not pursued, is the possibility that *both* are ideological, rooting allegory willy-nilly in historical and political necessity. Elsewhere in the collection J. Whitman takes a rather different view of the process of *alieniloqum* saying that it allows one to illuminate the 'One' by indicating many (NH: 73). In contrast to Boucher who is more concerned with the difficulty language has to discuss the material world, Whitman considers allegory a 'consolation', something potentially subversive but always able to 'reconstitute the very order it seems to disrupt' directing the mind 'from deception towards truth' (63). What is accepted, and dangerously so, without question or modification, is the desirability of consolation and the possibility of achieving truth. Neither theorist pays much attention to the reader and so neither is stimulated to pursue the implications.

The separation between literal and referential as material and ideological provides Quilligan with the basis for her distinction between allegory and *allegoresis*, which does bring in the reader in a significant role. Allegorical narratives 'unfold as investigations into the literal truth inherent in individual words' (Q1: 33). But by literal is meant an activity between word and object which is in opposition to the referential, expected, assumed, ideological relationship for which *allegoresis* searches. The truth investigated in allegory is not a definite end but the difference from the habitually associated meaning of *allegoresis*. . In turn, allegorical plots evaporate when the literal interrupts the metaphorical to alert the reader to the fictional nature of the reading (65). The narrative comments on the pretext at the same time as it enacts its claim 'to be a fiction *not* built upon another text' (98). This polysemic movement between construction and deconstruction is a voice of the fictional narrator, Booth's implied author.

Such a writer has a radically different role to the author who explicitly hands the reader a code. As Quilligan says, if there is one thing that allegory is not, it is 'mechanically decodable speech' (Q1: 29). The writer of allegory may directly address the reader but the primary signification is 'by all he does not say, thereby inviting the reader's active interpretation' (252). But by the time the essay for the Bloomfield collection is written, Quilligan clearly feels a need to insist that *allegoresis* is a specific kind of reading that continually deconstructs the text and forces disjunction between word and meaning on it. As a corollary 'true allegorical narrative' pursues a 'goal of coherence' that persuades 'the reader of the ethical efforts of interpretations; right reading is ethical action' (Q2: 185). It appears that the spectre of continual interpretation, endless dismantling, has moved the theorist into a different emphasis – on the final unity of the pretext rather than the process of polysemic interpretation. This has the unfortunate side-effect of restricting the positive application of *allegoresis* to all kinds of ideological interpretation – including the rigidly formalistic – by limiting it to the deconstructive. It diminishes the role of the reader, and begins to disguise the political implications of the stance.

Truth by opposition

In a different realisation of 'dialectic', Frank Kermode unhesitatingly takes on the possibility of continuous interpretation. Yet the foundation of his dialectic upon oppositional conflict leaves its politics complicit in all that it criticises. *Allos* and allegory become a question of secrecy of language (K: 144), and narrative is a necessary agent of that obscurity.

Narrative supplements 'logical' or rational and linearly causal relations, with its own coherence: It creates a paratactic structure. The repetition of this structure is not a matter of progress, but of the continual disruption of the movement toward an end. The apocalyptic intercalations into the text function by indicating not an end, but that more interpretation is needed (K: 127). One needs that 'opposition', that lack of consecutive narrative value (142), and to ensure it Kermode proposes an 'algebra' of opposition. The narrative is its own author. Its obscurity is the key to the overt rhetoric which questions itself and which keeps the reader interpreting (62). Such obscurity does not tell the reader what to think, instead it invites into interaction. Kermode suggests that the gospels are narrative augmentations of pre-existing fabula that do not direct the reader to explanations. They are non-reductive commentaries on the pretext that make necessary further interpretation (81). This is contrasted to 'institutional' readings which attempt to explain and clarify pretexts, because they fail to recognise the arbitrary nature of the authority they call upon. Institutional readings find it possible to be explicit in an explanatory manner because they operate within the 'fictions that give them value' (109). They explain pretexts according to the rules of their world and because the explanations fit those rules they are accepted as authoritative and true[22].

Kermode's analysis of institutional readings consolidates the dangerous but unexplored implications in the consolatory ideology of polysemous truth. But his insistence on oppositional conflict leaves him with only the private force of prophecy or apocalypse, that as we saw in the study of fantasy, is inherent in the oppositional conflict there. Several contributors to the Greenblatt collection make this complicity overt. Again drawn to that metonymy/metaphor duality S. Fineman analyses allegory as the poetic projection of the metaphoric (structural), onto the metonymic (temporal). He can claim that allegory brings together space with time, joins *langue* and *parole*, and he recognises that as such it becomes a 'hierarchising mode indicative of timeless order' (F1: 32), that is 'inherently' so, presumably because it is fixed, religious and political. Yet each of these oppositions is dependent upon the other. There is no way out of the vicious circle they inscribe and it is significant that finally he suggests that this kind of allegory is allegory as criticism, sinning because it pursues a specific 'thing' and left only with nostalgia, utopia and the apocalypse (51). Poetic allegory, in contrast, moves to silence, is always incomplete. Unfortunately Fineman's analogy for poetic allegory is desire, and desire such as this, arising specifically from 'neurosis', is highly ambivalent and exists in continual partnership with its twin, criticism.

The inclusion of an essay by Bersani in the Greenblatt collection is an indication of how close we are to fantasy. But here as in his book much quoted by by fantasy theory, Bersani goes out of his way to indicate the problems in the analogies. Once more, after reiterating the by now usual problems of *allos* as oppositional desire, in terms of masochism, death, representation, suicide and fantasy, he posits a third possible kind of desire. It is to make the object of desire or *allos*, 'productively unlocatable' (BE2: 161), and to be founded upon the socialising of the mother rather than the repression of the father. Techniques of repetition and replication would not be imitative but distancing, alerting one to difference and loss. Greenblatt's introduction to the collection begins by noting that allegory, in acknowledging darkness and the void, or loss, makes possible presentation in the absence of direct signification. And what is important here is that Greenblatt spells out the tendency of the entire system of opposition by saying that allegory in the end devoutly wishes 'the perfect, authoritative representation of the Truth' (AR: viii). Despite the insistence by all except Greenblatt that *allos* conceived in this manner will produce endless interpretation, in effective political terms of the critic who has to act, they are reduced to pursuit of Truth within the oppositional conflict of their analogies which inexorably moves them toward the fantasy of utopia and apocalypse.

Allegory as Material Difference: Stance

The necessary involvement of the reader
While the contributors to Greenblatt's book are all in one way or another concerned with difference rather than unity, they approach the question in different ways. On the one hand there is loss conceived of as the disappearance or lack of a possible unity, truth or god, in other words based on the fact of difference: and leading to oppositional frameworks. And on the other hand there is difference as a material condition that we have to deal with, bring into discourse, perceive as the location for our relationship with the external world. It is this latter approach that introduces the fourth set of definitions of allegory which are based on the attempt to discuss the ways in which human beings acknowledge the materiality of the external and in so doing generate value, in other words generate valuable relationships that reject the concept of a privileged subject or identity in their attempt to acknowledge the material.

Techniques for the discourse of allegory as an acknowledgment of the material, have fascinated writers throughout the centuries. But only in the post-Renaissance period with the invention of the subject necessary to new political and religious states, do these techniques get singled out as pejorative tools. A helpful index is the corresponding change in description of 'Mystic' or 'mystical', which is itself often defined as 'secret, allegorial' (*ET*). The activity of the mystic, the allegorical nature of mystical sayings, has been bound up first in discourse concerning power that operates outwith the control of human beings be it spirits, gods, God, the material; and second in the impossibility of representing that power and the problems of presenting the discourse, for that power could only be acknowledged in the activity of the discourse. The result has always been difficulty, deception, obscurity: But it can take two directions, toward wilful obscurity or rigorous 'experimentation' / attempt / activity to meet with and acknowledge that external power.

In English, the pre-Renaissance use of the word 'mystic' directed its reader to the idea of a necessary deception and story, as if attempts toward perfect description were 'licentious' acts of human control (*OED* : 816). With the Renaissance things change and the mystical moves from being a kind of deception which is a recognition of necessary human limitations, to a deception that is a wilful or neglectful failure to describe accurately. For example the *Oxford English Dictionary* lists the 1533 usage of T. Elyot, 'In the searching out of secrete and mystical things, their wuttes excellyd', *versus* a 1643 use 'while they mature ... such their mystical and pernicious designes'. By 1727 'mystical' speech is discourse that evades all 'Reason and Argument' (*OED* : 817). In this period 'mystical moves from the excellent and witty, to the pernicious, to the pejoratively illogical. Within the context of the histories of rhetoric and allegory, we can understand that since mystical discourse does not fall into a rational pattern or analytical argument it must indeed seem to lack all reason and argument. But metaphor does have reason and argument, as does oxymoron, enthymeme, analogy, metonymy and so on – a host of reasonable argumentative activities that lie outwith the restrictive demands of the new logic (H: 59–61).

The shift in the connotations of 'allegory' and its position within an ideological framework, is also detailed by W. Benjamin in a study of German tragic drama from the baroque period. Like Clifford he is concerned to distinguish modern or post-Renaissance allegory from its medieval forerunner, but unlike her he sees each as a stance for enacting the imperfections of human beings. Baroque allegory is a dialectic between nature and history which underlines the decay and lack of freedom of history as a philosophical truth – not, he emphasises, a factual truth but a practice and an awareness of material construction. There is no 'transcendent effect' which is often used to define art, but an attempt at 'the enigmatic and the concealed' (BEN: 181). He suggests that allegory collapses the beauty of totality by exposing the limitations of humanity, yet it achieves its own beauty in the grotesque ruin of subjective identity that it exposes.

During the Renaissance the pursuit of mystical discourse – recognition of external power – became sidetracked and split into diverse implications during the seventeenth century. Because of its attention to the material, it came to stand for attempts to communicate with forces external to human control that must by the definition of the new religious and political outlooks, necessarily be dark and malevolent. When denied access to the material, in an attempt to maintain purity the word took on an abstract, purely spiritual connotation, even coming to represent a desire to gain access to truth, often theological truth, other than by understanding. And later still, during a nineteenth century decadence of eighteenth century confidence in mankind's flowering autonomy, it came to be 'mystification': the cheap and sleight obfuscation of the simple, the wilful evasion, omission and hiding of the power of the external. In other words it became one with fantasy. Indeed it could be argued that this particular history of mystical allegory generated the rhetorical basis for fantasy and provided many of its techniques and strategies. But with this latter definition we have moved so far from an acknowledgment of the material as to make any functional connection between the two tenuous.

However, there have also always been voices that insisted on a recognition of the material: Coleridge for one, and Keats for another. Keats's description of negative capability – without the twist given it by Levin – remains one of the most thoughtful and positive statements of a materialist aesthetic that we have: an effect testified to by the sheer number of writers who return to it, and turn to it for help with this contemporary human dilemma. Throughout his early essays collected into *Blindness and Insight* (1971), Paul de Man introduces Keats as a touchstone for materialist philosophy, particularly in the essay 'The Rhetoric of Temporality' which begins with a description of 'Allegory and Symbol' to which we shall return. In *Allegories of Reading* de Man presents allegory as a writing which sets out to question its own truth or falsehood (DM1: 226). It uses 'rhetorical praxis that puts these statements into question' and results in a 'non-authoritative secondary statement ... about the limitations of textual authority' (98–9):

The general description provided means that allegory is quite different from the kind of process that moves to a specific end. Instead, the allegorical process continually repeats the 'confusion between figural and referential statement' (DM1: 116). Although reflecting Quilligan's separation between literal and referential, which allowed her to posit separate individual and ideological readings, de Man's figural and referential are not interruptions of each other. There is no room for rational logic which is held to proffer 'universal truth of meanings' (9), and to be method alone. But de Man also rejects the syllogistic dialectic of Quilligan and Kermode, and goes on carefully to extend the process of Honig's dialectical transfer and to reach his conclusion about the loss of meaning that leaves a 'non-authoritative secondary statement'.

de Man's presentation of allegory does however suggest an enigma lurking within its interstices, even a God existing where the figural and referential converge, although such an existence is impossible for human beings to know. Jonathan Culler provides a more distanced perspective on this by situating allegory neatly between the external world and subjective fantasy: it is the irreducible difference between the object 'as signifier and the meaning imposed by fancy of subject'[23]. Allegory indicates something 'precisely *other*' than 'the meaning of a form or object' as the result of a 'process of analogical reflection' (263). This is rephrased by Hillis Miller in the Bloomfield collection when he describes allegory's strategy as a necessary personification that reveals 'the eternal disjunction between the inscribed sign and its material embodiment' (HM: 365) so that 'naked matter shines through. It shines through as the failure of the idea to transform nature or thought' (365).

But in de Man's essay of the Greenblatt collection the concept of God lurking in the interstices is strengthened, almost becoming oppositional as he moves his prime analogy for allegorical activity from love to mathematics, coinciding with Kermode's notion of 'algebra'. The idea of zero as an usurpation that destroys the binary oppositions of justice (DM2: 20), of pleasure as seductive persuasion radically different from the persuasion to truth by proof (23), is highly suspect. Here once more is that collocation of words which fantasy exposed as inextricably connected. Truth as the desire of all seduction, Justice as the desire of all usurpation: the emphasis once more on ends not activities. The difference between truth and seduction in terms of Pascal's *Pensées* which is the topic of the essay, is significant and generative. But to elide into presenting difference as an analogy for allegory is misleading. It returns us to the split between realisable wish-fulfilment and ongoing desire in fantasy, both of which evade the material.

In *Allegories of Reading* de Man tries hard to present the activity of acknowledging the material in his development of the analogy of deceit. He states that allegory exposes the deceit of language (DM1: 116), that in allegorical writing the reader and writer are both unable to read, therefore the work depends on an agreement about referentiality which is broken again and again. Each time it is broken the rhetoric is questioned and this continual questioning becomes the allegorical text (204). The critic observes that writing which questions itself must have a fictional narrator (226), but this is far from meaning a specific 'figure' or character. What is necessary is an overt rhetorical stance. Wayne Booth restates the attitude in his insistence on the clarity of narratorial intention if the reader is to take up the full activity of the ironic mode. As a corollary, the reading of allegory is a mode grounded in a 'firm relationship between inside and outside' (DM1: 69). Virtually repeating Spivak's definition in terms of proper and literal meanings, de Man instead insists on a continuous basis for interpretation and denies the possibility of the iconic status. For him 'the allegorical representation leads toward a meaning that diverges from the initial meaning to the point of foreclosing the manifestation' (75).

To achieve this foreclosure de Man looks to repetitive structure which does not reproduce identities but, just because it is necessarily temporal can never coincide with the structure it repeats (DM3: 207). Similarly, the explicit speech of parables stresses the difference between word and object (DM1: 154) rather than a coded relationship between the two. In both cases the rhetorical stance is overt and invites the reader into a shared activity. As de Man points out, 'The narrator who tells us about the impossibility of metaphor is himself, or itself, a metaphor, the metaphor of a grammatical syntagm whose meaning is the denial of metaphor' (DM1: 18). An allegorical text 'simultaneously asserts and denies the authority of its own rhetorical mode' (17). Only by doing so can it maintain the dialectical transfer, the activity of the text.

Rhetorical Implications: Interaction

de Man implies that the construction and deconstruction is maintained within the writing itself rather than being generated only through the interaction of the reader with the text. In contrast the distinctions made between the secret and institutional readings, between allegory and *allegoresis*, extend this definition by technique firmly out into the realm of the reader. Quilligan summarises a number of techniques for response, listing the direct address to the reader, shifts between the literal and referential, wordplay, internal commentary making the actions self-reflexive, and the construction of the narrative as an activity parallel to reading (Q1: 254). Yet all have different aspects to them depending upon the stance which will direct the reader's response.

The critics of fantasy were particularly concerned about the reader because, for the most part, they were aware that the active engagement of the reader in the change to the alternate game world was essential to the conscious gamesmanship involved. In a number of cases, because a conscious audience was desired, it was simply defined as such. Little attention was paid to the possibility of it being submissive and of the alternate world being imposed. In the criticism and theory of allegory the reader is again important. But the emphasis on the reader's role is more complex. Awareness is not assumed, but discussed as a measure of the activities of the writer as well. The main difference to the techniques of fantasy, is that allegory attempts continually to alert the reader to the artificiality of the fiction proposed. It is not an initial jump followed by a necessary acceptance of the rules of the game, nor a sequential leading into the artificial so that its fictiveness is ignored. In allegory the techniques are all aimed at maintaining continual interaction.

The quality of continual interaction with the reader has led some critics to compare allegory with translation and *vice versa*. For example George Steiner in *After Babel* notes Kafka's description of the anagogic purpose of allegory in communicating the impossible. In the same context he mentions Walter Benjamin's presentation of translation as the interlinear truth revealed in the passage from language A to language B[24]. For Steiner translation is a dialectical testing of the relationship between an 'intractable alieness and a felt 'at-homeness''; it is a 'tension of resistance and affinity' (393). Here Steiner is specifically referring to communication between two languages, but implicitly he depends upon a parallel with the interpretation necessary within a single language, the activity between word and object, word and word. Translation and interpretation each convey differing approaches. For Steiner, exact communication is impossible; translation implies continual activity to different kinds of truths: correspondent, coherent and semantic. But when a critic says that poetry or prose is not translatable, there is the implication that optimally translation has specific end[25]. Similarly Susan Sontag sets off hermeneutic translation or interpretation as precise meaning carried out according to a code, against Nietzschean interpretation which is continual.

Depending upon the approach to translation and interpretation, the definition of allegory and the kind of interaction it requires will change. The assertion that 'allegory ... is a function of the reader's interpretive powers'[26] is open to divided effects. On the one hand allegory and its interpretations are seen as inseparable: Allegory is 'not a paraphrase of something capable of alternative expression' (C: 53). Todorov reverses de Man's conclusion about loss of meaning by defining allegory as one thing signifying another by way of a proposition with two senses one of which then effaces the literal, and he insists that this effacement,

> est indiqué dans l'oeuvre de manière explicite: il ne releve pas de l'interpretation (arbitraire ou non) d'un lecteur quelconque. (TO: 68–9)

On the other hand, it is commentary: 'an attaching of ideas to the structure of poetic imagery' (FR1: 89). From the perspective of translation, allegory can be viewed as the spiritual aspect of communication rather than the literal [27], or as the critical function which allows for 'detachability'[28]. Quilligan even opposes translation to interpretation, saying that the former assumes an accessibility of the text and hence imposes meaning, generates *allegoresis* (Q1: 235); while the latter recognises the difference between words and objects.

Here as previously the definitions are often at cross-purposes with each other, but two different approaches emerge one focusing on the reader reading to an end and the other on the activity of the reading. The possible existence of absolute translation, set interpretation, critical rather than literary writing, ideas rather than poetry, the accessibility of the text and imposition of meaning, all depend upon the possibility of a precisely representative language and literature. They spell out a determinable, fixed representative referential function of the word to object activity.

This possibility also lies behind the stance of fantasy, but adds a further dimension hinted at by Culler's location of allegory between the object as signifier and the meaning imposed by the 'fancy of subject'. The subject is not only the writer but also the reader. Because fantasy tends to be thought of as a genre with specific elements, or at the least as a defined attitude to knowledge and perception, its theorists neglect the possiblity that the reader can impose meaning upon a text, just as a writer.

Recent critics of allegory, anxious to differentiate between the interaction with the material and the imposition of value on it, have tended to discuss the stances from the point of view of the reader. Hence the descriptions of allegory and *allegoresis*, the spiritual and the carnal, as two different ways of reading rather than writing. However Quilligan's separation between allegory and *allegoresis* as horizontal and vertical movements, as interactive and imposed meaning, later becomes primarily a separation between writer and reader. In *allegoresis* we find the literature of literary criticism that looks for a meaning hovering over the words of the text (Q1: 26). Generally criticism is held to be a hunt for correspondences and codes (32). Instead of a radically different 'other', the reader remakes the meaning into a subjective 'sacred' text (140). The activity is simply a game; *allegoresis* is the reader imposing his rules upon the text.

This reversal of the accepted situation in the fantasy stance, highlights more clearly the questions raised by the concept of games. Fantasy theorists assume that if the audience is consciously playful there will be no problems over the ethics involved. But if it is, whose game is it? Someone must invent the rules; is it the writer or the reader? Someone aims toward a solution: whose is it to be? The writer's excuse is that she or he makes up clear rules which the audience recognises as obvious and consciously plays by. But the audience has no such excuse. The writer has no redress to the reading even though the work may be constructed to limit it. The writer can never be conscious of the rules the reader imposes.

Quilligan suggests that the 'proper' reader will always be willing to entertain a religious response, in other words to recognise the radically separate 'other' of the pretext (Q1: 223). Indeed she claims that the difficulty of allegory lies in the position of the reader as the central character. The stance continually alerts the reader by drawing attention to the language being used. Allegory aims to put the reader in a constant position of 'self-defining self-consciousness' (20). The reader reads by learning how to read, whereas readers of *allegoresis* are members of an elite who already know how to read (227). The allegorical reading generates a conscious responsibility that enables the reader to make evaluations, as opposed to creating a dependence upon the author and an avoidance of personal assessment (235): which Quilligan sets up as ethical *versus* aesthetic readings.

The separation between allegory and *allegoresis* is dependent upon the role of the reader. The work itself is allegorical, and Quilligan does not concern herself with the possibility of texts themselves as *allegoresis*, in other words as fantasy. She can treat the matter as distinctly separate in this way because of the concept of a sacred pretext, the pretext to which the text always refers and which provides it with a 'balance of interpretation' (278). The *allos* in this theory of allegory is always an object, the specific pretext of the Bible. Without it, the critic suggests that allegory becomes the infinitely regressive movement of the Derridean sign (239). But the Derridean sign need not be thought of as regressive. Although in constant movement, it has its own pretext which is language itself. Simply because we cannot grasp the materiality of language, does not mean that the pretext is not there.

A more complex theory of the separation between kinds of response permeates Kermode's *Genesis of Secrecy*. He recognises that the pretext as an object is not the *allos* in allegory, but that *allos* is the enigma revealed in interaction with the pretext. The criticism starts off once more with a concentration on the reader. The rather circular argument begins by distinguishing carnal readings which are all much the same, from spiritual readings that tend to be different. Carnal readings are fully institutionalised interpretations. They generate submissive responses that can become literal and take the alternate world as real as they tend to do within many political rhetorical stances. However, while spiritual readings try to be different, they are in effect bound to the institutional, subject to prejudice (K: 3), historical limitation and change, they are taught as if to an elect. Having proposed that spiritual readers attempt readings beyond those of the norm, based on the knowledge of their elect which is an 'inside understanding' (18), it becomes clear that all interpretations are bound to remain outside the text, bound to fail, because 'the original event of disclosure' (39) can never be captured. The point is that one should attempt to resist the coherence of the text, and to resist the oppression of any control within the text (54). As Kermode notes, it is all too easy to 'slip back into the old comfortable fictions of transparency, the single sense, the truth' (123).

The final essay in the Greenblatt collection does open out the discussion of the reader and the relation to value in a far more interesting if problematic manner. In it, Michael Holquist presents Bakhtin's dialogism as a study in the activity of reader, writer and writing. *Langue* and *parole* as separate constructs give way to a continuum of activity that generates social meaning, from a constant tension between 'canonization and heteroglossia'. Although ideology permeates that activity there are different degrees of ideological sharing, so that it becomes impossible for the individual to position her or himself. There is a 'necessity of bad faith, the inescapability of false consciousness'. The only way that position can validly be made is through 'the care they exhibit in their deeds for others and the world. Deed is understood as meaning *word* as well as physical act: the deed is how meaning comes into the world, how brute facticity is given significance and form' (HO: 176), because 'human existence is the interaction between a given world that is already there ... and a mind that is conjoined ... to this world through the deed ... of enacting value' (172). But this 'meaning' is not just a function of the writer, it is a main part of the reader's own institutionalising.

As Jameson notes, allegory may be practised as if the reader searches for a master narrative. In this sense:

> interpretation ... demands the forcible or imperceptible transformation of a given text into an allegory of its particular master code or 'transcendental signified': the discredit into which interpretation has fallen is thus one with the disrepute visited on allegory itself. (JA2: 58)

Yet it is only implicit that allegory may enact another role. Jameson clearly notes the primary reversal between medieval and modern allegory where the moral and anagogic change emphasis. He suggests that in medieval allegory the moral is individual and the anagogical is collective, while in modern allegory, through Frye, the moral is communal and the anagogic is individual and apocalyptic. He then goes on to look at what happens to the allegorical 'levels' in a system which rejects both the master narrative and pluralism.

If history is antiteleological, an absent cause, then pluralist readings become all too possible. But Jameson claims that all history passes through 'prior textualization, its narrativization in the political unconscious' (35). To avoid turning this textualisation into a master narrative the reader needs to turn to the three 'horizons' of semantic content: political history, society and 'history'. The three are parallel to symbolic act, ideologeme and that 'field of force' in which genre provides the formal effects of absent cause by textualising the 'determinate contradiction of the specific messages emitted by the various sign systems which co-exist in a given artistic process as well as in its general social formation' (99). Whereas fantasy reveals the ideologeme, by implication this practice of reading 'horizons' can be 'detected and allegorically articulated' (99). However, while the corollary is that much of the reading within *The Political Unconscious* is allegorical practice, Jameson is not concerned to separate precisely between the reader's recognition of ideologeme (fantasy) and articulation of 'history' (allegory) – possibly because his idea of value, although the one thing necessary to allegory, is inadequately developed.

Paul de Man proposes another proper reader in *Allegories of Reading*. This reader is not bound by institution nor toward a sacred pretext, and the related characteristics are revealing – if possibly misleading because they do not take into account much practical experience. Reading for de Man is the getting inside a text, making oneself familiar with it not by imposition but from being within it. In more abstract terms, the reader must have both literalism and suspicion to actively engage with the text. There must be an ability to separate between the referential and figural (DM1: 200). Most of all, as the critic observes in a comment on the work of Proust, reading:

> must acquire the power of a concrete action. The mental process of reading extends the consciousness beyond that of mere passive perception; it must acquire a wider dimension and become an action. The light metaphors are powerless to achieve this: it will take the intervention of an analogical motion stemming from a different property ... (63–4)

Significantly, metaphors in this theory underwrite the value of the 'secluded reading' and its imposed meaning, because they are substitutive and representational, while analogies indicate a different value for the direction of power.

5 THE ANALOGIES

allos, metaphor/symbol, money/exchange, desire/love, algebra/zero, deceit/truth and radioactive decay

All theorists of allegory eventually turn to metaphor and in doing so define their primary analogy for allegorical writing, for the *allos* of the text. The minutiae of these discussions more than any other set of strategies document/describe the attitude toward the material world being enacted. The crucial pivot for this terminology within the dominant Anglo-American tradition under scrutiny, is Coleridge. It is eloquent testimony to his ability to instigate readings that generations of critics/readers have commented on his presentation of metaphor and its surrounding cluster of related techniques: metonymy, analogy, symbol, association and others. Sorting out the mess often appears to be the central activity of contemporary theorists on allegory, although the attempts just as often betray the stance by trying to fix definitions.

The one thing that most commentators agree on, at least initially, is the activity of metaphor toward providing a substitute, a replacement identity. This becomes the first statement in several if/then triads of logic that attempt to explain its activity. The other key connection is metaphor's relation with symbol, which provides the second logical statement. And the result is usually extended out to allegory. For example Levin sets up metaphor in contrast to symbol, as a device toward unity in contrast with one toward difference. The drive of his definition is to present allegory as something that achieves identity; hence the alliance of allegory with metaphor which can be claimed as part of the Quintilian tradition, perceiving allegory as extended metaphor. But as we have seen, Clifford allies metaphor with symbol, suggesting that both move toward unity in opposition to allegory which works analogically to indicate difference.

The logical triads become far more sophisticated in other hands. Quilligan sets up metaphor's drive to unity, against the difference indicated by metonymy. The distinction allows her to separate *allegoresis* from allegory by allying the former with metaphor and the latter with metonymy. The former speaks to the referential, the ideological and finally the critic's imposition. The latter enacts the literal, the material and the reader's activity. The introduction of metonymy is part of the huge debt that theorists owe to Jacobson and which they pay back with little rigour. Boucher incisively demonstrates that metonymy in allegory can move both toward the simple replacement action of typology that is certainly ideologically defined, and toward the complex action of *alieniloqum* in personification. One cannot, as Quilligan seems to want to do, separate typology from allegory and place it wholly in *allegoresis* as a metaphorical construct. At least, if one does so, one has to be prepared to acknowledge that the 'difference' metonymy moves toward is not necessarily one of radical separation, generating distinct hierarchies. Both metonymy and metaphor may connect to the ideological. There may be no absolute way of separating between allegory and *allegoresis* or reader and critic in this ideological manner. And Quilligan silently acknowledges this in her comment that the social world derives from an interconnection/movement between the literal and referential, the metonymic and metaphoric (Q1: 86).

Paul de Man also sets up an initial separation between metaphor allied with symbol, as against allegory. The distinction is seen in terms of a structural or spatial device in contrast to a temporal one, the former attempting a unity that ends in the nostalgia of desired ends and the latter moving toward the difference of repetition. The reader/critic is a single unit responding to the allegorical alone; no description is provided for the audience of metaphor and this may be because de Man is uninterested in that response or that he considers it impossible. Indeed he returns to complicate the division, to over read or overwrite it pointing out the political praxis for literature in the space between the figural and referential (DM1: 150): exactly where that enigma of the material lurks. The rhetorical activity of allegory becomes a series of metaphors that deny their own possiblity as structured identities.

Fineman takes up the structural versus temporal in terms of metaphor versus metonymy, and suggests that using Jacobson's definition one can define allegory as the one mapped at right angles onto the other. But this mapping, which also intersects *langue* and *parole* as the historical and the ideological, in criticism becomes a hierarchical, ideologically bound response. He analyses this response carefully, revealing much in common with the preceding description of fantasy. But his response ends in 'sin'; it cannot describe the poetic reading which leads to silence. Far more interesting is Hodgson's account of Coleridge's contrast between allegory and symbol which he lays parallel to that between metaphor and synecdoche. With a fine sense of impossibility of isolated activity, he notes that metaphor is necessary to describe symbol and thus becomes implicated in it. One cannot separate cleanly between devices of identity and/or 'reality' – by which I take him to mean the material. The article presents the detail of Coleridge's later thoughts on these devices, and discusses the activity of determined metaphor within allegory, and analogy within symbol, as 'cognate', if also rhetorically distinguishable.

Behind many of these theories is the belief in metaphor as an agent of identity, that makes formal and explicit the representative urge of fantasy – which activity Todorov is so confident of having faded. Some of the theorists valorise the alliance between metaphor and allegory as promoters of identity, and those who do so end by exposing the dangers of fantasy. Angus Fletcher conflated allegory into a theory of a symbolic mode which took both metaphor and metonymy as teleologically defined and exercised authoritarian power, moving to fixed ends. Other critics have assumed that allegory's connection with unity-seeking metaphor reduces it to a powerless exchange of typology. In both cases allegory is allied with ideology alone, fixed criticism, the institution, nostalgia for unchanging order. For them *allos* is a specific external power, requiring clearly defined alternative worlds to explore, constructed from a rational, linear logic that ensures that the grounds of current ideology are not challenged, and spoken through an authoritative narrator who presents the reader with a code for the work.

But most theorists either ally allegory variously with metonymy or analogy in contrast to metaphor, or they explore the interconnection between the two. In the former case allegory is

clearly directed toward indicating an *allos* which cannot be
precisely identified or an *allos* generated by the conflict between the
literal and referential: the polysemous unity of Quilligan, or the
secrecy of Kermode; and in the latter stress on interconnection,
allos moves toward the material that exists between them. The
former requires repetitive and episodic structures of syllogistic
dialectical logic, that provide interruptions or disruptions of
movement, addressing the reader through what is unsaid or
bringing that reader into the conflict of the text. The latter
describes repetitive structures that question structure itself as they
move through time, operating with a dialectical ordering of
analogy that positions the writer and invites the reader into the
text. But as the more overt analogies of love, deceit, money and
desire make clear, most commentators do not, or are at a loss as to
how to break out of the circular movement that the shuttle between
time and space describes.

The analogy of money or exchange is the most crude form of this
shuttle, and lies behind the one-for-one coded definitions of naive
allegory. But even Holquist can begin an otherwise sophisticated
discussion with this figure. The idea of purchasing desire or getting
a commensurate reward for love is a fundamental principle of
much fantasy writing, not only in terms of creating satisfying
consolatory identities with specific literary devices, but in terms of
the ideology represented in the work and the ideology of the
politics and economics of the book. Theorists of allegory, although
they often speak of love and pleasure instead of desire and try hard
to break out of the infinite exchange of I/thou personalities that
fantasy presents, have precious little to offer.

Bersani holds out explicitly to allegory what he holds out
implicitly to fantasy: the idea of desire based upon the socialising of
the mother rather than the repressive privacy of the father.
Fineman suggests the infinite 'allegory of allegory' in
psychoanalysis as an extension of the 'allegory of love'. Beginning
with a slightly different figure, Durling tries to escape the
involution of the digestion of food that makes the body the
container of the soul which is also a container, by 'trusting' in the
voice of love – but cannot be precise as to its implications. de Man
specifically describes this involution as the erotic pleasure-
principle as self-seduction (DM1: 243) that encapsulates the
human being within a narcissistic world. Just so Nietzsche says that

looking for truth or fixity in the world is only possible by enclosing oneself, placing oneself under the domination of desire or pleasure[29]. But de Man shifts his emphasis in the essay contributed to Greenblatt's collection, allowing that pleasure may be an activity quite different from proof, rather than simply its other side.

In the later essay de Man also shifts his attitude to mathematics. Initially he provides a sharp contrast to Kermode's suggestion that 'algebra' is an appropriate metaphor for the activity of the reader of mystic texts. *Allegories of Reading* repeats Rousseau's warning that 'number is par excellence the concept that hides ontic differences under an illusion of identity' (DM1: 154), – that although it may be effective as a metaphor, it does provide the most complete and fully deluding basis for a fantasy world. In the later essay, he concentrates on Pascal's concept of zero as a possible analogy for the curious multivalency of allegory, which recalls Coleridge's notes on the mathematics of Jacob Boehme[30] – Pascal's near contemporary – and the fascination of the seventeenth century with the idea of cypher, a number that is not a number but secret writing, able to stand in for any number[31]. It is possible that the activity of allegory may be extended by pushing it out to incorporate the eastern philosophies from which the Arabic cypher or zero derives, but as it stands within a Western European geometry/arithmetic/mathematic it provides but a tenuous alternative.

One of the most problematic analogies for these concerns of power and value, at present running through the theory of allegory is that of deceit and by corollary, truth. We do not often think of truth as an analogy or figure, but like mathematics, that is because we allow it to define its own grounds. Quilligan insists that we must be aware of the activity of discovering truth or it will control us (Q1: 63). Presumably this is because if language can discover truth, it can aim at an absolute and a fixity. Polysemousness becomes a new structure for language, through which human beings offer themselves innumerable designs. But the infinity of design should not delude us into thinking that it can provide the answer. The moment we do, the moment we control it, we make it possible for the concept to control us, just as fantasy ensnares us within the world we make it into.

Significantly, Quilligan concludes by saying that allegory moves toward the acceptance or rejection of meaning as truth or untruth, and that it is an ethical rather than an aesthetic activity (241). The separation between the two is made possible by the impetus in her polysemousness toward a specific end. By contrast de Man calls allegory an ethical activity as well as an aesthetic. The values of the writer and reader meet in the text and in the process of interpreting the text (DM1: 206). He also notes in his study of Rilke that the attempt at pure figuration lying outside normative and ethical coercion must fail because of the materialism of language. If a rhetorical stance overtly recognises its own deceit, it presents its incompletion in the face of the materialism of the external world. de Man suggests that the specificity of human beings is rooted in linguistic deceit (156), that all deceit, all attempt at truth is necessarily incomplete. Durling makes the same argument for Dante saying that he differs as a deceitful narrator from the deceivers of Malebolge in the *Divine Comedy*, in that he is aware of the impossibility of extricating himself from his own deceit; he can take on the arrogant role of prophet knowing it is arrogant (DU1: 86). de Man separates between forms of deceit using a genre device as an analogy: if a riddle is an enigma it is said to yield deceit, but if it has only the solution of a puzzle it is merely clumsy (DM1: 203).

In de Man's definition of literature, language and evaluations are structural relationships between words and things that are capable of error (237) and deceit. Yet he has a rigid concept of the word 'morality' and thinks of it as the fact or the lie itself, as a thing rather than the acknowledging process of deceit (112–7). He also comments that if truth is a property of entities then to lie is to steal truth away (291). The process of lying exposes a true sense of the subject without this specific 'truth', but the lie by itself becomes the possessor of its rigid meaning or 'morality'. Lurking beneath the surface here are the residual effects of absolute specific truths and defined moralities. They are so prevalent that even Klause's exposition, in the Bloomfield collection, of George Herbert's development of *kenosis* as a 'self-diminishment that involves a deliberate departure from truth'[32] does not stress adequately the value that resides in the process of power relations active in acknowledging the material world.

The problem with most of the analogies that try to extend the reward-system of a fantasy stance into the materiality of the allegorical, is that they retreat from the active involvement of writer, reader and text at the same time. They forget that metaphor/metonymy may be teleologically directed and that it may not be. Most of the analogies are so firmly constructed by current ideology that they impose a retreat into the epistemology that the writers elsewhere explicitly reject. de Man asks 'why is it that texts that attempt the articulation of epistemology with persuasion turn out to be inconclusive about their own intelligibility in the same manner and for the same reasons that produce allegory?' (DM2: 2). He proceeds to pair epistemology with proof, and persuasion with pleasure and the concept of zero, thereby importing his own ideological distinction that separates epistemology from persuasion, fact from value. But the question is pertinent and takes us right into the confusion between fantasy and allegory.

Allegory, as fantasy, is a rhetorical stance refracted through epistemology and ideology; their effective difference is educative. The stance of fantasy attempts to persuade to truth by hiding its artifice, denying its rhetoric. It becomes tied to its hidden epistemology and ideology because of a need to convince about plausibility. But the stance of allegory, by being overt about its writing and specifically directing us to question epistemology and ideology, can engage any reader in the reading. Although hierarchy has been a focal topic, and has through this importance provided some critics with a means to map allegory onto fantasy, in the end it is a red herring. It is the enigma of material rather than hierarchy that lies at the core of allegory. In Quilligan's thesis it centres on the Christian religion, in Kermode's on awareness or partial glimpses of the mystery during the activity of secrecy and in de Man's in the possibility of the literal and referential converging, inscribing the material within the interstices of language. In effect, expression of belief about one's position in the material world, has always been the location for the constant enaction of positive rhetorical stance: But precisely because it is powerful and may be directed toward the authoritative or the material, there is always a tendency to fix it, to institutionalise it, make it hierarchical, turn it into a negative rhetorical stance.

A resilient analogy for allegory comes from Walter Benjamin who defines allegories as 'in the realm of thought, what ruins are in the realm of things'; here 'history does not assume the form of the process of an eternal life so much as that of irresistible decay' (BEN: 178). Allegories are neither fixed nor progressively evolving to something better. Instead, to go back to that radioactive envelope, they become the radioactive emission that indicates all material production and the current position of the material. All things emit radiation, sometimes from unstable chemicals which release their energy at dangerously high levels, but often at a constant level acceptable to life. We are all radioactive ruins. The stages of our decay indicate both the history of production and the current position of the material.

The acknowledging of the material world, without imposing upon it authoritatively, means that one must take account of history because one has to place oneself, position oneself within the discourse to announce at least some of the bias of one's humanity. An allegorical rhetorical stance allows one actively to locate that position – whereas a fantasy stance tries to make it impossible to do so actively. The stance of allegory is remarkably complex. Not the least because there is as yet no substantial body of discussion directed to it. Those who attempt to do so here, by viewing allegory as a material discourse, often get swamped by the 'chinese-box' effect. But allegory is a stance that can adequately incorporate the reader, adequately de-authorise the writing and adequately discuss text and history. One is tempted to suggest that the probings of the late 60s and 70s into this area, because they were carried out with little political commentary alongside, despite their concern with power, simply left readers/critics with an enormous burden of relativism seen in the fluctuating analogies, and which is difficult to support within any political persuasion. This suggestion gains some support from the overtly political/implicitly political: European/American divide, which infuses the academy of the West.

4 Modern Allegory and Fantasy

I DISTINCTIONS

Genre and technique, Mode and epistemology/ideology, Rhetoric and stance

To distinguish between fantasy and allegory a number of confusions must be recognised. There is the use of the words fantasy and allegory to refer to specific genres as well as their application as descriptive modifiers of, or modes within, a number of different genres. But more interesting is the interchangeable use of the words by different people referring to the same writing, or even by one person referring to the one piece of writing.

In the first case the confusion appears to be a matter of allegory and fantasy being used indiscriminately to indicate both generic and epistemological elements. The confusion arises because certain generic elements may, because of prevailing attitudes to perception lend themselves to a particular stance. For example, in fantasy the essential element is to posit a plausible rhetoric for the denial of rhetoric within a perspective that assumes that the external world is without power and that our control over it can be complete. Any generic element that encourages the control of imposition will lend itself to such a stance as does the narrative isolation of the island or the country house, the controlled game of a puzzle, or the definition of an apparently self-created language. Similarly, in allegory the stance encourages an active involvement by indicating the interaction with language and leaving it for the reader to engage in activity and assess the implications. Generic situations allowing for comparison and augmentation of the narrative such as parataxis, digression, or the open-ended mystery, will lend themselves to the allegorical stance.

Furthermore allegory like fantasy cannot be limited to attitudes to perception and knowledge however much their presence may affect the realisation of stance. For example, an epistemological change in the eighteenth century which shifts the focus of control, leads to the incorporation into fantasy of a phenomenally different world of the supernatural, whereas previously it had been solely 'naturalistic'. But there is no change in its basic attempt at the neutral activity of providing a complete alternate world – in the same way that the presence of a different epistemology combined with a different belief about the external world made attempts at control in the pre-Renaissance period full of danger and magic rather than neutrality and fantasy. Just so, the presence of an epistemology which looks on the world as neutral and controllable, is an anathema to the allegorical stance which focuses on the resistance of the world to control because of its material difference. The generic features apropriate to allegory in the pre-Renaissance world of a specific theological hierarchy become devalued and mechanical in later times, yet the stance surfaces again in different epistemology and in the rather different genres of modern literature. In effect 'naturalism' is just as available to an allegorical stance as to fantasy, only it is far more difficult to realise in the former. The difference between the two is not primarily one of literary elements or of knowledge and perception but of belief and value.

For example, in pragmatic terms the naturalistic novel has often been judged as a complete world, representing or reflecting this one and therefore finding it difficult not to conform to present standards. David Lodge observes that the form of the novel encourages one to separate between what is said and how it is said[1], laying the emphasis on the former. Yet the only distinction preventing a novel from 'dating', from being stuck in the grounds of its own chronological framework, is its difference from the actual world, the difference which is the result of the external materiality of that world, its resistance, its enigma, which requires an allegorical stance. Kermode has suggested that narrativity is a means of obscuring the ideology of one interpretation alone, and that as the narrativity develops from maxim to parable to novel it develops a more complex movement of obscurity (K: 25).

Narrative generates gaps in interpretation and then provides characters to fill them (85). Here the novel becomes the agent of allegory rather than fantasy.

Limiting these writings to formal genre restricts one's ability to pursue their effects in a number of different media such as television, scientific literature or mathematics. In omitting the commentary that these media make upon the literary 'canon', we hide the activities that modify genre. Yet even when those activities are recognised, if they are restricted to their effects within the current epistemology the broader questions about relationships to the external world which inform the power structures that move our ideologies, are hidden.

Despite its scope, Quilligan's work on pure allegory as a generic mode which combines most of those elements that sacralise language into something theological, clearly illustrates the unnecessary limitation and confusion. In twentieth-century writing there are active and involving stances which do not theologise language and are hence not in her terms generically allegory. She excludes Kafka and Borges for example. Yet these writers are among those most often cited as allegorical, and in terms of non-generic elements of rhetorical stance they are: their sacralisation of language is identical with that of Quilligan's allegorical writers but they do not theologise.

If we turn now to the confusions arising out of the interchangeable use of the terms 'fantasy' and 'allegory', we find that it often arises from the similarity in many techniques used by both. To take an example that has already been mentioned: the riddle. Much of G.K. Chesterton's critical commentary turned on devices related to the riddle: crossword, acrostic, puzzle and enigma. He used it to distinguish between different stances in detective stories. There are those within fantasy that find a complete solution and employ puzzle to do so, and those within allegory that glance off enigmas, pose incomplete resolutions. While this neatly presents the different directions that may result from a single device, it does not discuss how these directions or stances are taken. One element is ideological – definitions for devices change and shift with ideologies as we have seen with the working of personification. To complicate things critics may or may not choose to adopt a definition from ideologies of different chronological periods which in turn twist and distort when reflected by our own.

But the main reason for people taking issue over whether one work is either an allegory or a fantasy is to do with the nature of rhetorical stance: that it involves rhetoric, belief and value. Stance is realised not in narrative elements but in a text which combines writer, reader and work. Just as an attitude to language may affect the way that belief manifests itself in the values of writing, so that attitude may affect the way a reader reads. Plato feared that written language would not have a unique audience and would therefore not generate active involvement but arbitrary imposition of the opinion of the author. The first answer to the fear is that genre and mode create expectations that do define a unique audience. Involvement arises from the interaction with what the text actually does in realising those expectations, which describes rhetorical stance.

In effect it is not whether something is spoken or written that is important, but the stance refracted by ideology that any medium of text realises. Not only does the writing manifest stance, but also the reading. If the reader or listener assumes exactness of language, concern for active involvement in the text will be less prevalent; it will also be easier for the writer to convince that reader of the 'truth' of an opinion because the rules are being specifically set and the reader is less likely to question them. If the reader disagrees it is probable that she or he will do so by disagreeing with the end opinion rather than the activity of the persuasion which has been hidden. However, it is at all times possible, even if not exactly favourable, to disagree on the basis of stance. Disagreement with Tolkien's fantasy may either be in terms of opinion when a reader dismisses its moral naivety, or of stance when a reader laments the pretentiousness of the prose which destroys a positive interaction with value.

The converse also functions. An allegorical stance encourages involvement in the process of the text, and while necessarily stating position, does not impose it. Disagreement with such a text will normally result in discussion which is a condition of *acknowledgly* imprecise communication. But if, despite all, the allegory is read as if directed toward the opinion, the text may simply be accepted or rejected. The acceptance or rejection of a work solely as opinion indicates a fantasy stance on the part of the reader; it indicates a desire for defined answers and ends that underlines an ideological framework that is set toward control by imposition of the external world. This focuses on my own experience of reading *The Lord of the Rings*, and the revision of it subsequent to T. Shippey's analysis. His suggestion is that within the work there is another position precisely to do with history and language and its contradictory power relations that are quite different from the absolutist power structure spelt out by the surface opinion of the writing, which position generates an allegorical stance, an invitation to engage actively with the text.

The point is that one reader may read an allegory as if it were a fantasy while another will read it as an allegory, depending upon their own stances. George Orwell's *Nineteen Eighty-Four* may be a pessimistic, negative dystopia, a failed vision of the failure of human beings if it is read as an opinion and neglecting that language has other activities than conveying precise information or emotive value in opinion. Or the work may be an indication of what is at fault in rational humanism, an illustration of the weakness of its underlying assumptions, not just that it has failed but why and in that an instigation to possible alternatives. Such a reading is gained from participating in the values generated by the text, not simply agreeing or disagreeing with an opinion but learning and attempting individual position in commentary.

Lurking beyond this is the suggestion that critical confusions between fantasy and allegory are to do with whether the person using the words considers the text from a positive or negative stance. A fantasy stance, because it denies rhetoric, is confined to the generic and epistemological. Not only can fantasy never examine its own bases because its rhetoric is constructed to make that examination unnecessary, but it can never recognise the activity of allegory as more than a rigid code because it cannot read rhetorically. An allegorical stance, because it is primarily concerned with drawing attention to its rhetoric as one involving activity, can at least recognise that there is a choice to be made. However an allegorical reader can never enjoy a fantasy in the same way as the reader with a fantasy stance, because she or he will be aware that the opinions posited are open to discussion and can never provide consolation.

But why in the end should we be concerned about whether *The Lord of the Rings* is recognised as only a short-term escape, whether Mills and Boon or Harlequin romances are seen as the temporary worlds they are? Part of the answer lies in that stress upon the short-term that all justifications of fantasy turn to. As studies of negative political rhetoric indicate, the extension of the short term into the long term or the skilful meshing of one short term with another, provide the ideal strategy for imposition of opinion and abuse of power. But, again, just how seriously can we view the implications of a fantasy stance in literature? Is it reasonable to extend them into situations parallel to those of World War II which are often used as personal illustrations in studies of rhetoric particularly of negative stance? The habitual nature of most lives in the Western European world, means that people look at their newspapers partially aware of discrepancies, watch their televisions with the residual knowledge of distortion, and may possibly even read the average book consciously aware of the temporary nature of it consolation. But how many people question the 'facts' of science, the 'truths' of mathematics or even the 'rules' of law? Coleridge's comment that eighteenth century science, specifically 'physics', was inspired by fancy is appropriate here[2]. This fancy 'enables us to present to ourselves the future as the present: and thence to accept a scheme of self-love for a system of morality' (424).

We seem to need consolation, although this may be an assumption so deeply ingrained in this civilisation that we cannot see beyond it. But we should perhaps learn from the more obvious restrictions of mathematics and science, from the pragmatic effects of political propaganda that to assess our consolations, to ensure their temporary nature, we need consciously to choose them, to read them allegorically. For the consolations of fantasy perpetrate more serious divisions: those that inhibit our ability to learn, evaluate and interact with the world.

2 DISCUSSION

The most important question raised by the criticism is why should we be concerned to separate between the two terms? Why not accept that they offer different experiences and that at one time or another we may choose fantasy or allegory? Why not simply enjoy the consciously acknowledged entertainment of fantasy? However, the confusion in the criticism indicates that the entertainment is not often consciously acknowledged, that we rarely do choose actively between the two. To be fully conscious of the choices offered by fantasy it must be read allegorically, and yet its entire rhetoric aims toward preventing the reader from doing so.

Here, rather than analogy, let us begin with anecdote. C. S. Lewis in an essay 'On Stories' discusses different ways of reading and writing and suggests that some books lend themselves to being read in one way and not another, yet readers may read the same story in different ways [3]. He bases his ideas on a discussion with a student who reads fantasies primarily for adventure, suspense and escape, and not for 'the whole world to which it [the story] belonged' (91). Lewis himself reads for this 'other world', for him it is the spiritual beyond the story. He suggests that such works combine free-will and destiny and show it in operation, in other words make their strategy clear; they can be read many times for the ideal perepeteia. The mass populace on the other hand is held to read such works for immediate excitement, and the stories can be read only once if they are to generate this reaction. Lewis goes on to describe other techniques of fantasy in creating its alternate world, complete in 'every episode and speech'. He also notes that the internal tension between plot and theme invariably fails. Yet the stories come close to being the 'other' they indicate, and this identity Lewis finds desirable because he knows it can never be achieved.

However, he has only looked at one side of this writing: from his own conscious allegorical reading that attempts the wholeness of the 'other'. The point of view of fantasy is considered inadequately. He begins by saying that the student presented him with the escapist reaction, but proceeds to state that such a reaction is one of the uneducated masses. As an uneducated reaction, it is either the entertainment of the 'recurring tension of imagined anxiety' or 'certain profound experiences' (101), but since the masses are inarticulate it is impossible to say which. What has been ignored is that his student is neither uneducated nor inarticulate. And what the student says about his experience is that it is not profound, but enjoyably escapist. What neither of them considers is the strain toward populist writing that both descriptions indicate.

The anecdote indicates that certain writings incorporate techniques that are read differently depending upon the modal refraction of individual epistemology and ideology – historical specificity. Lewis's allegorical reading is truth-seeking and overlaps to a large extent with the techniques and strategies of fantasy. He knows that truth cannot be specifically articulated, yet the similarities in genre and mode to the student's end-directed, entertaining, fantasy reading cause him confusion, frustration and anger. If he were to accept the action of the consolatory enjoyment of fantasy readings he would be in a better position not only to argue the limitations of its other face, but also recognise the limiting tendencies of his own stance.

Women's writing about alternative worlds: fantasy or allegory?

Similar complexities arise, in a more obvious and pertinent way for contemporary readers, with the increasing number of women's writings about alternative worlds, and their growing audience. Serious critical response to these writings has by and large been dismissive or confused, partly because the critics fall into the trap of a simplistic fantasy reading[4]. End-directed readings, desire for satisfaction or solution, are fantasy stances; and writings that employ historically specific strategies and techniques inviting the reader into such a collusion, tend to generate 'good' and 'bad' valuations dependent on the basis of the opinions about their topical ends and goals. Writings about alternative worlds are made problematic as we have seen with Tolkien because their technical construction is conventionally recognised as an invitation to escape, so that the reader rarely makes the effort to read beyond the ideologically confortable.

Women's writings about alternative worlds are often doubly problematic because even the ideologically comfortable may be strange. I am thinking here of the high proportion of women's writings which dwell on child-parent relationships or sex-gender distinctions rather than the more usual topics of quest or contest or empire. The epistemological and ideological set to individual readings may fail to take into account women's community structures or language, and there is an overwhelming tendency to read the strangeness of these alternative worlds as utopian. There is little doubt that in some instances it is utopian, but there is also little doubt that in many others the entire group of related genres and modes from satire to pastoral to romance is indicated[5]. Their position on the ideological boundary combines with both their current popularity and the mixed critical response to make them a fruitful area of study for readings of fantasy and allegory.

There are several points here. The first is that women's alternative worlds, even when clearly inviting a fantasy reading directed toward utopia, are often rejected because the readers are out of step with the topics under consideration. For example there is the frequently made charge that women cannot deal with political reality in their utopias because they do not understand 'control'. Invariably, what is overtly or covertly implied, is 'party political' control. But the concept of a 'state', let alone a 'state run by parties' is an ideological construction which societies may question, and which in any case lies alongside different constructions for society within many groups, which have different attitudes toward control. To dismiss questions of 'who is going to make the tea/look after the baby' as being uninterested in social and political control, is an indication of severely blinkered ideological and epistemological vision.

A second point is that utopias do tend to depend on a fantasy stance. They emerge as genres within western literature during the same chronological period in which the stance is forming: the Renaissance; and they are based on the same desire of human beings for authority over the external world. If these alternative worlds are read as utopian there is little chance that the reading will be allegorical. Furthermore, if the techniques and strategies are not used in the conventionally satisfying, end-directed utopian manner, the reader may well simply assess the writing as 'failed' – whereas they may often have been directed toward an allegorical reading. Being out of step with the topics under consideration and the specificity of their modal and generic realisation, not only prevents the occurrence of allegorical reading but generates perverse assessments of the writing which limit the practical applicability of their values.

One of the most common assessments for 'failed' utopias is that they are relativistic, encourage loosely-deconstructive readings that have no moral value. This is a clear misunderstanding because end-directed fantasies always offer specific standards for action; it is impossible to have a relativistic utopia[6]. At the same time the interaction of allegorical readings, often inadequately perceived as relativistic offers explicit analogies for value-generating activity. Fantasy offers defined means and ends, but allegory does not separate between the two. While I have suggested that readers may read any writing as an allegory or as a fantasy, given the historical specificity of mode and genre, writings will always invite or tend in one way or another.

It is possible to read a nineteenth-century novel as an end-directed fantasy. However, the 'psychological' development of character, tied as it is to our contemporary perceptions of the private individual, means that unless the novel is very conventional as with the later detective story or romance, the satisfactions and solutions will not be sufficiently constrained to satisfy our desire for an end. Dorothea in *Middlemarch* may be read as a desirable solution to a female dilemma, but such a reading is problematic because the techniques and strategies are recognised to be attempts at setting out an isolated subject. The character is more interesting for the description of active ideological relations it presents – the interactions between individual and society. But one doesn't usually read a Harlequin romance for ideological assessments. We read it for what it offers or gives us in the way of permanent solutions[7].

Writings that offer alternative worlds, whether they be utopias, science fictions, supernatural or magical worlds, are particularly prone to the fantasy stance. As I have suggested, it is not the reader alone who decides on stance because the writer has rhetorical techniques and strategies which may be brought into action to encourage or discourage the end-directed reading. Whether hidden or acknowledged it is always an interaction of reader, writer and words, so one cannot make definitive statements about the specific ends of technique. But what we can do is say that within our own ideology and epistemology certain modes and genres of writing invite certain end-directed readings. It has been noted that the structural isolation of the island, the country house and the future time, the development of techniques of verisimilitude, and the deployment of step by step rational and analytical logic, are conducive to establishing the necessary pattern of recognition and simultaneous rejection within fantasy. It is this generic definition by technique that has allowed fantasy theorists of the last 30 to 40 years to pin down so definitely what makes writing invite fantasy activity. What is less clearly articulated is that readers within a fantasy stance move toward accepting or rejecting a work on the basis of the topics or ends of the writing, because they are systematically coerced into collusion with the necessity for hiding the process by which these ends are offered as 'given'. The distinction is particularly important to make, given the tendency for much recent feminist criticism to distinguish the techniques of alternative worlds from those of romantic fiction, as positive from negative[8].

The writings of alternative worlds that I am going to discuss, none of which are utopias, are Margaret Atwood's *The Handmaid's Tale*, Marge Piercey's *Woman on the Edge of Time*, Joanna Russ's *The Female Man* and Ursula Le Guin's *The Dispossessed* : each of which has gained, largely for reasons of publishing practice and distribution, a popular audience. Out of the group the last falls most precisely within definitions of fantasy, and the fantasy stance which characterises readings of Le Guin has come to overshadow many other writings about alternative worlds. Le Guin's alternative world is in effect two worlds, Annares and Urras both of which exist in the future, each with a specific socio-political structure. Annares is a working but regressing social anarchy, while Urras presents the usual excesses of a capitalist state. The worlds are in isolation from each other, each confined to a single planet, and in isolation from the contemporary reader through time. Considerable effort has gone into the creation of a number of psychologically realistic personae, primarily Shevek the main character or hero. Furthermore, the detail of both worlds is consistent and within the bounds of a western cultural imagination. Few if any fundamental technological, biological or scientific changes have taken place.

The primary difference lies in the structure of the societies, particularly that of Annares. The reader is led by the realistic character development, the careful verisimilitude of detail, and the knowledge of isolation which makes the difference acceptable, to understand and feel sympathetic toward its original social pattern of life. For Le Guin there are ends in view: we are told quite clearly that we can live differently. Although there are drawbacks to the private individual and the problematic influence from Urras, the reader can say at the end of it that it is an interesting description of working social anarchy, with subsidiary points such as agreement that the society would have to be maintained by inculcating the children with other standards until they reached adolescence – all the more acceptable since that is what we do in our own society anyway. At the same time, just because of those ends, we can also criticise the book for being limited, contradictory, repressive and inhuman. To the extent that the isolation between the future worlds and our own breaks down, we begin to notice the cracks and faults in the alternatives offered[9].

While these cracks and faults seem to emerge despite the narrative, Atwood's *The Handmaid's Tale* clearly signposts the problems of the future alternative. This proposed world is constructed by extending a variety of present day feminisms to an extreme point. A backlash among both men and women, against attempts to radically change the position of women, joins forces with religious fundamentalism and a right-wing power base that controls the economy. The result is a rigidly hierarchical structure in which women are assigned roles which derive from their biological suitability for reproduction, and are maintained in their positions by constant surveillance and isolation.

Published in 1985, the alternative world proposed by *The Handmaid's Tale* also begins in the mid-80s. There is no pretence to a naturalistic evolution from our present state, yet the writer carefully provides narrative links that progress from our time to the proposed alternative. The result is that one of the fundamental devices of the structure is to use verisimilitude and the familiar, profoundly to shock rather than to cushion. The insistence on the construction of all writing, both within the novel in discussions of pornography or in the 'historical notes' that present the entire 'Handmaid's tale' as a found manuscript, ensures that the catalogue of fantasy devices – neologism, attention to visual detail, rationally logical progression, completely consistent internal world – is foregrounded. The writing provides no contained alternative but a vision of claustrophobic oppression that acutely sums up the dangers of fantasy. Just so, the proffered ends or goals of this world are clearly not reccommended, and signify the limitations and problems in an array of current political initiatives.

We cannot say with the same definitiveness that Piercey's *Woman on the Edge of Time* is either a great study of how we could live differently, while not perfectly, or a restricted outline of the reactionary politics of private arbitrariness and institutional totalitarianism – although both of these stories are present. The construction of Piercey's work is significantly different from Le Guin's and Atwood's. In the writing, there is a present and a number of isolated future worlds. Part of the future is much 'better' than our own, but there are still wars; and it exists beside other future cultures which are apparently much 'worse' than our own. The evaluation of 'better' or 'worse' is controlled by the reactions of the main character from the present world when she enters the future, and is dependent upon our empathy with her responses.

If we take the future world on its own, as a world isolated from us and largely isolated from the other future cultures, it behaves as a fantasy. The construction is consistently realistic, and the reader comes to accept it by following the response of the character from the present, Connie, to whom we have previously been introduced. She initially finds the future world alienating and strange but comes to appreciate the qualities of tenderness, passion and care which are blatantly missing from her present life. Simply in this manner the reader follows a linear progression toward acceptance of the parameters in the future world. The main difference between the present and the future is that sex-gender relations have been restructured by liberating each sex from the necessity of motherhood and child rearing. Foetuses are now developed in artificial wombs and child care is a common responsibility. Utterly strange at first, although underwritten by actual developments in our own present world's biotechnology, the procedure comes to make sense.

The key to accepting the future world is Connie. She is constructed with many of the conventions of a nineteenth century realistic novel. We see her progressing through a part of her life, changing and flexible, surrounded by enormous social and psychological detail. Her world is immediate, and in effect almost as strange to me as a middle-class reader, as the future world. Yet we are shown Connie within an institutional world of social care, prison and mental hospital, which throws into relief the power relations of capitalist state politics. On its own this institutional world may be read as a fantasy, yet once thrown into comparison with the future world we can recognise all too quickly the features that define our current ideology. Just so, that comparison lifts the fantasy reading of the future world into a clear political commentary on the sex-gender relations of our own time which are part of Connie's repressive treatment. However, when put in tandem, the two worlds also imply a solution. The first is that there can be an improvement in gender relationships in the future, and the second is that this future can be achieved through private acts of violence.

To the extent that the reader dwells on these proferred solutions, rather than the process of comparison, they define the two responses to *Woman on the Edge of Time* as a fantasy. But to describe the writing in terms of these given solutions leaves too much out. Even more so, attempting to describe *The Female Man* in this way is to miss the point of the book. Russ presents us with many alternative worlds, in future and in space, none fixed and none wholly satisfactory – not because they include changes alien to our contemporary ideology that we do not like, but because they do not appear to have solved many of our own outstanding problems. More important are the alternate character-worlds, each character being divided and irreconcilably separate yet necessarily part of the one person. There is no alternative world 'better' than ours. The separate worlds impinge on each other; they jumble up and continually prompt the reader to be aware of inconsistency.

There is no attempt to persuade of the standards of any one alternative. There is no attempt at verisimilitude in the sense of 'this is a real world', to decrease the clashes between our world and the other. The writer provides characters with almost imperceptibly different speech patterns, adds descriptive details at a minimal level that serrates the smooth edges of our expectation, constructs outlandish personifications and overt technical structures in the logic of the plot. There is no steady progression or abrupt change, into the alternative world, but a continual movement back and forth from section to section within each part of the book. The sections are of uneven length and no regular narrative development, sometimes consisting of a single sentence. The result for a fantasy reading is that one either warms to a presentation of the impossibility of any solution, or one condemns the book for being totally dependent on the inability to make up one's mind, with no relevance to real life. Either way the reader is looking for an end.

Now Le Guin is fairly adequately described by a fantasy reading in that we can be positive about many of the techniques and strategies: the genre is science fiction and the mode is heroic. She is excellent at 'posing the problem'. But she also encourages us to think that she's doing more than that in the construction of heroic 'leaders' such as the original anarchist, Odo, or the present one Shevek. These heroic individuals are presented as people who will solve our problems, not, granted, in an absolute sense but still capable of finding the 'best way' for the time. As we have seen, Atwood's work is also firmly rooted in fantasy and and as such may be read as as a savage satire upon contemporary feminisms taken to their extreme. Piercey's writing which combines science fiction and novel in a realistic mode, can be described by a fantasy reading but the two responses it generates sit uneasily together. The implication in the writing is that the futures, both 'better' and 'worse' than our own, are dependent on our own. The 'worse' future can be seen as an evolution from our present institutional authorities, and the 'better' as one which has arisen from human beings interrupting that evolution with acts of violence like Connie's. While the notion of evolution as 'natural' is not addressed, neither are the implications of private acts of violence which collude with institutional force. But the writing that is quite inadequately described is that of *The Female Man*. This too is technically science fiction but in a disruptive parodic mode. Either result of a fantasy reading evades the definition of specific topics emphasising the relativist nature of the offered solutions, and valuing or disparaging them: both being highly unsatisfactory.

All of these readings move beyond restrictive technique-based kinds of genre to the epistemological and ideological strategies of mode. In doing so they provide useful short-term strategies that achieve specific interpretations. However they also hide the activity of stance and fail to assess the works on the basis of long term value-generating activities. Hence they are incapable of dealing with the problems of 'heroic' solutions, the compromises of satire or the circle of private and institutional violence, and have no way of making any sense of *The Female Man* without leaving it on the shelf as a woolly form of deconstruction[10].

Assessment of short-term goals differs from discussion of long-term activities, not in the opposition of order or control to arbitrary mess. It is not an either/or distinction. What it does mean is assessment of control based on pre-determined assumptions, desires or rules, differing from discussion of control based upon working toward generating policies with what is at hand – the historical specificity of human beings and materiality of the world. There is no doubt that short-term strategies are very effective but reading from the long-term in an allegorical stance does not concentrate on the end in mind but on the values generated by the activity involved. In our own epistemological and ideological framework, we have the whole problem of the prophet or revolutionary simply changing one repressive order to impose another. There are effective means of doing this both in politics and in writing: seductions, addictions, coercions, collusions; but the need to find other ways of interacting, which involve activity and policy is difficult to speak of in theory because the two are inseparable.

Can we for example read any writing in an allegorical stance and move toward appreciation of activity and aims in the single process of reading? Le Guin can be read against convention, and Odo's actions or Shevek's become a kind of analogy for our own engagement in society: In other words that we can have social interaction not because it is something someone tells us to do but because it is an activity in which we all enact policy toward a social reality. This moves from *The Dispossessed* as a story about the failure of revolution, to one where the importance lies not in the ends of revolution alone but in the activity that instigated it and carried it out. *The Handmaid's Tale* allows the reader to do this without strain, it actively encourages awareness of convention. The procedure of the writing is to call attention to the fantasy construction, and in doing so expose the analogous constructions of social and political power that are being presented. In a rather different manner one can read the sex/gender questions in *Woman on the Edge of Time* as an invitation toward thought about our own constructions of those questions, and one can read the politics of the function of the institution as serious commentary on the frustration, despair and arbitrary violence of the individual within the state. As long as we break the apparently causal connection between the two worlds which compromises both, they act as constructive analogues for each other.

The two worlds of *The Dispossessed* stay separate and isolated even within an allegorical reading; each contains a discrete system of human relationships. The worlds in Piercey's work encourage the reader to intercomment and in this way produce a description of human relationships that the reader may assess. In contrast, Atwood's worlds are intimately related through the foregrounded devices of fantasy, and make the reader question the present, albeit directed by the tightly controlled recognition of convention. But the worlds in Russ's *The Female Man* are significant precisely for their interaction. They sharpen our awareness of the enigmatic resistance of time and space to explanation, of our ignorance of history and the variety of ways that language and writing can approach that ignorance and resistance. The jumbled narrative structure, juxtaposed plot interactions, intangible character overlays engage the reader into a series of activities that make us choose, decide, act upon our involvement in the text. While there are no specific solutions, there are value-generating activities which are directed at certain things Russ evidently sees as desirable – for example feminism, lesbianism, moral responsibility. At the same time these concerns are placed in specific historical periods, and it is not only the concern itself but also recognition of how to assess it that is important. From an allegorical stance, Russ directs us toward decisions about problems specific to our history. But even the present in her novel is not the present of our time so she also makes it possible for us to engage in an activity which may be directed toward any set of problems due to ideological stagnation. In an allegorical reading, the disparity of alternate worlds is far from offering numerous solutions. Instead it asks quite definitely for decisions about the enaction of human relationships with which these worlds at the same time present and engage the reader .

Allegory produces the least happy reading in Le Guin's work because the activity runs so against the grain of dove-tailed, painstaking convention. The hidden controls of the writing have to be exposed to make possible an alternative response; and in just the same way as one explains a joke and watches it crumble, the system becomes wooden and creaky. It is as if the writer uses the genre unselfconsciously to pursue the topics. Piercey is for more susceptible to an allegorical reading but the writing is compromised by the naturalism of the novel. The overt power relations between men and women work well and engage reading as do those between the individual and the institution, but the relationships outlined by the development of a political evolution have to be excavated – leaving skeletal remains of a highly abstract kind. Indeed the contradiction arising from Piercey's work suggest that for a generous reading it needs neither allegory or fantasy as stance. Atwood however, indicates the ease with which a skilled writer can move fantasy through one degree into allegory, by consciously using the fantasy devices to comment upon the topics, subverting the implicit subversion of the unsaid. I would argue that Russ too is happy within this stance of allegory, where ends and desires are quite evident but are not the only thing. We engage in activities we can apply not only to an assessment of her ends, but also to our own. While Atwood's stance gives us a skill to understand current structures of communication and power, that of Russ attempts to explore the possibility of different practices.

To return to the concrete: Each of these writers concentrates on family structure, particularly parent-child relationships. They each reflect a particular North American concern with the use and abuse of family relationships not only on an individual basis but by strong forces within American political movements. Le Guin is quite clear that family structures must be changed while retaining what are shown to be the positive aspects of the traditional structure. But the answer is overtly presented as a series of short-term political actions. Family, and ultimately social change on Annares, have depended upon an artificial separation from the actual practices of capitalist society as seen on the planet Urras, and are crumbling as we see it described. The agent for revitalised change is individual political action, and much of the story follows the emergence of these individuals. This heavy dependence on the conventional structure of 'good' and 'bad' political systems, what Orwell called politics for the nursery, makes the writing simpler to read because it fits in with ideological expectations. However, at the same time its dominance weakens and downplays any constructive statement about changing family and social values.

For Piercey the family structure of the alternate world is similarly changed but is curiously parallel to the community structure of the people in the institutional hospital. The question of war or of conventional power politics is not central; and it is easy for a reader, not finding them, to dismiss the writing as pure escapism without realising that the community structures are offered as alternative political systems equally concerned with power and society but not in the same way. Fundamental to these suggested community structures is a way of interacting with people, but the writing does not address itself fully enough to the activity of human relationships that sustains the structure. The writing does not hide the comparisons between the two worlds that make our commentary possible, but neither do the strategies actively encourage the reader to engage.

The Handmaid's Tale addresses itself to the implications of extending some of the contemporary solutions to the development of the family. As fantasy it contents itself with depicting the negative, all the problems and shortcomings of those solutions. The pragmatic end of the narrative is a barrage of criticism against the traditionalists and the trendy, with very little in a positive tone but for the intensity of the mother-daughter relationship that has been disrupted. The long-term help that is offered lies in the lessons about recognising the power structures of communication, and how these form the base for all contemporary solutions.

With Russ however, the future alternate world is almost incidental as an answer. The chronological detail of how that future came about is certainly incidental to the way that people respond in specific historical situations. All the family structures in each alternative world are different, and this along with the lack of expected political structure becomes a way of condemning the book as relative. Indeed when a central character arrives from the future on a Pentagon office desk, displaying all her incomprehension and controlled disgust at the sight of these people in charge of the politics of the nation, the scene can be misread as a naive jettisoning of party politics rather than the constructive comment it is on the narrowness of much national policy. Russ is very much more demanding than Le Guin or even Piercey. The writing keeps away from naturalistic conventions for portraying a working alternative community, except in the descriptions of Whileaway that are riddled with minute details calculated to enrage a contemporary reader expecting some kind of utopia. At all times the reader has to read not for conventional use alone but for the running against convention, the breaking up, the parody, irony and finally allegory of its segmented structure. For example, it is easy to fix the work as feminist ranting – indeed Russ does this for us toward the end of the book in an interpolated catalogue of handy phrases. But this would be to miss the often vicious parody of a whole range of modern feminist reactions – the reversal of gender roles or the opposition to men to the point of elimination – portrayed as historically necessary for particular periods but definitely limited.

What emerges is the divided life of all human beings throughout the alternative worlds, their dealing with the problems of individual and community relations in different ways. Beyond this, the common factor of intimate evaluation, the need continually to be prepared to lose part of the construction of self if change is to come about. These are the real political lessons. Questions of 'who makes the tea/looks after the baby' are far more important than 'who pushes the nuclear button'. 'Who pushes the button' is an 'on-off' question already based on decided truth as to good and bad. It is a question made necessary by short-term policy, and one which demands a considered answer. But the other questions are those we make every day, all day. They require continual reassessment and invitation to moral action, in which activity long-term policies can be effected.

One is left too often only with the negative: fantasy as rigid and repressive – which is ungenerous and does not acknowledge the pragmatic short-term use or entertainment; or allegory as relativistic and loosely deconstructionist – which is a limited and unhelpful reading of long-term practical skills. While fantasy is justly feared for its powerful effects, it is often pragmatically necessary given our western state systems where effects are expected within a short time – usually four to five years of a government's span. However, while not all relativistic writing is allegorical, to condemn all allegories as relative is simply failing to engage with what they can offer – which is long-term policy based on human interaction within a specific historical period or set.

Rhetorical stances lie outwith ideology and epistemology in activities that relate to the material world, although contemporary strategies will refract and deflect any common stance through a social convention, a mode or genre. The problem with reading these works of alternate worlds is that as writer or reader, the less one is aware of conventions bound to epistemology and ideology the more entrapping they are.

The writings of these women if rather more pointed are directly analogous to that of Tolkien and Orwell and the responses to the alternate worlds they too offer. *The Lord of the Rings* is most often read as either 'good' or 'bad' for proposing certain authority structures; but it may be read as the joy of language holding out the possibility of analogous action in our relationship with past histories. *Nineteen Eighty-Four* can be read as pessimistic liberalism or as active pursuit of the weaknesses of liberal humanism and encouragement to alternative action. But the stances extend to readings of works completely out with the genres of alternate worlds. Keat's 'Ode on a Grecian Urn' for example, may be read within convention as a declaration that Beauty and Truth are indeed all we need to know. On the other hand it may be read within the context of the stasis of the life being described on the urn as an ironic comment upon that ideologically stagnant history. The activity of the former is to read toward an end or answer, while that of the latter is to read toward an active engagement with the historical context both of our own and Keats's time.

It does seem to be the case for our own history that reactionary strategies attempt to hide ideological and epistemological limitations, while radical strategies attempt to reveal them and open them out to assessment. While one can appreciate the gamesmanship of the former, it is not reasonable to expect people to enjoy being counters in that game. Hence within a fantasy stance people find it necessary to look to new and different strategies of desire and design to protect themselves. But an altogether more helpful approach might be to extend upon the attempts of radical strategies to open out toward evaluating activities.

There is a central problem in the tendency to be uncritical about the ways in which one reads fantasy. But far more important is discussion and extension of the allegorical stance. There have been a number of attempts to provide a vocabulary, a strategy and even a rhetorical basis for allegory, of which this essay is one, but despite its elusive, firmly material activity, there needs to be far more. It is from allegory that contemporary values can be generated and assessed.

It is difficult work because the analogies always prove insufficient:

> No sharp boundary can be drawn round the cases in which we should say that a man was misled by an analogy. The use of expressions constructed on analogical patterns stresses analogies between cases often far apart. And by doing this these expressions may be extremely useful. It is, in most cases, impossible to show an exact point where an analogy begins to mislead us.[11]

Fantasy has self-sufficient systems to maintain the analogies of neutrality and purity, games, desire, neurosis, obsession. They will always prove misleading to all but their inventor. But those for allegory – deceit, money, food, love death – are necessarily inadequate. The allegorical stance continually assesses its own analogies, searching for that point where we become misled. But it is from this activity that value, for this contemporary western society, can be generated.

Notes

ABBREVIATIONS FOR FREQUENTLY CITED WORKS

AMS   *Allegory, Myth and Symbol* ed M. W. Bloomfield (London, 1981)

AR   *Allegory and Representation: Selected Essays of the English Institute 1979–80* New Series no 5, ed S. Greenblatt (London, 1981)

AU   W. H. Auden *Secondary Worlds* (London, 1968)

B   M. W. Bloomfield 'A Grammatical Approach to Personification Allegory', *Modern Philology*, 60 (3) 1962–68

BE1   L. Bersani *A Future For Astyanax: Character and Desire in Literature* (London, 1978/76)

BE2   L. Bersani 'Representation and Its Discontents', in AR

BEN   W. Benjamin *The Origins of German Tragic Drama*, trans J. Osborne (London, 1977)

BL   S. T. Coleridge, *Biographia Literaria* eds. J. Engell and W. Jackson Bate (Princeton, 1983)

BO   H. Boucher 'Metonymy in Typology and Allegory, with a Consideration of Dante's *Comedy*', in AMS

BR   C. Brooke-Rose *A Rhetoric of the Unreal, Studies in narrative and structure, especially of the fantastic* (London, 1981)

BRE   D. Brewer '*The Lord of the Rings* as Romance', in SCH

C   G. Clifford *The Transformations of Allegory* (London 1974)

CA   E. Cammaerts *The Poetry of Nonsense* (London, 1926)

CRI   *Tolkien and the Critics: Essays on J. R. R. Tolkien's 'The Lord of the Rings'* eds N. D. Isaacs and R. A. Zimbardo (Notre Dame, 1968)

D   W. Davie 'The Gospel of Middle-Earth according to J. R. R. Tolkien', in SCH

DM1   P. de Man *Allegories of Reading: Figural Language in Rousseau, Nietzsche, Rilke and Proust* (London, 1979)

DM2   P. de Man 'Pascal's Allegory of Persuasion', in AR

DM3   P. de Man 'A Rhetoric of Temporality', *Blindness and Insight* (London, 1971)

DU   R. M. Durling 'Deceit and Digestion in the Body of Hell', in AR

E   R. C. Elliott *The Shape of Utopia: Studies in Literary Genre* (Chicago, 1970)

ET   *An Etymological Dictionary of the English Language* ed W. Skeat (Oxford, 1910)

F   A. Fowler, *Kinds of Literature: An Introduction to the Theory of Genres and Modes* (Oxford, 1982)

FI   J. Fineman 'The Structure of Allegorical Desire', in AR

FL   A. Fletcher *Allegory, The Theory of a Symbolic Mode* (Ithaca, 1964)

FR1   N.Frye *Anatomy of Criticism* (Princeton, 1957)

FR2   N. Frye *The Secular Scripture, A Study of the Structure of Romance* (Cambridge, 1978/76)

G   C. Guillen *Literature as System: Essays Toward the Theory of Literary History* (Princeton, 1971)

GE   R. Gerber *Utopian Fantasy: A Study of English Utopian Fiction since the end of the Nineteenth Century* (London, 1955)

H1   L. Hunter *Rhetorical Stance in Modern Literature* (London, 1984)

H2   L. Hunter 'James Barrie: The Rejection of Fantasy' *Scottish Literary Journal* 5, No 1 (May, 1978) pp. 39–52

H3   L. Hunter *George Orwell: The Search for a Voice* (Milton Keynes, 1984)

HE   P. Hernadi *Beyond Genre, New directions in literary criticism* (London, 1972)

HI1   E. Hirsch *Validity in Interpretation* (London, 1971/67)

HI2   E. Hirsch, 'Past Intentions and Present Meanings' *Essays in Criticism*, 33, No 2 (April, 1983), pp. 79–98.

HM   J. Hillis Miller 'The Two Allegories', in AMS

HO   M. Holquist 'The Politics of Representation', in AR

HOG   J. Hodgson 'Transcendental Tropes: Coleridge's Rhetoric of Allegory and Symbol', in AMS

HON   E. Honig *Dark Conceit: The Making of Allegory* (London, 1959)

HU   J. Huizinga *Homo Ludens: A Study of the Play-Element in Culture* (London, 1949/44)

I   W. R. Irwin *The Game of the Impossible: A Rhetoric of Fantasy* (Chicago, 1976)

J   R. Jackson *Fantasy, the Literature of Subversion* (London, 1981)

JA1 F. Jameson 'Magical Narratives: Romance as Genre' *New Literary History*, VII, 1

JA2 F. Jameson *The Political Unconscious* (London, 1981)

K   F. Kermode *The Genesis of Secrecy: on the interpretation of narrative* (London, 1979)

KR M. Krieger'"A Waking Dream": The Symbolic Alternative to Allegory', in AMS

L   C. S. Lewis *Allegories of Love: A Study of Medieval Tradition* (Oxford, 1936)

LE   S. R. Levin 'Allegorical Language', in AMS

M1   C. Manlove *Modern Fantasy: Five Studies* (Chatham, 1975)

M2   C. Manlove *The Impulse of Fantasy Literature* (London, 1983)

MA P. Marinelli *Pastoral* (London, 1971)

N   A. Nuttall *Two Concepts of Allegory* (London, 1967)

OED *Oxford English Dictionary* (Oxford, 1933)

Q1   M. Quilligan *The Language of Allegory: Defining the Genre* (Ithaca and London, 1979)

Q2   M. Quilligan 'Allegory, allegoresis, and the Deallegorization of Language', in AMS

R   E. S. Rabkin *The Fantastic in Literature* (Princeton, 1976)

S   R. Scholes *Fabulation and Metafiction* (London, 1979)

SCH *J. R. R. Tolkien, Scholar and Storyteller: Essays in Memoriam*, eds M. Sah and R. Farrell (London, 1979)

SH1 T. Shippey *The Road to Middle-Earth* (London, 1982)

SH2 T. Shippey 'Creation from Philology', in SCH

SP   G. Spivak 'Thoughts on the Principle of Allegory', *Genre*, 4 1972

T   T. Todorov *Introduction à la littérature fantastique* (Paris, 1970)

TO   J.R.R. Tolkien 'On Fairy-stories' in *Tree and Leaf* (London, 1964)

W   G. Whalley *Poetic Process* (Westport, 1973/53)

WH J. Whitman 'From the *Cosmographia* to the *Divine Comedy* an Allegorical Dilemma', in AMS

NOTES TO PART ONE

1. All references to frequently cited books will appear within brackets and consist of an abbreviation of the writer's name followed by the page numbers. The abbreviation is taken from the list of *Abbreviations for frequently cited books* to be found immediately preceding these footnoted references. Thus (F: 272) is taken as : A. Fowler, *Kinds of Literature* (Oxford, 1982), p. 272. Within each paragraph, references to a book immediately following a bracketed reference to that book, will indicate page numbers only. Thus after (F: 272), an immediately following reference to *Kinds of Literature* will simply be presented as : (311).

2. A. Einstein, (London, 1947) pp. 341, 343, 350.

3. R. P. Warren, 'Pure and Impure Poetry', *Kenyon Review*, V, 2 (Spring, 1944), p. 242.

4. A. E. Poe, *The Complete Poems and Stories of Edgar Allan Poe*, intro A. Quin, bibl E. O'Neill (New York, 1946) p. 1026.

5. W. Pater, *Studies in the History of the Renaissance* (London, 1873) p. 205.

6. A. C. Bradley, *Poetry for Poetry's Sake* (Oxford, 1901) pp. 19–20.

7. See Fowler, p. 27, and his discussion of Moore's neo-classical definition.

8. F. de Saussure, *Course in General Linguistics*, eds C. Bally and A. Sechehaye with A. Riedlinger, trans W. Baskin (London, 1960) p. 88.

9. L. Wittgenstein, *The Blue and Brown Books* (Oxford, 1958) p. 77.

10. S. Sontag, *Against Interpretation* (London, 1967) p. 42.

11. Kenneth Burke reduces it to the division between the self-protective and the suicidal ethos, *A Rhetoric of Motives* (New York, 1950) p. 35.

12. Each of R. Barthes, I. Murdoch and W. Booth – among many others – have attempted a re-examination of 'value', see H1.

13. B. Croce has been one of the most forceful proponents of this view.

14. W. R. Winterowd, *Rhetoric, a Synthesis* (USA, 1968) p. 29.

15. *Ibid.*

16. M. L. Ryan, 'Towards a Competence Theory of Genre', *Poetics, 8*, p.3.

17. W. Booth, *The Rhetoric of Fiction* (Chicago: 1961).

18. Booth's attitude to this common location for poetic and rhetoric has since changed; see his address to the International Society for the History of Rhetoric, Oxford 1985.

19. T. Kent, 'The Classification of Genres', *Genre*, XIV, 1.

20. K. Burke, 'Lexicon Rhetorica' in *Counter-statement* (Los Allos, 1931/53) p. 147.

21. See H. Rose and S. Rose, *Radical Science, Ideology of/in the Natural Sciences* (London, 1976), especially R Lewontin and R. Levin 'The

Problem of Lysenkoism'. Evolution cannot be used as a straightforwardly self-evident analogy.

22. M. Hodgart, 'From *Animal Farm* to *Nineteen Eighty-Four*' in *The World of George Orwell*, ed M. Gross (London, 1971).

23. A. Zwerdling, *Orwell and the Left* (London, 1974).

24. C. Small, *The Road to Miniluv: George Orwell, the State, and God* (London, 1971).

25. See *The Times*, obituary on J. R. R. Tolkien in SCH, p. 14; E. Fuller, 'The Lord of the Hobbits: J. R. R. Tolkien', CRI, p. 29; H. Keenan 'The Appeal of *The Lord of the Rings*', in CRI, p. 62; and P. Kocher, *Master of Middle-Earth: The Achievement of J. R. R. Tolkien* (London, 1972) p. 16.

26. R. J. Reilly, 'Tolkien and the Fairy Story' in CRI, p. 142.

27. M. Kelly, 'The Poetry of Fantasy: Verse in *The Lord of the Rings*' in CRI p. 171.

28. R. J. Reilly, *Romantic Religion: A Study of Barfield, Lewis, Williams and Tolkien* (Athens, 1971) p. 212.

29. R. J. Reilly, as above in CRI, p. 139.

30. R. Helme, *Tolkien's World* (London, 1974) p. 115.

31. P. Spacks, 'Power and Meaning in *The Lord of the Rings*' in CRI, p. 98.

32. R. Helme, p. 84. 33. See for example several of the essays in SCH.

NOTES TO PART TWO

1. For example see S. Prickett, *Victorian Fantasy* (Hassocks, 1979).

2. This despite the introduction to K. Coburn's edition of the collected papers, BL volume 1, which says that Coleridge followed eighteenth century critics in reversing the earlier roles which were that fantasy was superior to imagination.

3. Plato, *The Sophist and Statesman*, trans and intro A. E. Taylor, eds R. Klibausky and E. Ancambe (London, 1961) p. 182, sections 266–267.

4. P. Sidney, *A Defence of Poetry*, ed and intro J. A. VanDorsten (Oxford, 1966/1595).

5. *Greek-English Lexicon*, ed N. Contopoulos (Athens, 1903), p. 484.

6. G. Puttenham, *The Art of English Poesie*, eds G. Willcock and A. Walker (Cambridge, 1936/1588) p. 18.

7. A history of 'normality' and 'madness' is well-documented throughout the work of M. Foucault; see also the progression in OED, p. 171.

8. S. T. Coleridge, *Logic*, vol 13, ed J. R. Jackson (Princeton, 1981) p. 284.

9. I. A. Richards, *Practical Criticism* (London, 1929).

10. W. Porter, as above, pp. 211 and 209.

11. L. Hunter, *G. K. Chesterton: Explorations in Allegory* (London, 1979) chapter 10.
12. D. H. Lawrence, *Phoenix II*, coll and ed with intro and notes W. Roberts and H. T. Moore (London, 1968) p. 395.
13. See for examples HU: 15,20,107,134. 14. See L. Hunter, *G. K. Chesterton: Explorations in Allegory*, as above, p. 25.
15. W. Booth, *Modern Dogma: A Rhetoric of Assent* (Chicago, 1974), p. 173.
16. I. A. Richards, *Practical Criticism*, as above, p. 261.
17. G. K. Wolfe 'Symbolic Fantasy', *Genre*, VIII, 3, 1975, p. 205.
18. H. Kaplan, *The Passive Voice, An Approach to Modern Fiction* (Athens, 1966), p. 5.
19. F. Kafka, *Metamorphosis*, trans W. and E. Muir (Penguin, 1961), p.9.
20. W. Brandt, *The Rhetoric of Argumentation* (USA: 1970).
21. W. Booth, *A Rhetoric of Irony* (Chicago, 1974).
22. S. Freud, *Beyond the Pleasure Principle* trans C. Hubback (London, 1922), p. 71.
23. D. Suvin, 'Science Fiction and the Genealogical Jungle', *Genre*, IV, 3, 1971 p. 259.
24. Plato, from *Republic*, II 378, quoted by J. MacQueen in *Allegory* (London, 1970) p. 13.
25. It is with Machievelli's Renaissance that the power circle of authority and totalitarianism becomes dominant among the emerging national states of Europe.
26. See for example David Lodge's discussion of repetition in literature in *The Language of Fiction: Essays in Criticism and Verbal Analysis of the English Novel* (London, 1966).
27. See R: 66 and H. Kaplan, *The Passive Voice*, p. 10.
28. See GE: 55 and AU: 144.
29. E. M. Forster, *Aspects of the Novel* (London, 1917), p. 144.
30. M. Foucault, *The Order of Things* (London, 1970/1966), p. 320.

NOTES TO PART THREE

1. See FR2: 'modern romance'; C: 'modern allegory'; or M. D. Springer *Forms of the Modern Novella* (Chicago, 1975), 'apologue'.
2. See for example M1: 168–9, allegory narrowing book to rigid skeleton; J: 16, allegory conceptualises relations; S: 110, allegory concerned with value as a fixed thing; or FR1: 90–91, on 'naive' allegory.
3. D. Lodge, *The Modes of Modern Writing: Metaphor, metonymy, and The Typology of Modern Literature* (London, 1977).
4. See bp Nichol, *love, a book of remembrances* (Vancouver, 1974), and his volumes of *Martyrology* (Toronto, 1977 and onward).

/ 5. See KR; P. Grimaldi and M. B. Riggio in AMS.
6. See respectively: R. Cawdry, *A Table Alphabeticall* (Florida, 1966/1604), p. 14; J. Bullokar, *An English Expositor* (Scolar, 1967/1616); T. Blount, *Glossographia* (Scolar 1969/1656); E. Phillips, *The New World of English Words* (London, 1658); E. Phillips, *The Moderne World of Words* (London, 1706/1686); and J. Kersey, *A New English dictionary* (Scolar, 1969/1702).
7. See FL and C, for comments on the contribution of Goethe and Coleridge respectively.
8. SP: 349; see also G. M. Spivak, 'Allégorie et histoire de la poésie', *Poétique*, 2, 1971, pp. 427–441.
9. A. Strubel '"Allegoria in factis" et "Allegoria in verbis"', *Poétique*, VI, 1975; see for example the account of Bede, p. 351.
10. M. D. Springer, as above, p. 19.
11. D. Richter, *Fable's End: Completeness and Closure in Rhetorical Fiction* (Chicago, 1974).
12. S. Sontag, *Against Interpretation* , p. 13.
13. S. Sacks,, '*Fiction*' *and the Shape of Belief* (Berkeley, 1964), p. 8.
14. R. M. Davis, 'Defining Genre in Fiction', *Genre*, II, 4, 1969.
15. J. MacQueen, *Allegory*, p. 68.
16. W. Booth, *A Rhetoric of Irony*, p. 265.
17. D. Richter, as above, p. 82.
18. W. Booth, *A Rhetoric of Irony*, p. 208.
19. *Greek-English Lexicon*, p. 347 and p. 7.
20. As opposed to symbolic, emblematic, ritualistic, etc. referentiality.
21. W. Empson, *Seven Types of Ambiguity* (London, 1947/30), p. 124.
22. *Ibid.*
23. S. Fish has also explored this area thoroughly.
24. J. Culler, 'Literary History, Allegory and Semiology', *New Literary History*, VII, 2, 1976, p. 263.
25. G. Steiner, *After Babel: Aspects of Language and Translation* (London, 1975), chapter 2.
26. For example, see D. Lodge, *The Language of Fiction* p. 25.
27. D. Heron, 'The Focus of Allegory', *Genre*, III, 2, 1980, p. 178.
28. P. Szandi, 'Introduction to Literary Hermeneutics', *New Literary History*, V, p. 1.
29. M. Bloomfield, 'Allegory as Interpretation', *New Literary History*, III, p. 311.
30. Nietzsche, quoted by Heidegger, *The Will to Power as Art* I, trans D. F. Kreel (London, 1981/61), p. 112.
31. S.T. Coleridge, *Marginalia* ed G. Whalley (Princeton, 1980).
32. See especially T. Blount, *Glossographia* (Scolar, 1969/1656) p. 264.
33. J. Klause, 'George Herbert, *Kenosis*, and the Whole Truth' , in AMS, p. 214.

NOTES TO PART FOUR

1. D. Lodge, *The Language of Fiction*, p. 36.
2. S. T. Coleridge, *The Friend*, ed B. E. Rooke (Princeton, 1969),p. 447.
3. C. S. Lewis 'On Stories', *Essays Presented to Charles Williams* (London, 1947), p. 90.
4. See for example *Women and Utopia: Critical Interpretations*, eds M. Barr and N. Smith (London, 1983).
5. This is an aspect not sufficiently addressed by the otherwise useful *Women in Search of Utopia, Mavericks and Mythmakers*, ed and intro R. Rohrlich and E.H. Baruch (New York, 1984).
6. See for example 'Recent developments in English Studies at the Centre', English Studies Group 1978–9, in *Culture, Media, Language*, eds S. Hall, D. Hobson, A. Lowe and P. Willis (Hutchinson, 1980); which points out the potential for opposition in popular romance.
7. A thorough study of this phenomenon may be found in J.A. Radway, *Reading the Romance* (London, 1984).
8. N. Rosinsky's study of *Feminist Futures* (Ann Arbor, 1982) approaches the difference between topic and process in terms of women's alternative worlds alone. Her vigorous criticism notes the tendency to associate authorial writing with gynocentric essentialism and the writing of active participation with feminist androgyny (non-essentialist). But she also points out that this is not always the case. The possibility that authorial writing may at times be necessary politically, and the possibility that non-essentialist philosophies may have their own authority structures, is not pursued.
9. See U. Le Guin, *The Language of the Night*, ed S. Wood (New York, 1979), for clear accounts that Le Guin has given in interview, about the ends of her work.
10. N. Rosinski, *Feminist Futures*, p. 66.
11. L. Wittgenstein *The Blue and Brown Books*, p. 28.

Index